MAKING SENSE OF MARKETS

MAKING SENSE OF MARKETS

AN INVESTOR'S GUIDE TO PROFITING AMIDST THE GLOOM

KEVIN GARDINER

palgrave
macmillan

First published 2015 by
PALGRAVE MACMILLAN

Palgrave Macmillan in the UK is an imprint of Macmillan Publishers Limited,
registered in England, company number 785998, of Houndmills, Basingstoke,
Hampshire RG21 6XS.

Palgrave Macmillan in the US is a division of St Martin's Press LLC,
175 Fifth Avenue, New York, NY 10010.

Palgrave Macmillan is the global academic imprint of the above companies
and has companies and representatives throughout the world.

Palgrave® and Macmillan® are registered trademarks in the United States,
the United Kingdom, Europe and other countries.

ISBN: 978–1–137–47138–3

This book is printed on paper suitable for recycling and made from fully
managed and sustained forest sources. Logging, pulping and manufacturing
processes are expected to conform to the environmental regulations of the
country of origin.

A catalogue record for this book is available from the British Library.

A catalog record for this book is available from the Library of Congress.

CONTENTS

LIST OF ILLUSTRATIONS

FIGURES

TABLES

ACKNOWLEDGEMENTS

I am indebted to the many individual investors and clients whose interest since 2008 has convinced me that there is an audience for these ideas and helped me organise my thoughts and presentation.

More generally, my understanding of economics and markets has benefited over the years from the experience, example, feedback and help provided by able and generous colleagues and friends, including (in approximate chronological order): Iain Saville, Nigel Jenkinson, Ian Harwood, John Shepperd, Nigel Richardson, George Hodgson, Darren Winder, Richard Urwin, Reg Ammon, Rob Ellis, Stephen Roach, Ravi Bulchandani, Barton Biggs, Byron Wien, Joachim Fels, Richard Davidson, Tim Harris, Michael Quach, Bill McQuaker, Paul O'Connor, Garry Evans, Robert Parkes, Janet Henry, Vivek Misra, Alen Mattich, Aaron Gurwitz, Greg B. Davies, William Hobbs, Fadi Zaher, Christian Theis, Petr Krpata, Amie Stow, Tanya Joyce, Henk Potts, and the Ullapool school of Dr E.W. Davies, T.S.T. Key and K.C. Wall. Special thanks are due to Pete Baker at Palgrave Macmillan, and to William Hobbs and Simon Key for reading the manuscript. All these, and my various employers, are of course absolved from responsibility for the views presented here, which are my personal opinions only. Royalties will go to the United World College of the Atlantic.

Lastly, thanks are due to my wife and daughters, and to my mother and late father, without whom my work and this project would have been neither possible nor as meaningful.

INTRODUCTION: WHAT WE TALK ABOUT WHEN WE TALK ABOUT MARKETS

The best lack all conviction, while the worst
Are full of passionate intensity.

– W.B. Yeats

You don't often read about the important investment lesson from the great panic of 2008/2009. Many pundits failed to spot it at the time, and still haven't. When the next crisis breaks it may be forgotten, as was a similar lesson after smaller scale affairs in 1987, 1992 and 2001. This book is an attempt to write it down before that happens, in the hope that readers will be able to derive some reassurance – and useful investment advice – from it. Conversations with many individual investors since 2008 have convinced me that there is a readership for it – a silent majority perhaps who are tired of being told that the economy is doomed, that pensions are unfinanceable and that investment returns will be negligible.

What the great panic and its more muted predecessors shared was a financial shock, and one that was seen as a harbinger of bad times to come. The biggest financial shock ever seen – the Wall Street Crash of 1929 – was followed shortly by the Great Depression, a prolonged slump that hurt economically in a way that no subsequent economic downturn in a major industrialised economy has come close to doing, and so recent unease has been understandable. It would be foolish to deny the possibility of another Depression, and if it hadn't been for the prompt actions of the authorities in late 2008 we might have come a lot closer to one than we did. However, the tendency for the public debate to focus only on the potential for disaster, and to overlook the possibility (arguably, the probability) of a less catastrophic "muddling through", has been striking. The interaction of the markets and media, the reasons for the collective preoccupation with what might go wrong(er), and the varying (but undeclared) interests of the talking heads who play a role in that public debate, have passed largely unnoticed. More recently, warnings against over-optimism are commonplace: we are being alerted to new bubbles almost every day it seems. In October 2014 a sudden swoon in stock markets showed the "wall of worry" to be firmly intact as analysts queued to say "here we go again" and "we told you so". Warnings against routine pessimism are less common.

The important lesson from the panic and its modern precursors (including the stock market crash of 1987, the UK's expulsion from the ERM in 1992 and the collapse of stock market valuations after 2000) is that received wisdom often becomes overly pessimistic, and can lead investors astray. The main message in this book is that contrary to that consensus, the routine drivers of growth are not primarily financial, and the prospects for the global economy (and particularly for the developed West, where expectations are most downbeat) may be brighter than feared. What people thought was a crisis of aggregate solvency was really one of liquidity: it had to be. It is still worth investing.

If you accept too easily the popular explanations for financial shocks, and if you think that finance is a more important driver of the economy than it really is, then you may miss portfolio and business opportunities. The book will show why much recent received wisdom can be too pessimistic. But it will also offer some perspective on the way in which that public debate is conducted, and on how much economic and financial knowledge is formed and disseminated, in order to encourage readers to question the consensus view, particularly at times of crisis. It is human nature to seek a convincing narrative when trying to explain dramatic events, to try to "make sense" of markets. Sometimes we try too hard, and end up making the wrong sort of sense, or we infer meaning and causality where there is none. The book will help readers guard against making these mistakes. It blends some of the insights of behavioural finance with a common sense questioning of the logic and data that informs the gloomy consensus.

At the time of writing, in late 2014, the renewed expansion in the US economy – still the most important single driver of global investment trends – has lasted for five-and-a-half years, a little longer than the typical upswing of the last half-century or so (if there is such a thing as a "typical" business cycle). The US stock market has tripled since its March 2009 low point, despite widespread assertions beforehand that we are in a "low return environment", and the Federal Reserve and Bank of England have started what looks set to be a long and gradual process of normalising monetary conditions. In the US, quantitative easing (QE) has been tapered and (as of October 2014) stopped, and money markets are expecting policy interest rates to start rising in the year ahead. In the UK, the Bank of England has long since stopped its QE, and two traditional cyclical warning signs are flashing amber: house prices are embarked on another surge, encouraged (again) by misguided policy, and our international payments are even more imbalanced than usual.

That investment lesson – the knowledge that the global economy need not be doomed, that received wisdom is lazy, and errs on the side of pessimism – has been a very profitable one these last few years, and it may now be a little late to put it fully to work in the current cycle (which may have matured still further, or even ended, by our publication date). Even the gloomiest pundit is aware that disaster has been avoided for five years or so at least. Stocks are not as inexpensive as they were in the crisis and its immediate aftermath. Nonetheless, if you know how to look, you can see the signs that the lesson has not been fully learned, and that suggest it will quickly be pushed to the back of our collective minds when market volatility spikes next (as we saw during that market swoon in October 2014, for example).

There is no single rule, valuation tool or statistical technique that will help you implement the book's main message. Rather, it requires approaching financial markets and investment with an open mind, and being willing to ask not just what it is that we are being told, but by whom we are being told it, and why? It also requires that you think carefully about what it is that you want from your investments. This book will show some of the ways in which such a stance can be cultivated, and will illustrate clearly just how mistaken much received wisdom can be. It will also suggest what can reasonably be expected from a typical, balanced investment portfolio – and what can't: investment is worthwhile, but will probably *not* make you rich quick, and thinking that it will is a mistake. The post-crisis climate offers a once-in-a-lifetime (here's hoping) opportunity to clear the air, and to be frank about what financial analysis, and investment advice, can and can't offer.

An awareness of the wider context within which the market debate is taking place; a recognition of the spuriously precise and unconvincing nature of much of what passes for economic knowledge; an acceptance of the insights gained from behavioural finance into the unrealistic assumption of rationality in decision-making; and above all, an acceptance of the possibility that investors may not necessarily get paid for taking risk, in contrast to the central tenet of the "modern portfolio theory" that has dominated thinking on markets since the 1950s – this all suggests that the approach outlined here can perhaps be termed a "postmodern portfolio theory". In place of the perfectible, precise search for the best, optimised portfolio, we recognise that practical investing is about *satisficing* – settling for an approximately weighted, acceptable portfolio from amongst a probable plethora of similarly attractive alternatives.[1]

We can be sure of little. We know less than we think we do about the economy and markets, and there may be less to be known than we imagine. This doesn't sound very helpful, but when so many pundits are asserting loudly and authoritatively that: growth is shackled by debt; we can't afford our collective pensions; our children will be poorer than us; the dollar, the euro and the West are doomed; we are about to run out of food, metal, oil and/or water; the geopolitical situation is especially precarious – well, simply knowing that none of these things need be true is both reassuring and potentially profitable.

I follow my own advice in my personal savings, and in helping shape the investment policy of the endowment fund at UWC Atlantic College, where I am a trustee. The aim here is to try to take a long-term view, to focus more on absolute than relative returns, and to hold a multi-asset portfolio focused mostly on conventional assets, not "alternatives", and one containing more stocks than bonds and cash – not because you necessarily get paid for taking risk, but because business is likely to grow over time, and unless shares are obviously expensive, owning a small portion of it is likely to be more attractive than lending to it, or to the government. Low-cost tracker funds can be a good way to implement this approach, particularly when gaining exposure to more competitively researched markets and many bonds: performance is uncertain, fees aren't. But so too can a higher-cost discretionary solution if you decide that you'd simply like someone else to do your diversification and worrying for you.

This is a practitioner's account of issues encountered in analysing, and advising on, the macroeconomic climate and investment markets. My experience in wealth management suggests that it will appeal to many individual savers who are simply interested in hearing about whether their portfolios can continue to muddle through in the face of all that pessimism. I hope it will also be useful to many students, teachers and finance professionals as well as to a wider readership. I have tried to avoid jargon, there are no equations, and the language is (I hope) simple, clear and occasionally provocative. References are few, and largely non-academic. The ideas are grounded solidly in economics, but the most valuable insights I gained from my lecturers at the LSE and Cambridge were delivered in words, not symbols. The

economy and markets are less sophisticated than the statistical and mathematical techniques inflicted upon them.

Part I of the book makes the case for investing. It sets out the conventional account of our economic and financial predicament, and then suggests
an alternative, less threatening account, illustrating exactly why some of our
biggest fears – debt, demographics, Western decadence, resource depletion
and geopolitical danger – may be overstated. It offers some guidance on how
to take the wider perspectives that help unearth investment opportunities,
and are often missing from narrower, consensual views. Finally, it offers
some tongue-in-cheek advice on raising the financial signal-to-noise ratio,
and suggests why it is that we are so inclined, in macroeconomic matters, to
look on the dark side.

Part II suggests how best to invest given the insights in Part I. It stresses
the importance of having a realistic personal investment policy, of not aiming too high, and of not paying too much for financial advice (which in practice means avoiding many "alternative" assets, keeping the more ambitious
claims made for emerging markets at arm's length, and using passive security selection when appropriate). It shows clearly why there are no infallible
valuation models for stocks or bonds, but some useful rules of thumb nonetheless, and it suggests that private investors avoid "weighting in vain" –
there are no uniquely optimal portfolios, and many "benchmarks" should
be ignored or left to institutional investors. It offers some guidance on how
to gauge whether the prospective returns suggested (not promised, I hope)
by investment advisers are plausible, and argues that a multi-asset portfolio
in which stocks represent the largest holding is likely to be a better risk-
adjusted long-term investment than cash.

The conclusion argues that it is still worth investing, that investment
portfolios should be constructed simply and inexpensively, and that the lasting damage done by the richness of embarrassments that culminated in the
great panic of 2008/2009 has been to the financial services industry – and to
conventional economic and financial analysis.

Part I

THE GLASS IS HALF FULL

1

WHY IS EVERYBODY SO GLOOMY?

It ain't what you don't know that gets you into trouble. It's what you know for sure that just ain't so.

— Mark Twain (attributed)

In March 2012, the Financial Times carried a front page story headlined "Years of struggle for a jinxed generation". It stated that "For the first time in half a century, young Britons embarking on their careers cannot expect to be any better off than their parents".

This was a remarkable thing to be saying, but has since become part of received wisdom. For as long as we can remember, each peacetime generation has enjoyed a better standard of living than the one before it. Of course, the pace at which living standards have risen has ebbed and flowed. Occasionally, they have fallen for a year or two, usually when recessions have temporarily shrunk the economy. The Financial Times here however was stating flatly not just that economic growth might slow, or that a recession might lie ahead, but that an entire generation's living standards, their incomes after tax and inflation, would fall short of those enjoyed by their predecessors – and noticeably so. Our children, it suggested, will be worse off than us.

The article's style was almost as remarkable as its content. In contrast to most statements made about the future, there was little qualification or equivocation. Its conclusions were assertions, rather than hypotheses, offered confidently and clearly, almost as matters of fact – which of course they weren't, because statements about the future can't be. The Financial

Times is usually the most analytically-minded of the UK broadsheets. It is arguably also the most objective. And it wasn't August – there were plenty of other things to be writing about.

The article's message and mood was in fact very much in line with the prevailing consensus – it was a particularly authoritative-looking statement of what many other media, market and academic commentators were saying, and still are. In 2014, a radio programme titled "The Future Is Not What It Used to Be" also presented that consensus very eloquently. Since 2007, the economic world has been hit by "one damned thing after another". Most dramatically of course there was the financial crisis, and its economic fallout, that erupted in late 2008/early 2009. The euro's existential angst surfaced in 2010, and deepened – amidst rising unemployment – through into 2012. There have been high-profile downgrades to the credit ratings of supposedly safe governments including the United States (2011), France (2012) and the United Kingdom (in early 2013), and amidst the single currency's soul-searching, Greece defaulted on its debt in 2012. Geopolitical tension has been simmering, most visibly at the time of writing around Ukraine, Syria and Iraq. China's trend rate of economic growth is slowing, and there has also been a marked faltering in the progress of Brazil, India and (particularly) Russia, the other members of the high-profile BRIC quartet of emerging economies for whom hopes have been high. Meanwhile, in the background, unemployment in the United States and the United Kingdom has fallen only slowly even as the immediate crisis has eased; the jury is still out on whether "Abenomics" will avert a third "lost decade" for Japan's economy, whose troubles are seen by many as a harbinger of what awaits the West; central banks have been engaging in "unconventional" measures including buying government bonds ("Quantitative Easing") and offering "forward guidance" designed to keep interest rate expectations low; interest rates have indeed been negligible, and well below inflation rates; and the annuity rates that many UK pensioners still depend upon (but which future retirees no longer have to buy, as of 2014) have been falling. Finally, while stock markets have risen, there has been no accompanying sense of optimism: instead, perhaps because most pundits have missed the boat, there is widespread acceptance that they have been driven by monetary froth, and have become overvalued – some even talk of another bubble. All this has created the perfect emotional storm, a gale force gloom. Who will be willing to invest – or hire – in this climate?

The case for pessimism looks pretty convincing. These were the most dramatic and frightening financial events of our working lifetimes by far, and it has been one of the worst economic climates too. To return to the

Financial Times article, young workers have seen their living standards fall markedly recently, and by more than the average person. Why did all this happen, and what might happen next? The accepted explanations for these events are not so convincing, but in the current mood are being largely taken at face value, and are colouring our view of the future, not just the past. We are driving with our gaze on the rear-view mirror – and objects in that mirror may not be quite what they seem.

This happens a lot in the world of investing. A shocking event happens, and we rush to explain it with a convincing narrative that shows why it had to happen – and why, because of it, things will never be the same again. Having driven our car into a big hole in the road that we didn't spot in advance, we explain why it was inevitable that we would in fact fall into that hole – and why we'll never be able to get out of it. In reality, we fall into these holes because we do indeed often drive by looking in the rear-view mirror, and not at the road ahead; and at the risk of stretching the analogy, we then doubt we'll ever get out of them because, still looking in the rear-view mirror, the side of the hole looks pretty steep – and we fail to notice that ahead of us, perhaps, is a negotiable slope leading upwards and out of it.

All forecasting, not just in the realm of economics, suffers from the same problem: what we know is in the past, and our understanding of the past depends upon our perspective. Niels Bohr, the physicist and Nobel laureate, famously quipped that "Prediction is very difficult – especially about the future". The future is simply, but profoundly, unknowable: things can happen that have never happened before, and models and knowledge built on past experience are of limited use. To reason from the past into the future is to risk committing the fallacy of induction – of arguing from the specific to the general. For example, to use the analogy most recently popularised by Naseem Taleb, just because all the swans we've ever seen have been white, that doesn't mean that black swans don't exist; similarly, just because the sun has risen every day in the past, that doesn't mean that it will do so forever. Note that this simple point applies as much to pessimistic outlooks as to optimistic ones: expecting recent bad news to continue forever is just as prone to error as believing that the sun will always rise – a point overlooked by many commentators, who tend to think that only optimists are capable of the logical fallacy.[1]

The problem is particularly pressing in the case of economics, though, because making sense even of the past is often difficult. The precise, empirical regularities that characterise science are elusive, because in economics the moving parts are people, and it is hard to quantify many of the key variables and concepts. And the importance of perspective, and interpretation, becomes correspondingly greater.

Also, and as an economist myself it is embarrassing to acknowledge this, much economic and financial analysis itself can be misguided, and poorly conducted. We resort too quickly to the satisfying axiomatic security (or perhaps *seeming* security[2]) of mathematical abstraction, we are spuriously precise in our commentaries, and we do not question enough our raw data and what it is that we can reasonably expect to know. There is not enough focus on that practical world in which people, companies and governments use their capital, effort and ingenuity to finance and make, and then sell or otherwise distribute, the wonderfully vast and continually evolving array of commodities, products and services that make up "the economy", and on why it is that some individuals, companies and countries seem to fare better than others.

Macroeconomic analysis in the twentieth century was given its momentum by the insights of the brilliant British economist J.M. Keynes, who chose to focus on aggregate spending – consumption, capital spending and exports – in explaining the business cycle, a focus that remains dominant today. The total spending in an economy, less imports, is just another way of looking at the total output of all those goods and services. The same is true of total incomes – wages, profits and other income, another view favoured often by macroeconomists. But it is not clear that it is any easier or more meaningful to explain why we consume rather than invest, or why profits rise or fall relative to wages, than it is to explain why we produce the mix of goods and services that we do. We lose a lot of empirical relevance, and explanatory richness, with those spending and income-oriented perspectives.[3] And we can also miss out on investment opportunities, which present themselves not in terms of GDP or consumer spending, but as products, businesses or borrowing plans.

More topically, this lack of attention to practicalities meant that in 2008, many bank economists were not familiar with the product range and operating processes even of their own industry. We collectively lost a lot of time belatedly swotting up on the financial process called "securitisation", which had by then been around for almost forty years. We collectively discovered that central banks like the Bank of England or the Federal Reserve don't always control short-term interest rates or the money supply – particularly if those central banks don't happen to have responsibility for supervising banks as well as for the operation of monetary policy.[4] We also realised that policymakers who didn't have formal responsibility for monetary policy could nonetheless have an influence on the monetary climate through their regulation of banks – through the introduction of deposit guarantees, for example. Later in the book I will argue that while the economy itself may not be permanently altered by the crisis, our faith in conventional economic and investment analysis should be.

So what does this particularly deep hole in the economic road look like – what are the reasons for the litany of bad news resounding since 2007? From a grandstand seat I have been able to watch events closely, and have had the privilege of being able to speak extensively with many investors and other market and media participants about their concerns. There are several themes that feature regularly whenever the conversation turns to what went wrong, or is still going wrong, in the economic world. For example: too much debt means we (the developed world) can't grow. Too many old people means we can't afford our pensions. Too many aspirational consumers in China will compete away the employment we're left with, and use up all our scarce resources. Too many rogue countries and a disenchantment with the excesses of liberalism threaten to replace the old Washington consensus with anarchy. Too many stock prices have risen too far, and too many of those lucky enough to have savings to begin with will see them destroyed by renewed financial volatility and negative real interest rates.

These worries are not new, but they have been given added potency by these recent events – the trauma of 2008 in particular. This is not the place for a full account of those events,[5] but in a nutshell, rising tensions in the credit markets from the spring, and the collapse of the Lehman Brothers investment bank in September of that year (and the near collapse of the insurance giant AIG at the same time), effectively froze much of the global money market, leaving banks afraid to lend to each other for fear that they would not get their money back.

The fear was contagious – and in financial markets, in which there are so many transaction points, where prices are instantly flexible and there are numerous information providers competing to get those prices and their stories in front of traders, contagion is rapid. It was also self-fulfilling. Any business whose suppliers think it is in difficulty will stop supplying it with goods to sell, its shelves will empty and, with nothing to sell, it is indeed in difficulty – and in the capital markets, such a self-fulfilling panic can (and did) take just hours to become established. If a bank's peers think it has a problem, it does have a problem.

Fear in financial markets is hardly new. The panic was particularly difficult to dispel in 2008 however because banks' assets had become extremely complex, opaque and interdependent as a result of the latest wave in a rolling tide of financial innovation dating back to the 1970s (and largely overlooked by much economic research). The massive growth, from a standing start little more than a decade earlier, in instruments providing insurance against default on bonds – Credit Default Swaps (CDS) – had helped to foster a belief that the credit cycle had been tamed.[6] CDS were used routinely to hedge banks' and investors' holdings of bonds – and in some cases their holdings of shares too. Loans were parcelled up in complex tranches (Collateralised Debt Obligations) that allowed them to be insured more easily, and those complex, increasingly hard-to-value parcels were then distributed widely through the long-established process of securitisation mentioned earlier. Securitisation allows banks to bundle and effectively sell on, or make into securities ("securitise") the loans that they've made, typically mortgages, into the wider investment markets, with the result that the ultimate owner of the loan – which might be another bank, or a hedge or pension fund – often has little detail on the specific circumstances of the borrowers whose interest and principal payments they have bought.[7]

In a conventional bank run, depositors have a pretty good idea what they are worried about. The bank with whom they've placed their cash might have made some bad loans to local businesses, property developers or homeowners, and the anxious account holders can get some feel for the order of magnitude of the losses they might face by taking a view on the collateral involved – by kicking the tyres themselves, as it were. When the assets of the bank include loans made in another area, or even in another country, parcelled up in a complicated way that makes it difficult to know exactly what the collateral backing them is, and when the package is further wrapped with some insurance of uncertain value issued by a third party whose creditworthiness is also difficult to fathom, then depositors and other lenders to the bank can't find the tyres to kick.

As banks scrambled to stay liquid in the face of the panic, bank customers in turn started to lose access to the everyday working capital needed to finance business. Solvent companies with solid order books as far away as Asia found routine credit lines such as overdrafts and export finance drying up, and had little alternative but to cut back on their own spending and employment plans. The economic seizure delivered some dramatic falls in industrial production across the world. In the United States and the United Kingdom, two of the countries whose banks had been particularly innovative and reckless in their lending, industrial output fell by 16% and 12% from their respective pre-crisis peaks to their troughs. In the case of Ireland, whose banks were less innovative but even more reckless, industrial output fell by 11%. Almost ironically, perhaps, industrial production was hit hardest in two big exporting countries some way from the epicentre of the crisis but whose economies are traditionally sensitive to global trade: German industrial production fell 20%, and Japan, whose banks had been largely keeping themselves to themselves, saw a fall of 32%.

Sudden falls on this scale in industrial production had not been seen since the Great Depression of the 1930s, and took place against a backdrop of large falls in stock prices (the US stock market, already down by 20% from its all-time closing high reached in October 2007 at the time of Lehman's collapse, would eventually fall a further 46%, for a compounded decline of 57% when it bottomed in early March 2009), and faltering public confidence in the banking system (in the United Kingdom, confidence had already been shaken by the run on Northern Rock in September 2007). As policymakers struggled to keep up, for a while we faced the prospect of financial and economic implosion, and a possible return to barter, deflation and mass unemployment – or at least it seemed so, and few of us would have wanted to find out for real.

Some analysts had been arguing since well before the noughties, and its attendant financial innovation and recklessness, that the global economy was a house of cards, ready to collapse at any instant. They now proclaimed that they had indeed told us so, and that The End was Nigh. More balanced voices were drowned out in the tumult. The price of gold, the "barbarous relic" that frightened savers turn to when they feel that financial disaster is looming – hyperinflation, banking collapse or both – soared: it had already risen a long way in the previous decade, and would go on to more than double between Lehman's collapse and September 2011. For many of the more apocalyptically-minded it was the breaking of the link between modern money and gold that had created the house of cards to begin with: specifically, the suspension of the dollar's convertibility into gold that marked the formal ending of the "gold standard" way back in 1971. It was widely and loudly asserted that the crisis was rooted not in a shortage of liquidity, but somehow in a general insolvency.

Of course, the absence of a direct link between money in circulation and gold does not lead inevitably to economic ruin. Those apocalyptic commentators are misguided. "Money" has always been a bit of a confidence trick. Many different materials and objects have been used as money in the past, and for something to be a credible medium of exchange and store of value requires simply that people believe it to be so: the faith that many people arbitrarily place in gold could in theory be placed in something else, and that something needn't be tangible – it could even be something like bitcoin, for example.[8] The key to that confidence in turn lies in making the supply of that "something else" look as if it is reasonably stable, just as the amount of gold seems to be. Governments, central banks and commercial banks do not always do a good job of this, and central banks currently have indeed – as the "gold bugs" point out – been taking some risks with those experiments in

"Quantitative Easing", which might yet lead to a big increase in the amount of money in circulation, and inflation. "Fiat" money – money that is not backed by a specified totem – can never "run out", because governments and the banking system can just create more of it (we shall discuss this further in Chapter 2). As noted above, however, governments do still enjoy huge power over the economy and its citizens, and this gives whatever they decide to call "money" a head start in terms of credibility – even if it is just a piece of paper or plastic, or an array of binary digits in an electronic ledger somewhere. Meanwhile, the amount of monetary gold available is not as rigidly fixed as its champions claim, and its usefulness as an insurance against inflation is overstated.[9]

Not all the monetary doomsayers had been fixated on gold. The modern "fractional reserve" banking system, in which only a small amount of depositors' funds are available for withdrawal at any given time, with most being used to fund banks' lending to third parties, was another alleged contributor to the supposed day of reckoning. So too was the related notion of "borrowing short to lend long", which sounds obviously and needlessly risky. In practice, like fiat or non-metallic money, these arrangements can be sustainable – and in the case of banks using short-term deposits to fund long-term loans, they are positively desirable in many circumstances: that is exactly what we want business-friendly financial intermediaries to do. But looking back from the uneasy high-tide vantage point of the crisis, many nervous investors remembered that the break with gold had been followed within a decade by the first flows in that long tide of financial deregulation in the United States, the United Kingdom and elsewhere; that deregulation had fostered a bigger scale of fractional reserve banking; and that in the noughties at least, banks had mismatched the maturities of their liabilities and assets to an unusual extent. There was also, in the large balance of payments deficit run by the United States over many years, and in the huge accumulation of reserves by China and Japan, a very visible international dimension to much of this borrowing that looked unsettling. The massive expansion of financial balance sheets after the 1970s seemed, with hindsight, to suggest clearly that there was now indeed just "too much debt", that we had become collectively insolvent.

This conclusion was given some influential academic corroboration with the impeccably timed publication in September 2009 of the book *This Time It's Different: Eight Centuries of Financial Folly*, by Carmen Reinhart and Kenneth Rogoff, professors of economics at Harvard (Rogoff is also a former Chief Economist at the IMF), based on earlier work that pre-dated the crisis. In a daunting display of scholarship, they compiled a massive database of financial crises, and suggested that banking crises tended to be particularly traumatic and cast a long shadow economically and fiscally, typically being followed by surges in government debt as the public sector bailed out the private banks. In a related paper they subsequently argued, with this in mind, that a public debt level of 90% of GDP seemed to be a threshold which, once exceeded, had been associated statistically with significantly slower economic growth.

The claims made (often by others, to be fair) for Reinhart and Rogoff's work always looked a little excessive, and their threshold analysis in particular was shown in April 2013 to have been overstated. In drawing stylised conclusions from a mass of very different historical episodes, they had to cut a lot of corners, leaving little room for a careful analysis of cause and effect. Comments on the level of Ireland's indebtedness for example had suggested a high-altitude tendency to use some inappropriate data. The title of their book cited an oft-used excuse for ignoring conventional rules about overvalued investments: "It's different this time". In financial crises, however, things are subtly different *every* time, and the likely lessons from "eight centuries of financial folly" for the current situation were in fact limited. Nonetheless, the book itself was (is) a tremendous compilation and reference work, and its publication was seized upon by financial commentators as an immediate "explanation" of why we were in crisis, and why we should expect there to be a lasting economic fallout.[10] The revelation that some of the subsequent policy inference at least was statistically mistaken did not reverse this instinctive broadsheet response: the emperor may have been wearing fewer clothes, but the crowd still liked the fashion statement.

Meanwhile, attempts to rescue the markets through the winter of 2008/2009, made difficult by the sheer complexity of the capital markets in the late noughties, were further hindered by political equivocation and brinkmanship. The US congress and public were torn between fear of financial collapse on the one hand, and deep distrust of both Wall Street and Big Government on the other. Eventually, however, the public sector on both sides of the Atlantic showed itself capable of considerable financial innovation, and managed to stabilise the situation using, amongst other things, an improvisory mix of lowered official interest rates, easier access to central bank funds and lines of liquidity, direct support of bond markets, partial bank nationalisation, controls on short selling, and extended deposit insurance. Each stage of the evolving rescue process had its very vocal critics, but after a final lurch lower in March 2009, the US stock market began to rally (from a level little more than two-fifths of its pre-crisis high of 1565 reached in October 2007). Economic indicators had by then begun to stabilise.

The rescue left many observers sceptical that anything more than the financial equivalent of a sticking plaster had been applied. By pushing interest rates towards zero (and firmly into negative territory when allowing for inflation), by boosting government borrowing, and by directly buying government bonds in the market place ("Quantitative Easing"), the solution to the crisis seemed to involve the creation of even more credit in a world seemingly awash in it to begin with. The authorities seemed to be addressing the symptoms, not the underlying illness. Then in late 2009 and again in early 2010, on the other side of the Atlantic but in the same nervous capital markets, we learned the incoming Greek government had discovered that the outgoing one had been borrowing far more than it had previously admitted to (or, more generously but more scarily perhaps, more than it had known about[11]), and while Greece itself is only a tiny portion of the euro area, those still-stretched nerves and an awareness of the interconnectedness of the euro and global capital markets helped reignite fears about the fabric of the global financial system. There were good reasons for concern, because the single currency's economic, financial and political architecture had been only part-built: this had always been known, but in the newly nervous climate, with the fragile US economy still at risk from a "double dip" recession, it assumed greater significance. It focused attention on public sector borrowing and balance sheets not just in the large peripheral Eurozone countries of Italy and Spain, but in more traditionally creditworthy countries including the United States, the United Kingdom and France.

This next phase of the perfect storm would be less intense (at least to date), but longer lasting, than the immediate crisis of 2008/2009. Again, policymakers intervened to stabilise the situation – by settling nerves, stabilising deposits and by lending directly to the troubled governments in Greece, Ireland and Portugal. Greece would go on to default on its debt in 2012 (and in late 2014 is still capable of unsettling markets), but by buying time (or "kicking the can down the road", as sceptics saw it) the authorities helped ensure that the impact proved containable. In the United States and the United Kingdom, faced with disappointing economic recoveries, the Federal Reserve and the Bank of England added further to their purchases of government bonds, thereby helping keep long-term interest rates low and boosting bank liquidity (and, potentially, the supply of money, though to date there has been little sign of that liquidity leaking into wider circulation).

As noted, the crisis certainly had a big impact on the wider global economy. The Great Depression feared by many did not materialise, but the US downturn has become known as the Great Recession. In the United States, the economy shrank by 4% between late 2007 and mid-2009, the largest fall in GDP since 1945–1947, and a setback that pulled the country's rolling ten-year trend growth rate down to 1.6% in 2010, also the lowest level in more than half a century. The US housing market, where banks' greed and reck-lessness had given us the so-called NINJA mortgages made to sub-prime borrowers with no income, no job and no assets, imploded, with sales col-lapsing and housing starts dropping to half-century lows (many of the mort-gages themselves of course had been repackaged, "insured" and sold on as part of the process described above). Unemployment more than doubled in the United States, to 10%, and more recently surged to a record 12% in the euro area (and a striking 26% in Spain and Greece, though the data there are not directly comparable, despite being labelled as "standardised"). Even China slowed sharply in 2008, and aggregate global GDP actually fell for three successive quarters from the middle of the year, a cumulative decline of 3% and the first material fall since comprehensive quarterly data have been available.

Despite the difficulties in the Eurozone, the wider picture has in fact improved since 2009. Recovery has been patchy and lacklustre, and in the case of the euro area and Japan, less obvious in GDP data. But while many components of output fell sharply in late 2008 and early 2009, the global economy as a whole didn't shrink for long – indeed, it began to grow again in the second half of 2009. It helped that the emerging world had not been rely-ing on funds borrowed from the world's capital markets in the run-up to the crisis, and after the initial seizure, their banks were able to start function-ing again relatively quickly. Further support came from the many and vari-ous public spending and other fiscal initiatives introduced by governments across the world, even though the stimulus they provided added to those debt totals. Growth since mid-2009 has fallen short of what we've seen in recover-ies from previous recessions, but at almost 4% per annum, after inflation, it has firmly outpaced the increase in the world's population, which has grown by a little more than 1% per annum over the same period. Here perhaps is a first hint that in some respects at least, the gloom has been overdone. Global GDP in late 2014, adjusted for inflation and changes in exchange rates, was some 20% higher than in mid-2008, *before the fall*, while the global popula-tion over the same period rose by an estimated 8%. As a result, per capita GDP – a proxy for global living standards – rose by around 12% to a new all-time high. This is not just a reflection of the continuing gains made in the emerging world: real US GDP per capita has also rebounded back above its pre-crisis high (as of mid-2013).[12] The United Kingdom has, as noted, been lagging behind, but even here real per capita GDP is back at its pre-crisis peak, having slumped by 7% to its autumn 2009 trough.

(Arguably, this is a more impressive result than it sounds. If the pre-crisis peak was unsustainable, because it was flattered by reckless and excessive borrowing, then to be at or above those levels now – without any renewed outbreak of recklessness – is not a return to normal, but genuine progress. This is one of the many inconsistencies in the public debate: if the economy was in some sense ahead of itself before the crisis, then to criticise the recovery for not matching those levels more quickly might be a little harsh.)

If you ask a representative group of private investors whether the global economy is in good shape, few – if any – will raise their hands (I have tried this myself with a total sample now reaching into the thousands). Many people will be amused even to be asked the question: of course the world economy is not in good shape! But if you then ask whether the group can think of a time in recorded history when the average human being has been significantly better off in material terms, more hands may start to rise, but will quickly falter and fall back, the net result being very similar to the answer to the first question. The point being made is that a short-term focus on disappointing growth, frustratingly slow improvements in labour markets, and volatile financial markets can cause us to forget that the underlying levels of some key indicators of human welfare and corporate efficiency are historically very respectable – because as those global GDP data suggest, average human living standards have likely never been higher. Posing these two questions illustrates how a simple change in perspective can make a big difference to the way we feel about the economy, and can make investors a little more receptive to a "glass half full" outlook – of the sort fleshed out more carefully in this book.

Sceptical readers may think that this is all well and good, but that the scale of the bad news of late is such that even though it may be relatively short term and incremental in nature it is surely only a matter of time until it begins to impinge upon those global income levels – or, even if the global picture remains historically healthy, until the developed world at least will see its slice of the global pie shrink, and our living standards fall (notwithstanding the fact that, as noted, the largest developed economy – the United States – has seen per capita GDP levels reach new highs). The narrative that has been constructed to explain the crisis and its aftermath seems so entrenched and plausible. Individuals, companies, governments and banks all borrowed a lot of money, and have still barely repaid any of it. All that debt, viewed alongside the volatility of stock markets and the historically low interest rates that have resulted from policymakers' financial firefighting since 2008, in turn seems clearly to further threaten the pensions needed by our very visibly greying populations, and is depressing prospective investment returns. As the aging, debt-encumbered developed world flounders, China and the rest of the emerging world, whose workers are paid so much less than we are, seem obviously poised to exploit our weakness and siphon more of our budget conscious spending away from our own companies and workers. And tension in international trade can surely only aggravate further the rising geopolitical risk so starkly visible since 11 September 2001 and now simmering most obviously in the Middle East and Eastern Europe. We read and hear all this in the media, and some brilliant academic minds are backing it up. Who in their right minds would want to save and invest against this backdrop?

This view is mistaken. The accepted explanation of the crisis and its aftermath is a caricature, and a damaging one. It has encouraged many employers and investors to think that business can't return to normal until all that debt has been repaid, those pensions have been refinanced, our real incomes have dropped to China's levels and so forth. But we didn't fall into that hole in the economic road for the stark reasons popularly given. National balance sheets, the funding of Western pensions, the drivers of international trade, trends in geopolitics and the determination of interest rates and stock prices are all much more finely nuanced than the conventional accounts suggest.

Below I offer a quick alternative account of what went wrong. The rest of the first part of the book will then flesh this out a little more carefully, focus on each of these widely held concerns in turn, and I hope place them in their proper perspective – briefly, without resorting to jargon, and keeping footnotes and references to a minimum. The second half will conclude by offering some practical thoughts on how to invest if there is indeed Life After Debt. It will also suggest that the way in which we think about economics and finance may need to change.

In my view, the financial crisis was exactly that – it had economic consequences, but it was essentially a *financial* crisis, not an economic one. It was simmering for a long time before it boiled over – in the next chapter I will suggest that it can be seen as the culmination of a series of capital market embarrassments and accidents stretching back for more than a decade – but not for as long as the gold bugs would have us believe, and for different reasons to the ones that they give. In my view, these financial embarrassments and the culminating crisis were triggered by seizures in *liquidity*, not a lack of underlying *solvency*. This contrasts with the widely held view in 2008/2009, but as we shall discuss in Chapter 3 it is not clear whether the system as a whole can be "insolvent" in any meaningful way.

The good news is that because there may be little fundamentally wrong with the global economy, it can likely move back towards business as usual, doing what it does increasingly well – that is, feeding, clothing and housing

the average human being, and lifting the living standards of most participants (including those in the already wealthy but currently dispirited developed world). It can do that because the drivers of sustained prosperity are
not financial in nature, but are such things as the labour, natural resources,
accumulated capital and organisational and technological skills that we have
at our disposal. These real "factors of production" were not suddenly augmented when the capital markets were exuberant, but equally they have not
now been materially diminished. And because the background crisis to the
crisis predates 2008, some parts of the global capital markets have emerged
from it sooner than the idea of the "Great Deleveraging" seemed to permit.
As noted, the future is profoundly uncertain, but this can cut both ways: just
as few forecasters predicted the nature and scale of the events that unfolded
after 2007, who is to say that the conventional, gloomy outlook is not setting
itself up for a surprise now – this time in the opposite direction? As noted,
Rogoff and Reinhard may be mistaken, their brilliance notwithstanding –
not because it's different *this* time, but because it's potentially different *every*
time, and applying a template based on the past to the future is of limited use
(the fallacy of induction, remember).

The bad news for some of us is that because it was indeed a financial
crisis first and foremost, the financial sector itself will be one of the last to
recover. Much received financial wisdom may not recover at all.

2

AN ALTERNATIVE ACCOUNT – A RICHNESS OF EMBARRASSMENTS

A history in which every particular incident may be true may on the whole be false.

– Macaulay[1]

There is an alternative interpretation of the journey that led us into that financial pothole, and it leads to a different assessment of our chances of escaping from it, and of the likely rewards from investing. On this reading, the growth in global living standards in the last half-century or so has not been built on sand: the banking system is not doomed, the dollar (or euro) may not be about to collapse, we have not necessarily borrowed "too much", we are not too old or uncompetitive, we are not about to run out of natural resources, geopolitical anarchy may not lie in wait, interest rates can rise and stock prices may not be in a bubble. The crisis may not have been inevitable, and its causes may not have been profound. It might be seen instead as the culmination of a rolling series of financial accidents and policy mistakes dating back a decade or so at least, each characterised by the interaction of extrapolative expectations (the assumption that recent trends will continue) and feedback loops (self-reinforcing effects) with increasingly liberalised capital markets. A particularly prosperous episode in economic history has been characterised as an "embarrassment of riches":[2] perhaps we have recently witnessed a "richness of embarrassments" for liberalised capital markets. As with the conventional account, those embarrassments might

have their roots in the wave of financial liberalisation of the 1970s and early
1980s.[3] While they may share the same origins, however, their implications
are much less profound.

Only a little more than half a century ago savings and capital markets
were tightly controlled, to an extent barely conceivable now. Residents in one
country could not always change their currency into another, or could do
so only in small quantities (with a record of the transaction being stamped
on your passport – if you had one). Businesses looking to raise capital were
largely confined to local sources of funds. On both sides of the Atlantic,
access to personal credit was tightly restrained – and not just in the case of
big ticket transactions such as buying a home or a car. BankAmericard was
launched in 1958, Barclaycard in 1966, but general credit cards as a source
of routine or "revolving" credit did not gain widespread acceptance until the
1970s and 1980s (and in some developed European countries, even later). In
the meantime, for individuals seeking credit, a bank loan, or a "hire purchase" agreement with a specialist credit company or store scheme, specifying a deposit and a repayment schedule, was commonly used for bigger
purchases. Admittedly, in the immediate aftermath of the Second World
War, other markets – notably food – were also tightly controlled in many
countries, but restricted access to international liquidity and to borrowed
funds generally was the norm, and stayed so even when post-war business-
as-usual resumed.

Then from the 1960s, the growing and inflating global economy, led by
the industrialised group centred around the US, Germany, Japan and the
UK, began to burst free of those international constraints – most visibly when
the dollar's convertibility into gold at a fixed rate was suspended in August
1971, and most big countries allowed market forces a bigger role in determining their exchange rates, which "floated" more freely as a result. Domestic
corporate loan and personal credit markets similarly began to be loosened.
Landmarks included the birth of the eurobond market in 1963, which orig-
inated as a tax minimisation arrangement for European companies looking to borrow in dollars but which grew into arguably the first significant
international capital market, and the advent of large scale securitisation with
the issuance of mortgage-backed securities by the US Government National
Mortgage Association in 1970. In the UK, one of the first acts of the radical
Conservative administration led by Mrs Thatcher, which took office in 1979,
was to abolish foreign exchange controls; hire purchase controls were ended
in 1982; and the cartel that effectively rationed mortgages was ended in 1983.
Meanwhile, the number, diversity and complexity of specialised financial
instruments whose value derived from obligations and opportunities linked

to existing currencies, bonds and stocks expanded rapidly. The notional value of these "derivatives" collectively would eventually exceed the value of the underlying securities, massively so in the case of credit insurance (an innovation of the 1990s).

The dismantling of financial controls, and the acceleration in financial innovation, was not part of some comprehensive coordinated policy pursued by the global monetary and regulatory authorities, but a piecemeal process driven in different ways, and for different reasons, across the developed world. In some cases, for example in the views of the UK government after 1979, it reflected a particularly strong belief that government should be as small as possible, and markets as free as possible, even if that meant taking some risks with the management of the economy. Nigel Lawson, Chancellor of the Exchequer from 1983 to 1989, was both an advocate and architect of many of the changes, but also aware that they were likely to complicate the operation of monetary policy and might result in a volatile business cycle, as indeed they did.[4] But in other instances the deregulation was more pragmatic, and was a response to altered financial circumstances. The gradual shift to floating exchange rates, for example, was actually resisted for a long time by governments from across the political spectrum, though few politicians or economists nowadays would seriously propose a return to fixed rates.

Whatever the immediate triggers, however, the result was a gradual opening up of the financial opportunities available to individuals and businesses. Financial balance sheets grew faster as more people borrowed, but because the starting point had been one of tight constraint, it was – and still is – impossible to say what their "right" size might be. More importantly, the wider economic significance of the trend is difficult to gauge – in particular, its underlying contribution to economic growth may not have been as potent as much received wisdom suggests.

Had liberalisation not occurred, growth might have been slower, but that does not mean that it was the prime mover of that growth. To return to a driving analogy, taking your foot off the brake is different from pressing the accelerator: a lack of access to credit can act as a brake, but access to it doesn't necessarily make the car move forwards. Viewing things in this way can make a big difference to the perceived possibility of normal business – and investing – resuming. If you believe, as some do, that floating exchange rates, fiat money and readily available credit have inflated the size of the global economy, and profoundly undermined its foundations, leaving it vulnerable to a sudden implosion of living standards and employment, then your view of the outlook will be a pessimistic one as long as that regime is in place. If you see financial arrangements as mostly facilitating economic development rather than causing it, you may be a little more open-minded. (Some of the other concerns noted above – the greying of the population, and a perceived scarcity of natural resources – are less financial in nature, and we shall address those in Chapter 3.)

Finance may be less routinely important to economic growth than the public debate suggests. As we've seen, when finance freezes, the impact can be catastrophic; but that does not mean that "money makes the world go round". If the brakes are suddenly applied at 70 mph, the deceleration will be dramatic, and the car may even go out of control and crash; but it is the engine that sets (and keeps) the car in motion.

Because financial markets can lead to an economic accident, because they are volatile, and shape our evolving individual fortunes, and are an obvious source of daily news, their intrinsic ongoing importance may be overstated. This is particularly the case here in the UK, where the City of London has always been a large and vibrant part of the UK's economy, since well *before* the industrial revolution of the eighteenth century.[5] In practice, however, financial liberalisation may have had less to do with the broad pattern of growth since the 1970s than is generally realised, and because the crisis may indeed have been first and foremost a financial one (albeit one that had painful short-term economic consequences), our economic and investment prospects may not have been permanently affected by it. The increased availability of credit, the widespread financial innovation, the shift to floating exchange rates and the acceptance of paper money all coincided, but they were more economic effects than causes: a growing and more integrated global economy was steadily pushing up against constraints imposed at a time when international trade was smaller, people were poorer, and faith in bigger government across the political spectrum was greater.[6] Financial liberalisation was arguably a consequence of growth, not a driver of it. For a while at least it seemed to be working fine, and on this view it need not be reversed for the global economy – and investment portfolios – to continue growing.

Viewing financial developments as a consequence of wider economic trends is not a new idea, but a very old one. The neoclassical economist Alfred Marshall, who introduced in the late nineteenth century the framework of notional supply and demand curves that still helps us organise our thinking today, listed land, labour, capital and organisation as the "agents" of production, the key inputs or factors that drive prosperity. Missing from his list is an explicit mention of finance: "capital" is the tangible and intellectual capital that is utilised directly in production. Arguably, some sort of monetary system might have been implicit as part of his "organisation". But Marshall paid most attention to such "real" magnitudes as labour and productive capital, and for good reason: financial balance sheets represent titles to ownership and obligation, but are not themselves productive capacity. A bank note or a stock certificate (or their electronic equivalent) doesn't directly produce anything. In a broad sense of course, the total value of a business is often described as its capital, but this tells us nothing about the way in which it produces its output. We will revisit the underlying drivers of growth in Chapter 3.

The unconventional monetary measures designed to fight the post-crisis fires have failed so far even to boost money supplies in the way that they could for precisely this reason: they have been trying to affect something that is itself usually a consequence, not a cause, of economic growth, namely, the amount of money in circulation. What passes for modern "money" may be defined and regulated by the authorities, but they do not control the quantity of it rigidly. The literal printing and distribution of a big increase in banknotes is not politically practical: instead, the way in which central banks have been trying to boost money supplies has been to buy bonds (a form of "Quantitative Easing") in the market, which in practice has mainly boosted banks' liquidity and balance sheets. This is often described as the equivalent of "printing money", but this is a convenient – and inaccurate – shorthand.

The liquidity injected into the banking system is most likely to get into wider circulation, and the measured money supplies, if banks use it to create loans, and they can only do that if people and companies want to borrow to begin with. Until they do, the direct impact of QE is mostly limited to its effect on bond prices and long-term interest rates. The modern money supply is thus largely "endogenous" – it is mostly driven by the wider economy and its interaction with the banking system, and is unlikely to be an independent ("exogenous") prime mover of anything.[7] This doesn't mean that monetary policy is powerless: changing the price of borrowing – interest rates – or its availability can of course still have an effect. But the "transmission mechanism" through which policy affects the economy is less direct than textbook models, and notions of "helicopter money" dropping on an unsuspecting public, often suggest.[8]

The prominent role played by lending in the money supply process explains why banking supervision is so closely linked to monetary policy, and why it makes sense for central banks in charge of the latter to have responsibility for the former (a point overlooked by the UK government when it took banking supervision away from the Bank of England in 1997, but learned anew during the crisis).

It also explains why debt is not always the macroeconomic ogre that many fear: debt and money are two sides of the same coin, as it were, and the credit expansion that facilitates growth is usually accompanied by an increase in the measured money supply. To quote the Bank of England, "Commercial banks create money, in the form of bank deposits, by making new loans".[9] Those loans cannot be created unless someone wants to borrow. Viewing debt as a counterpart to the money supply makes it potentially a force for economic good, not evil, a lubricant that loosens the brakes on growth. The financial revolution of the late seventeenth century, which saw the creation of the national debt and the Bank of England, facilitated not just the financing of the wars with France, but the expansion of demand that backed the industrial revolution.[10] (There are even more straightforward reasons for thinking that the threat posed by aggregate debt is much smaller than the conventional narrative suggests, and we discuss them in Chapter 3.)

The long, piecemeal liberalisation and expansion of financial markets really gathered pace, and borrowing behaviour changed most markedly, in the early 1980s: this is when the rate of growth in financial balance sheets really accelerated most visibly relative to the wider economy. It coincided with rising living standards, and occasionally fostered a faster growth rate than would otherwise have been seen (for example, when the sale of council houses and the relaxation of mortgage controls culminated in the UK housing boom of the 1980s). The proportion of household income that was saved rather than spent fell markedly in both the US and UK in the 1980s relative to the 1970s, suggesting that factors other than income were boosting growth over this period. The same was true of the private sector as a whole – businesses and consumers together – and of national savings rates and financial balances generally, at the expense of the international balance of payments. The greater availability of credit facilitated this. However, easier credit may not have been the only, or even the main, cause of the lower savings ratios and faster real growth that occurred in the 1980s relative to the 1970s. The rapid inflation and social unease of the earlier decade had pushed household saving ratios higher for precautionary reasons, even as real interest rates had turned negative, and the subsequent return to "normality" under the Reagan and Thatcher administrations likely reduced the perceived need to save as much (even as real interest rates turned firmly positive again). And easy credit is unlikely to have been the main driver of economic growth during the post-1970s period as a whole.[11]

After the initial surge in credit, and the most intense wave of monetary innovation, in the early 1980s, the pace of credit expansion and liberalisation slowed for a while in the US and the UK.[12] In the seven years to the end of 1986, for example, total debt in the US economy surged from 150% of GDP, a level that had been broadly stable since the early 1960s, to around 205%, a proportionate increase of more than one-third. In the next eleven years, however, the debt to GDP ratio rose more slowly, to 235%, a further proportionate gain of just one-seventh (see Figure 3.1). There were certainly plenty of dramatic events during the latter period. It included Black Monday (the stock market crash of 19 October 1987, which still stands – and by some way – as the largest single-day decline in US stock prices).[13] It also included the subsequent boom and recession associated with surging real estate sectors on both sides of the Atlantic, the US savings-and-loan crisis and chronic federal budget and current account worries – the "twin deficits" – with their attendant currency volatility; and shortly afterwards, the UK's Black Wednesday (16 September 1992, and sterling's effective expulsion from the Exchange Rate Mechanism), with the ERM itself being tested severely in 1993 (before eventual monetary union – the euro – became reality in 1999). However, in contrast to the predictions of those commentators who'd been warning constantly of imminent economic doom and stock market collapse since the end of the gold standard, the wider, systemic impact of each of these events proved relatively short-lived and (in retrospect, judged by the standards of subsequent embarrassments and the turmoil of 2008/2009) mild.

The initial deregulation of credit and the opening-up of global currency and capital markets, and the following hiatus, thus passed if not without incident, at least without obvious systemic damage. The economic climate was one in which growth and inflation were if anything a little more sedate than they had been during the more constrained period (inflation most obviously, since it had been boosted sharply by the surging oil prices, poor labour relations and excessively loose policies – fiscal as much as monetary – that characterised the 1970s). There was a lot more debt, and many more assets too, but the impact of larger financial balance sheets on underlying economic performance was not dramatic.

By the mid-1990s, the stage was set however for a second surge in credit creation, against a backdrop in the United States of the Clinton administration's encouragement of affordable housing. This helped first-time buyers who previously could not have obtained access to mortgage finance to do so, a development that led to rapid growth in the sub-prime, or less creditworthy, part of the market. At the same time, there was an attempt formally to repeal the sections of the important 1933 Banking Act – known as Glass Steagall – that had been introduced after the 1929 Crash to prevent banks becoming directly involved in the securities and insurance markets. Repeal did not happen until 1999, but it was significant because it reflected a belief that derivatives, securitisation and credit insurance had so blurred the line between banking, capital markets and insurance activities that the Act had become almost an irrelevance. It was a symbolic acknowledgement of the scale of the piecemeal liberalisation that had already occurred.

In the UK, the experiment in the late 1980s with exchange rate targeting, culminating in the brief membership of the Exchange Rate mechanism, had had the effect of reintroducing a degree of rigidity to capital markets, and its passing in 1992 effectively gave renewed impetus to liberalisation and financial innovation generally. In 1997 the independence of the Bank of England, and the enhanced credibility it gave UK capital markets, added further momentum, as did the growing importation of securitisation techniques – a process that was not slowed by the Bank being relieved of its responsibility for banking supervision at the same time.

The property booms of the 1980s had led to economic hangovers in the form of painful US and UK recessions in 1990, but these had in turn faded and economies were growing again, sufficiently so for the US Federal Reserve to start raising interest rates from their emergency levels (which in those days was 3%). The stage was set for first of those substantial embarrassments for liberalised capital markets: the emerging markets bust sparked by that normalisation of US interest rates from 1994.

The emerging economies were opening up to business just as institutional investors were looking for alternative opportunities after the heady developed world expansion of the 1980s and the recessionary hangover that hit in 1990. Despite being more volatile and less liquid, emerging markets' strong performance encouraged many to view them as one-way bets. However, as the Federal Reserve started to return interest rates to more normal levels, the inflows to emerging markets reversed. Mexico was an early casualty, with its "Tequila" crisis in late 1994; but eventually it was to be Eastern emerging markets that were hit hardest. Exchange rates had not been liberalised as fully as in the developed world, and as funds flowed back out, pegged rates needed to be defended, which triggered recessions, a region-wide crisis in Asia from 1997, and a default on some of its bonds by Russia in 1998 (whose predicament had been worsened by a slump in oil prices). The Asian crisis in particular was traumatic, with currencies falling by 30–40% (in one case, by 80%), and cast a long economic shadow in the region; it also brought political change, as democratically elected governments were ousted in South Korea and Thailand, and a long-standing authoritarian regime in Indonesia fell. Malaysia reintroduced controls on the movement of capital, with some support from the academic consensus, which noted the special difficulties faced by small countries in a world of freely moving capital in keeping their domestic policies on an even keel.

For a while it seemed as if the Asian crisis might have a wider impact. *The Economist* magazine carried a leader in mid-1998 warning that "Britain's next recession" could be imminent, partly because of the impact of Asia's slump on UK exports. In the event, the damage was largely contained. But the emerging markets' implosion led quickly to a second embarrassment for liberalised capital markets: the failure of Long Term Capital Management (LTCM), a US hedge fund whose collapse threatened wider monetary and economic disruption for a while in late 1998.[14] It followed closely on the heels of Russia's bond default in August 1998, and seemed to represent a greater systemic threat. It was stock market volatility that did most damage to LTCM, whose owners ironically included some of the cleverest and best-connected people in capital markets. LTCM had been able, in the more loosely controlled capital markets, to accumulate massive positions not just in Russian bonds but also to take a huge short position in equity volatility: specifically, it had bet that stock markets would stay stable by writing huge numbers of derivatives contracts that left LTCM exposed if volatility spiked, as it did. The returns that LTCM had stood to make if its bets had worked out would have been small, but by using borrowed funds to make them it was able to scale them up into (in theory) an attractive investment proposition.[15] Unfortunately, that leverage worked even more dramatically when things when wrong. And LTCM's brokers and bankers, eager to lend to one of their biggest customers, found themselves financially embarrassed: they hadn't realised – or had failed to check – that LTCM had been everybody's favourite customer.

As the scale of the seizure became apparent, the US stock market, which had previously largely shrugged off the Asian crisis, fell sharply, and at the start of September was more than 20% below its July peak. The Federal Reserve Bank of New York eventually organised a bailout by LTCM's main creditors and counterparties in late September,[16] and the markets stabilised and rallied – hitting a new high before year-end. Again, the wider global economy was ultimately little affected by the episode, though many thought that it might be.

As normal service resumed, a further consideration encouraged the Federal Reserve to err on the side of generosity in its money-market operations through 1999. The imminent calendar changes associated with the millennium were thought to pose a material risk (the "Y2K" threat) to computing systems generally, including those in the capital markets. The policy response of generous liquidity provision, coming hard on the heels of the Fed-assisted solution to the LTCM debacle, created the impression that the monetary authorities were effectively underwriting risk-taking: there was talk of a "Greenspan put", a put option being a derivative that offers insurance against lower prices. This impression coincided, unfortunately, with a big increase in the number of high-risk investment opportunities. The internet and mobile telecommunications were becoming a hot investment theme as technology – and government licensing – developed rapidly: the transmission and ownership of digital media, and the potential for doing business online, developed into the dotcom or TMT (telecom, media, technology) craze. Books were (quickly) written on the "new", "weightless" or "wired" economy; pundits talked of the internet abolishing scarcity; and sceptics were told they just didn't "get it".

The valuations of the TMT sectors in stock markets, and in some cases of more prosaic businesses that had quickly grown an internet or e-business dimension, rose through the roof, with a merger and acquisition frenzy adding to the euphoria. By early 2000, the market value of the TMT sectors in the US stock market had risen to 45% from just 22% only four years earlier, and the valuation of the overall market itself had risen to levels not seen before or since (there will be a more careful discussion of stock market valuation in Chapter 7). Pets.com and Boo.com quickly came and even more quickly went; a UK company called Freeserve briefly traded at valuations that implied it might eventually account for two-fifths of all UK retail sales; the UK government raised £22.5 billion (equivalent to more than 10% of GDP at the time) by auctioning five radio spectrum licences to 3G mobile telecom operators, an out-turn that was greeted by the boom's cheerleaders as suggesting that the operators must be even more valuable than investors had realised; Amazon, Nokia, Oracle, SAP and Vodafone seemed poised to take over the world; and a French sewage company did take over Universal Studios. It did all end in stock market tears, the third of those big embarrassments for deregulated capital markets, but one that again had little direct economic fallout. There was a US recession in 2001, but even amplified and prolonged by the terrorist attacks of that September it was still one of the shortest and mildest on record and in more recent data has subsequently been largely revised away. The UK and eurozone economies escaped with even less cyclical damage.

The TMT-driven stock market surge that peaked in March 2000 was followed by a prolonged slide that saw the US stock market lose half its value, with the TMT bloc shrinking by four-fifths, and European stocks falling even further. The US market was the first to stabilise, in late 2002, with the European market – which had been prone to even more fanciful thinking than the US – and the developed bloc generally following in early 2003. The wider rebound began without an obvious trigger as the second Iraq war was entering its climactic phase, a classic illustration both of how turning points do not always require an obvious catalyst, and of how bad news can be discounted in advance. As stock markets languished, however, and the scale of the earlier overvaluation became apparent, so institutional investors – still enjoying easy and historically inexpensive access to liquidity – began to look for alternative opportunities. Embarrassment number four was at hand.

A supporting role in this one was played, with the best of intentions, by accountants and regulators. Even before the debacle of the new economy, the UK pension industry, shaken by the Maxwell scandal in 1990 and subsequent changes in pension accounting standards, and encouraged by the trend towards lower inflation, had been viewing bonds more favourably. The TMT fiasco and "liability driven investing" gave added impetus to the trend. Conventional government bond yields had fallen a long way from the inflation-driven highs of the late 1970s/early 1980s, and pension fund and other institutional investors' attention extended to other "fixed income" assets – including corporate bonds and asset-backed securities (ABS). Again, liquidity conditions remained generous and capital flows mostly unfettered: even as the Federal Reserve again started to normalise monetary conditions from 2004, newly prominent hedge funds in particular found it relatively easy to borrow.

ABS are the securitised bonds encountered in Chapter 1. They had been around in modern form since the early 1970s, and had long been an important source of US housing finance.[17] They carried higher yields than government bonds, and their appeal now was strengthened as discussed in Chapter 1 by the new forms in which they were bundled, packaged and leveraged as part of the innovations in credit insurance. That credit insurance itself encouraged institutional investors to take more risk than they otherwise might have done, and the traditional safeguards on conventional corporate loans and bonds were gradually loosened in a climate in which financial risk seemed to have been tamed. Even stock market volatility faded markedly: implied volatility as measured by the VIX, the so-called fear index that tracks the cost of buying portfolio insurance, fell to a low of 10% in early 2007.

As noted, the US recession of 2000 had been a modest one, and the developed world economic climate – as opposed to the climate in stock markets – had by this time been benign for the best part of a decade. In the US in particular, economists labelled a decline in economic volatility "the Great Moderation", a phrase given wider circulation by Ben Bernanke in 2004 (he was to take over from Greenspan as Federal Reserve Chairman in February 2006). In the UK, the Governor of the Bank of England, Mervyn King, talked in 2003 of a non-inflationary, consistently expansionary (or NICE) decade, though he warned that it was unlikely to last.

Meanwhile, China's accession to the World Trade Organisation in 2001 had triggered a renewed wave of interest in emerging markets, popularised in Goldman Sachs' BRIC report (on Brazil, Russia, India and China). The emerging world's industrialisation, and its focus on commodities – epitomised by China's demand for Brazil's metal and energy – represented a further unconventional opportunity for institutional investors, and as central bankers became a little too complacent, and credit markets got more expensive and yields dipped ever closer to those on government bonds, emerging stock markets and commodity markets embarked on what were deemed "supercycles" of their own – embarrassments numbers five and six. The near-doubling of food commodity prices in little more than two years to mid-2008 rightly caused considerable political unease as the cost of living for poorer emerging world consumers was pushed higher as a direct result of footloose capital's single-minded hunt for returns. The gap between US ABS yields and government bond yields hit a low point in 2005 as their prices were bid higher (yield levels had dipped as low as 2.5% in 2004 – they have been recently lower again, but this largely reflects the post-crisis decline in the general level of interest rates and government bond yields); emerging markets outperformed developed markets by around 200% over the seven years to mid-2008; and the overall CRB spot commodity index surged by two-thirds in the three years to mid-2008, at which point, Brent crude oil prices stood at $140 per barrel, compared with less than $10 per barrel in late 1998, shortly after Russia's default.

The collapse of the credit boom, and the passing of the emerging market and commodities fads, takes us through to the eruption of the crisis itself, which began rumbling in early 2007 and of course erupted fully with Lehman's collapse – and AIG's near collapse – in September 2008. A downturn in the US housing market, where reckless borrowing from reckless lenders – encouraged by some reckless politicians – exposed the wishful assumptions and valuation defying complexity underpinning much of the new credit markets. The sub-prime segment was plunged into financial distress, with the consequences that reverberated around the world. Emerging stock markets and commodities for a while looked to be insulated against the freezing of developed world liquidity, but for a while only.

These successive episodes from the mid-1990s onwards, culminating in the panic of mid-September 2008 to mid-March 2009 – a period during which implied US stock market volatility averaged 51%, making the world's largest market for corporate control a lottery – were not the result of something gravely wrong in the engine room of the global economy. Many large, non-financial businesses sailed through the successive financial storms in good shape. There were of course some real tensions in the economy – most notably the imbalance in trade between the United States and China – and they attracted considerable attention (and had done for some years). Viewed in context, however, these tensions were manageable, and not the immediate cause of the panic (see Chapter 3). The world would have been poorer had the US not imported as much as it did.

Taking the post-liberalisation period as a whole, the big picture is not one of a developed world economy boosted giddily by the expansion of credit. The conventional narrative account, in which paper money and cheap credit created an inflationary boom that had to end in tears, is less convincing than the more episodic narrative of accidents and embarrassments, and doesn't sit as easily with the facts. Nominal GDP growth – output growth and inflation together – was more *muted* in the post-liberalisation world. Between 1979 and the peak year of 2008, the compound nominal growth rates achieved by the US and UK economies – the US being of course by a long way the single largest and most important driver of global economic and financial trends, and the UK being one of the largest developed economies and very much in the van of global financial liberalisation alongside the US – were three and two percentage points per annum slower respectively than those achieved in the previous 29 years. On closer inspection, both real output and the price level grew more slowly in the US; in the UK, output growth was similar to that in the earlier period, but inflation a lot lower. The scale of the slowdown is of course dependent on the exact points of comparison, but the key point is that there was no dramatic acceleration. The notion that the post-liberalisation era was a prolonged debt-fuelled spending binge is mistaken.

We don't know of course what might have happened had things been different: it is possible that without the surge in borrowing, real and nominal economic growth might have been still slower. As noted above, when we look at the behaviour of households on both sides of the Atlantic we find that the proportion of their disposable income that was spent was higher after 1979, and their savings ratios were correspondingly lower, which is consistent with a greater use of credit. Had these shifts not occurred, growth would have been slower. The macroeconomic climate in the 1970s had been tough, however, as we also noted earlier, and some of the decline in savings ratios likely reflected a smaller perceived need to save for precautionary reasons. Households felt able to relax as the danger of runaway inflation eased, the real value of their bank deposits stabilised, the risk of losing their jobs faded, and the real value of their other assets – homes and investments – began to improve (we will discuss the historical and balance sheet perspectives further in Chapter 3). A greater availability of credit was associated with the lower savings ratios, and helped facilitate them, but was not necessarily their prime mover: they might have fallen even if credit had not been easier to come by. At the economy-wide level, the behaviour of US and UK companies and governments didn't change as markedly, and the overall contribution to GDP growth from lowered national savings ratios in the US and UK between 1979 and 2007 was relatively modest, at *less than a quarter of a percentage point per annum on average.*

As Figure 2.1 suggests, the link between borrowing and economic growth is a loose and flexible one. From the 1970s, the global economy effectively burst free of the rigid constraints posed by the gold standard, fixed exchange rates and capital controls, and greater access to credit can be seen as part of the process – extra lubrication for a motor already in motion. In practice, however, credit can be used more widely than simply to transact the goods and services that enter GDP: it can be used to acquire and transfer assets. Much of the credit expansion of the 1980s, and of the late 1990s and 2000s, was associated with balance sheet transactions, most notably the acquisition of already existing houses and of savings plans. The prices of homes and of financial assets rose strongly over this period, but not without reason: rising household formation, declining interest rates and improved profitability were also working to push prices – and demand for credit – higher. And the

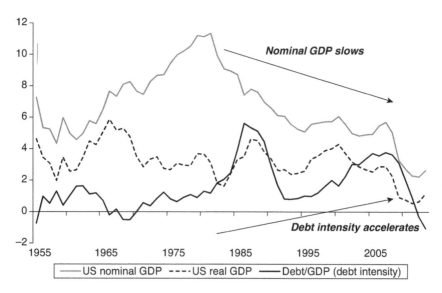

Figure 2.1   Growth in US GDP and debt intensity, 1955–2015, five-year moving averages

Source: Federal Reserve, Datastream, author's calculations.

direct economic impact of this balance sheet expansion on growth was, as noted, relatively modest.

Particularly after 1997, the surge in borrowing was not necessary for GDP growth and was not directly fuelling it – which is why, after 2009, a *lack* of loan growth has not prevented the global economy from stabilising and more than regaining the ground lost in the Great Recession. The expansion of financial balance sheets has coincided with rising prosperity, but has more likely reflected it than caused it: a greater take-up of financial services, like spending on service sectors generally, may simply be a characteristic of wealthier economies. Again, this is not to suggest that our banks are run as well as they might be.

Remember, this more ad hoc but benign account of the origins and nature of the crisis is at odds with the prevailing public mood and most other published accounts. If the panic of 2008–2009 can be seen as the biggest in a succession of financial accidents in a liberalised global capital market, and not as a sign that the global economy has been built on sand, the implications for investment (and the wider economic outlook) are potentially profound. The accidents were a consequence of financial liberalisation and innovation, and have done much to ensure that regulators and supervisors will now reverse some of it. Those of us who believe that markets are best left to themselves where possible can't now easily make that case for the financial markets. But that is not the same thing as saying – as many have been – that the global economy can't grow, that the developed world is bankrupt and that savers should keep their money under the mattress. Or that everything is hunky dory in the economics and finance textbooks.

3

FIVE BIG THINGS TO WORRY LESS ABOUT – OR WHY IT STILL PAYS TO INVEST IN THE WEST

I keep thinking there is bound to be something else. I could hear it sometimes, but I couldn't play it.

– Charlie Parker[1]

Often it seems there must be something obvious to be said about a particularly hot topic, only for us to find that things are actually a little more complicated than they seemed. All that debt; our aging populations; the competitive threat; the sustainability challenge; geopolitical tensions – these are all major and plausible concerns, and might be thought to point to some obvious (and pessimistic) investment conclusions. They needn't. Because they are all such big and embracing issues, on closer inspection they turn out to be more complicated and nuanced than the headlines suggest, and there are simply too many moving parts even for the brightest and best minds to disentangle. If Charlie Parker couldn't play something, it wasn't playable.

A book could easily be written on each of these concerns, and they are just some of the most pressing issues that have been worrying investors of late. However, in this chapter I will illustrate briefly why each of them is much more nuanced than it might appear at first sight, and why the best advice in each case – and in the case of a few secondary issues tackled in Chapter 4, and indeed in investing generally – is to try to keep an open mind.

If you focus unquestioningly only on the potential bad stuff, you will miss opportunities. It is a longer chapter, but perhaps the most important in the book, because it makes the case for investing at the most basic level. After all, if we're doomed economically, what's the point of saving?

LIFE AFTER DEBT

We worked through Spring and Winter, through Summer and
through Fall
But the mortgage worked the hardest and the steadiest of us all
It worked on nights and Sundays, it worked each holiday
It settled down among us and it never went away

— US folk song, 1890s

Debt has grown rapidly in the US and the UK as financial markets have been liberalised, outpacing their economies, and is central to the conventional narrative outlined in Chapter 1: it is probably the macroeconomic issue that has received more attention of late than any other. The concern is understandable. If you have a mortgage but no job, or your mortgage is large relative to your income; if you've borrowed to start a business and your customers are slow to pay; or if you are the finance minister of a small country whose predecessor borrowed recklessly, then debt can be a life-changing burden. Intuitively, it seems as if this must be the case collectively too: if it is bad for individuals, surely it must be equally bad when added up across the economy as a whole. Debt played a big role in the panic of late 2008 and early 2009, and the work of Reinhart and Rogoff, also noted in Chapter 1, has given added academic authority to the instinctive idea that debt is a bad thing, period.

However, what is true for individuals in this case does not hold to nearly the same degree at the global level. Debt does matter, of course; and in the short-term it can pose serious difficulties to the economy, as we saw. But the extent to which aggregate debt can be a sustained threat to collective living standards is routinely and hugely overstated.

Here are two typical comments on debt:

"Global Debt Exceeds $100 Trillion as Governments Binge." (Bloomberg, 9 March 2014)

"public debt allows the current generation...to live at the expense of those as yet too young to vote or as yet unborn." (Niall Ferguson, 2012)

Each begs the same implicit question: who has been doing the lending? If the world has borrowed more than $100 trillion,[2] to whom does it owe it? If our children will have to make good our borrowing, to whom will they repay it? We can't borrow from Mars – if we could, the syndication desks would surely have been out there back in 2005/2006 – so whoever has been doing all that lending is on this planet too. We may not realise that we are lenders as well as borrowers, but we are, because we own the banks from whom we've borrowed – or our governments do, and we collectively own those. And our children can only repay any debt they inherit – the public (or national, or government) debt, since most private debt formally lapses with the estate of the borrower – to others living at the same time, that is, to their own generation.[3]

For every borrower there is of course a lender: at the level of society as a whole there is no "net" debt. Insolvency refers to a situation in which outstanding claims exceed available assets: in aggregate, society as a whole cannot be meaningfully insolvent since its financial claims are also its liabilities – collectively we have no creditors. Almost all analyses of the debt crisis pay little or no attention to this rather important point. The failure of common sense to make itself heard on this and other topics is one of the main themes of this book: in Chapter 4 we'll suggest a few reasons why received wisdom so easily goes astray.

Debt directly neither reduces nor raises aggregate wealth: as the borrower's financial balance sheet has a liability added to it, the lender's gains an asset. If borrowers are more likely to spend than lenders, then spending fuelled by it, and any bank failures that result from it not being repaid and having to be written-off, can certainly have a potent short-term economic impact. One can imagine special circumstances in which that cyclical effect does some medium-term damage to the economic system, or in which a badly designed and public debt-funded infrastructure project leaves a legacy of inefficiency. The debt itself however does not represent a long-term constraint on the economy's ability to grow.

The crisis has been followed by a modest shrinkage in the amount of debt relative to aggregate incomes, but it remains at levels that are much closer to historic highs than lows, and the pessimists who believe that the global economy has been built on sand are as worried as ever.[4] But once we accept the validity of some borrowing – and few would suggest returning to the strict controls of the 1960s and 1970s – we have to recognise that it is difficult to know what the "right" amount of debt might be. The notional tipping point at which it becomes problematic is known as a "Minsky moment", after Hyman Minsky, an economist who studied the evolution of credit cycles, but there is no way of spotting one in advance.

Even a sudden seemingly sharp rise can be benign. Imagine you have left your wallet at home, find yourself short of cash in the lunch queue, and borrow £5 from a friend, acknowledging the debt to him with an IOU. The next day he finds himself in a similar position, and a third friend similarly lends him £5. The day after, the third friend is embarrassed, and borrows £5 from you in the same fashion. Total debt has risen by £15, total lending has risen by the same amount, and nobody is better or worse off than they would otherwise have been. They would however have been hungrier – and the canteen poorer – had the borrowing not occurred: the debt has acted as money and facilitated trade. In principle, IOUs could be extended like this without limit, and without the borrowing being used to buy anything.

Borrowing without a particular transaction in mind might seem point-less, and at some stage we would worry about the incidental costs imposed by the time spent arranging and swapping all those IOUs, but it would be diffi-cult to know at what point – if ever – the process itself directly threatened the business of getting lunch. Much of the modern financial system effectively consists of such overlapping and ultimately self-cancelling IOUs – gross bor-rowing that nets out to nothing, and which in many cases has no transactional point. This is hardly an advertisement for the system: like the high-frequency stock market dealing infrastructure that has tunnelled through mountains to allow trades to process a few milliseconds faster, you suspect that the resources might be better used elsewhere. That's not the point, however.

Our benign lunch queue arrangement can become problematic if one of the parties in the chain of IOUs becomes unable to settle their debt for some reason, leaving the lender short of funds and other lenders anxious to call in their own IOUs early for fear of the same thing happening to them. In our example, some of our friends might find themselves without lunch for a few days. In late 2008, investors who'd lent to Lehman Brothers, and who had assets in custody with them, suddenly found those assets frozen, and were themselves unable to keep their own promises. And beneath the moun-tain of complex gross exposures, some banks were made insolvent by the fall in the market value of the property held as collateral against their lending. Some small countries faced similar difficulties – Iceland's banks failed and its currency collapsed, and at a later date (and for different reasons) Greece saw its government debt restructured. But even as the decline in that US col-lateral, amplified and exaggerated by the impact of mark-to-market account-ing policies, exceeded $1 trillion, the Federal Reserve, the US Treasury, the Bank of England, the European Central Bank and other institutions – who were much criticised at the time for their improvisatory approach – man-aged to contain those insolvencies. Ultimately they were able credibly to do so because that mountain of gross debt had not affected the underlying pro-ductive potential of the US and global economy.

At the height of the panic, when faith in bank-created money itself seemed at risk, events could easily have turned out differently, resulting in a deeper downturn – luckily, as noted earlier, we didn't find out. The point is that it was impossible beforehand, or now, to know what level of gross borrowing is the "right" level – and if borrowing is controlled too tightly, too many people in our example may have to skip lunch. Bankers did not conspire to take us to the edge of the monetary abyss, but collectively the industry behaved stupidly and greedily. Much lending and borrowing was reckless, and needlessly complicated, increasing the chance that the gross borrowing would cause systemic difficulties when defaults occurred. Regulators and supervisors were clearly asleep at the wheel. Banks and CDS markets are facing tighter controls now, and higher equity ratios – tempering the extent to which banks themselves borrow – are being used to reduce the potential for future seizures.[5] But a Great Deleveraging that will shrink most consumer, corporate and government balance sheets back to some pre-crisis ideal has always been unlikely, and I suspect that the volume of financial instruments globally will stabilise and perhaps even start to rise again, relative to incomes, as economies continue to grow. The flexibility provided by access to borrowing and financial products generally may simply be increasingly demanded as people and economies get wealthier in real terms.

Because this is another effect of the focus on debt, and on financial instruments generally: it can make us forget that our collective wealth is not ultimately financial in nature. Financial assets and liabilities are entitlements and obligations: they do not directly produce anything, or yield the sort of direct satisfaction that tangible treasure such as art or jewellery might. In paying so much attention to financial balance sheets we overlook the fact that society's stock of productive capital in particular is high, and growing steadily. Its content is evolving – away from heavy industrial assets, and towards intangible technological know-how – but it is expanding most of the time. We'll discuss why that is shortly, but the point is that while there may be no net debt, there is real net wealth, a lot of it, and it is owned by households, as the ultimate owners and stakeholders of businesses and representative governments.[6] And it is productive capital that matters most for economic growth – and which is in turn itself augmented by that economic growth.

To illustrate the way in which gross and net debt, and economic and financial assets, can get so tangled up in the public debate, let's take a quick look at the United States. The US consumer is customer number one for Global Inc., and the American economy is still the most important driver of global capital markets. Its economic and financial data are not perfect, but they are amongst the best established and most comprehensive we have. It is also the country about which people take the most entrenched views: we are told often – and with relish – that the US is bankrupt, and that global capitalism's days are numbered accordingly. However, the popular perception is a caricature – and a massively misleading one.

Figure 3.1 features prominently in the debt debate. It is based on data available at the Federal Reserve's website: it shows total US debt as a proportion of GDP, broken down into the four domestic sectors – households, businesses, the government and banks. This chart is as far as most analyses of debt go. It shows that the total amount of US debt rose from around 140% of GDP in late 1963 to peak at around 360% in mid-2009, before falling back a little to around 330% at the end of 2013. Taking the 50-year period as a whole, total US debt grew at a compound annual rate of 8.5%, compared with nominal GDP growth of 6.7% (a relatively small gap, you might think, which illustrates both the power of compound arithmetic *and* the danger of spurious precision). The impression conveyed by the chart is that debt mostly grew in line with the economy through the 1960s and 1970s, when the line is flat; it accelerated markedly, and grew much faster than GDP, with the financial liberalisation of the early 1980s; the pace of increase in debt relative to GDP then slowed for a while, before reaccelerating in the late 1990s and the 2000s, and then falling back as noted – for the first time, but not far – after 2007. Indications currently are that it is stabilising.

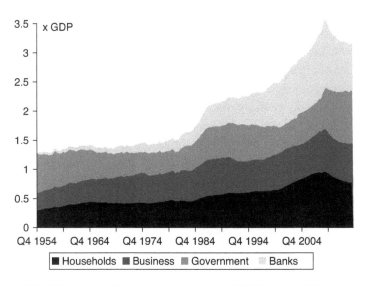

Figure 3.1   US debt outstanding, as a proportion of GDP, 1954–2014
Source: Federal Reserve, Datastream, author's calculations.

Within the total, each of the four sectors has seen its debt grow faster than the economy. Taking the period as a whole, it is the financial sector itself whose liabilities have expanded most, reflecting the increased layering and complexity of financial activity. Since 2007, as the private sectors' debt ratios have fallen, the government's have expanded, reflecting the economic firefighting role played by fiscal policy as it helped stabilise the economy.

The data in the chart include loans and mortgages but also bonds – borrowing in the shape of securities that can be traded, which is the form that most borrowing by governments in particular takes. But derivatives, which include debt-like obligations, and which would add hugely to total gross financial liabilities, are not included. Nor are some intra-sector liabilities – for example, much of US banks' borrowing amongst themselves. The chart thus shows only the underlying debt liabilities of each sector to the others, and to the rest of the world (the international borrowing that troubles so many commentators). Nonetheless, there is enough in the chart for it to appear unsettling.

However, while the four sectors are distinctively important economically, as we've noted, simply adding up their debts may not be a very meaningful thing to do. Governments issue bonds to consumers and banks; banks lend to consumers but also borrow and accept deposits from them; companies borrow from banks but also have deposits with them. But these cross-holdings – each sector's ownership of other sectors' debts and bonds – are ignored. Moreover, no account is being taken of the other assets held by each sector, which will include the bulk of the real economic capital of the US economy. The household sector for example owns most of the corporate sector and housing stock, and the value of its homes hugely exceeds the mortgages outstanding against them, but these assets are ignored. A more useful picture of the aggregate position requires more consolidated and complete data – but where do we draw the lines?

Figure 3.2 shows the evolution of US households' net wealth over the same period for which Figure 3.1 showed the US economy's escalating total borrowing – and tells a rather different story. Consumers' gross debt is shown – the same line as in Figure 3.1, but here with a negative sign to indicate that it is a liability. But above it, in positive territory, can be seen US consumers' financial assets, which alongside their holdings of cash and government bonds will include the securities and other equity investments that represent their ownership of the bulk of the corporate sector and its productive assets. Figure 3.2 also shows households' directly owned tangible assets – their houses and durable goods – and the sector's net worth, that is, the sum of its financial and tangible assets less the debt. Even as its debt has

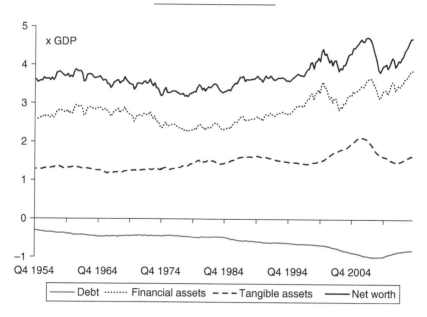

Figure 3.2 US households' aggregate balance sheet, as a proportion of GDP, 1954–2014

Source: Federal Reserve, Datastream, author's calculations.

risen, its net worth has risen too, and has remained firmly positive through-out the last half-century. In 2013 alone, the increase in US consumers' net worth, in absolute terms, was roughly equivalent to the GDP of China. Far from being notionally bankrupt,[7] the average US consumer is one of the wealthiest people on the planet – because they effectively own most of the US economy, one of its most productive assets. Its value can fall as well as rise of course; but even at the low point of the latest episode, that value was still substantial.

Of course, the distribution of US consumers' massive aggregate wealth is highly unequal – as is the distribution of their incomes. Big inequalities in wealth and living standards, particularly if they arise from unequal oppor-tunities, are unfair, and may need to be addressed through the political sys-tem. There is however no sign that the reported increase in inequality within the wealthier Western economies in recent years, described most recently by Thomas Piketty,[8] has had a material effect on US consumers' spending behaviour. And more progressive, redistributive taxes on individuals, if cho-sen by voters, might be designed so as to minimise any impact on growth.

Figure 3.3 shows the US net international position, including overseas borrowing by its government and banks, and its international investments in overseas business and other assets. The US is an international debtor – its

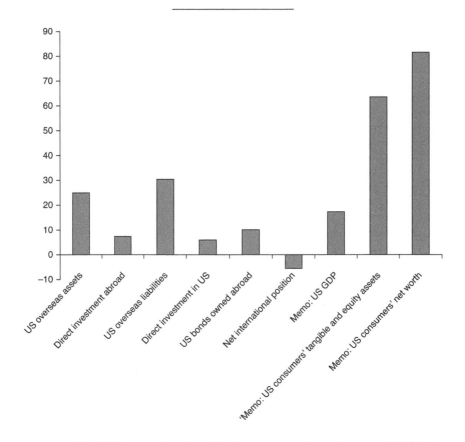

Figure 3.3   The US' international position in context: selected assets and liabilities, $ trillions, Q2 2014

Source: BEA, Federal Reserve, author's calculations.

identified liabilities to foreign lenders and investors exceed its identified overseas assets – but the balance, at roughly a third of US GDP, is modest when compared to the scale of the gross assets and liabilities, and even more so when set alongside US consumer wealth. Put bluntly, US borrowing from (amongst others) China is of little consequence when set against the size of US consumer assets (though the sheer size of the US means that its borrowing can occasionally influence international liquidity). It is the equivalent perhaps of someone with a large savings plan and substantial home equity using a credit card for incidental purchases. Moreover, US liabilities are largely denominated in dollars. A decline in the value of the dollar increases the relative value of US overseas assets, and reduces the burden of its dollar borrowings.[9] Its overseas assets also tend to be disproportionately tilted towards direct investment, which is more likely to grow over time, rather than bonds and loans.

Some of the household sector's net worth in Figure 3.2 is purely financial, and not directly backed by the ownership of a real asset: it includes cash, bank deposits and bonds. It also implicitly values the business assets held by consumers in line with the markets' collective appraisal of them, and as we shall see in Part II these valuations are far from fixed or incontrovertible. But the point is that there is (of course) much more to the US collective balance sheet than its gross debt, which includes massive double-counting, suggests.

Table 3.1 shows selected aggregate liabilities and assets for the US, the UK and Ireland. The massive financial sectors in the UK and Ireland illustrate clearly the short-term risks that can (and did) arise when assets and liabilities are not matched exactly, and declines in the value of the assets (a bank loan, say) lead quickly to losses that are large when compared with the size of the local economies. However, many of the assets and liabilities are the exact same instruments, which are simply being held in both economies' large and internationally open fund-management sectors. If a client's investment portfolio shrinks in value, so too does their fund manager's liability to them. And again, even the large losses on banks' riskier activities in 2008 looked less daunting when viewed in the context of underlying net worth or solvency.

In the UK, the Office for National Statistics has estimated the net wealth of the country as a whole: relative to the size of the economy, liabilities are massive, but assets are even larger, and UK households' net worth is on a par with their US peers. The UK also has a small net international liability (which is quite capable of being reversed by fluctuations in exchange rates

Table 3.1   Selected assets, liabilities and household net worth for the US, UK and Ireland

Trillions of $, £, €	US	UK	Ireland
Memo: annualised GDP	$17.3	£1.6	€0.2
Total financial liabilities	$190.2	£30.4	€5.1
Total financial assets	$198.3	£30.1	€4.9
Total overseas liabilities	$29.5	£10.0	€3.2
Total overseas assets	$24.0	£9.7	€3.0
Net international position	−$5.5	−£0.3	−€0.2
Household net worth[a]	$80.1	£8.2	€0.5

[a]Net financial assets, including ownership of business, plus housing assets (and in the US and UK, other fixed assets).

Note: UK data as of end-2013; for the US and Ireland, Q1 2014.

Source: UK ONS; US BEA, Federal Reserve; Ireland CSO, Central Bank of Ireland. Total financial assets and liabilities are not defined precisely the same way in each country: the table is a guide to orders of magnitude only. Note that GDP in Ireland is about one-sixth larger than its GNP, reflecting the large overseas-owned sector.

and stock market values). Consolidated total wealth data for Ireland are patchier, and its net international liabilities are substantial relative to the size of its economy – but again, they are only a fraction of the headline gross amounts that feature in the public debate. Irish consumers' net worth is also firmly positive, suggesting that they remain collectively solvent, though it's a closer call than for the two larger economies.

Whether official statisticians can ever really construct a convincing comprehensive national balance sheet is a moot point – even if they can accurately take stock of all the things that have a measurable worth, there is surely more to national wealth than that – but at the very least they remind us that balance sheets have two sides, and that the ultimate ownership of valuable real productive resources still largely resides with domestic households. Again, we are not arguing that debt doesn't matter, only that its aggregate importance has been sharply overstated by the current crisis-driven focus on gross financial magnitudes.

Today's low interest rates are a further reason for thinking that the aggregate debt burden is manageable: even though there is a lot of debt, the cost of servicing it is historically small (Figure 3.4). But we can't make too much of this. If financial balance sheets are not a major collective problem, then interest costs may be less macroeconomically significant too, and are probably not a major reason to be optimistic on growth. Interest charges, like debt, represent a transfer of spending power from one agent (the borrower)

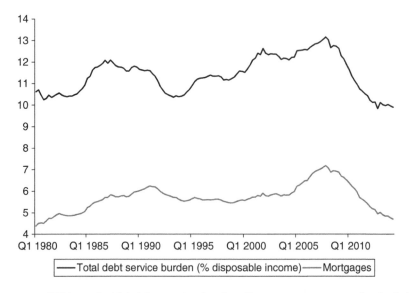

Figure 3.4 US households' debt service burden (interest payments and scheduled repayments), 1980–2014, % of disposable incomes

Source: Federal Reserve.

to another (the lender), not a net increase in the size of the economic cake – which is why they are largely netted off when official statisticians calculate GDP. By contrast, consumers' collective ownership of business assets brings with it a primary economic income, or value added, in the form of profits and dividends.

In practice, there is some net effect: borrowers are likely to spend more as rates fall, while lenders are unlikely to cut their spending by a similar amount (when rates go up, lenders save much of the increase, while borrowers cut back on spending). But most of the time, the redistributive impact of changes in interest rates on total spending is unlikely to make the difference between ongoing growth and stagnation.

In conclusion, then, debt represents a redistribution of current spending power from lender to borrower, in exchange for a promise that the flow will be reversed in the future. As we saw in Chapter 2 and in our example above, it can increase liquidity. Lenders and borrowers are often different people, but not always: in the example above, the lunch queue borrowers also have assets; and in the real world many people with a mortgage also have savings and pension plans, while companies often have cash in the bank at the same time as borrowing in the credit markets. A careful analysis of its redistributive and monetary impact is not, however, what the public debate has been about. That debate says simply and loudly that there is too much debt, and that it is an impediment to sustainable growth. This is too pessimistic. There must be some limit to borrowing for individuals, sectors, governments and smaller countries – but in practice the limits are likely to be loose, and to vary over time, depending on would-be lenders' willingness to lend. Levels of debt associated with the Great Panic may yet become commonplace – and new, as yet unscaled levels may perhaps be associated with the next seizure. A population whose living standards and tangible assets are growing steadily may have greater uses for the flexibility facilitated by debt – and by financial services generally – and use disproportionately more of it.

DEFUSING THE DEMOGRAPHIC TIMEBOMB

You don't object to an aged parent, I hope?

Dickens, "Great Expectations"

There are few things that can be predicted 30 years ahead with any confidence – remember the warning earlier about making forecasts – but the greying of the world's population is one of them. Fertility and mortality rates change only slowly, and most of the people who will be alive in 30 years' time are already born. The proportion of the world's population that is elderly is set to grow markedly.

Data compiled by the US bureau of the census (one of several credible sources for such projections) suggest that the proportion of the global population aged 65 and above will almost double, rising from 8% in 2011 to 15% in 2041. For Europe, the proportion is set to rise from 16% to 26%. France, Germany and Italy, the three largest Continental economies, will collectively see this age group grow from 19% to 28% of the population; the UK will see it rise from 17% to 25%. In the US, the increase will be from 13% to 20%. In Japan it will rise from 23% to 37%; in China from 9% to 24%; and in Russia from 13% to 23%. Countries and regions at the other end of the scale are India and Africa, where the over-65 group accounts for just 6% and 3% respectively of the populations to start with (though both groups are still likely to double in size).

The world's population, though aging, will still get bigger: over the next 30 years, it is projected to grow by around 30%, from seven billion people today to just under nine billion. Growth will be fastest in India and Africa, and to a smaller extent the US and UK. Continental Europe, China, Japan and Russia will however see their populations decline, which will make their aging of greater significance.

There are many reasons for this greying. Life expectancy has risen as the basic necessities of life – food, drink, shelter – have become more widely available, healthcare has improved, and lifestyles and working practices have become safer. Birth rates in some cases have fallen because of changes in government policies (as in China, with the one child policy it pursued for many years) and altered social norms (the greater availability of birth control, a fashion for smaller families). In many developing countries, they have fallen because people are better off, and no longer need as many children to look after them in old age. In many developed countries, the long-term decline in birth rates was interrupted for a while by the post-war "baby boom", which is leaving behind a particularly pronounced grey bulge as the boomers retire. Whatever their causes, these trends have long been worrying economists – and adding to our gloom.

There have been innumerable papers and books on what has become known as the "demographic time bomb". Here is the introduction to a particularly influential article published some years back:

The list of major global hazards ... includes the proliferation of nuclear, biological, and chemical weapons, other types of high-tech terrorism, deadly superviruses, extreme climate change, the financial, economic, and political aftershocks of globalization, and the violent ethnic explosions waiting to be detonated in today's unsteady new democracies. Yet there is a less-understood challenge – the graying (sic) of the developed world's population – that may actually do more to reshape our collective future than any of the above.

Unlike with global warming, there can be little debate over whether or when global aging will manifest itself. And unlike with other challenges...the costs of global aging will be far beyond the means of even the world's wealthiest nations – unless retirement benefit systems are radically reformed. Failure to do so, to prepare early and boldly enough, will spark economic crises that will dwarf the recent meltdowns in Asia and Russia.

> Peter G Peterson, "Gray Dawn: The Global Aging Crisis",
> Foreign Affairs, January/February 1999

Some of Peterson's other concerns are tackled in this chapter too. In case you think his account a little idiosyncratic, here is a more recent example:

From the fall of the Roman and the Mayan empires to the Black Death to the colonization of the New World and the youth-driven revolutions of the twentieth century, demographic trends have played a decisive role in many of the great invasions, political upheavals, migrations, and environmental catastrophes of history. By the 2020s, an ominous new conjuncture of demographic trends may once again threaten widespread disruption. We are talking about global aging, which is likely to have a profound effect on economic growth, living standards, and the shape of the world order.

> Neil Howe and Richard Jackson, "Global Aging and the
> Crisis of the 2020s", Current History, January 2011

Here is a more UK-focused warning:

Combined with improved longevity and falling annuity rates...lower contribution rates suggest that the next generation will enter retirement with a much lower standard of living than the current generation.

> *The Guardian*, 17 July 2012

Not for nothing is economics termed the "dismal science". Only economists could be dismayed at the fact that people face longer and healthier lives.[10]

This one would relish the prospect – even living in London and working at a bank, as I do. The worry, of course, is that an older population won't be able to afford all those pensions, particularly at recent low levels of stock market valuations and interest rates, fuelling the tension predicted by some of the more dramatic prognoses. Though not new, the theme is woven into the conventional narrative that explains why we're in such an economic hole currently. It is also very likely wrong, for three key reasons.

Before we look at these reasons, there is a conceptual point to clarify, relating to the role played by savings in funding pensions – a role that is frequently misunderstood, as in the third quotation above, for example. As noted, pensions worries have been given added urgency by the poor returns from stock markets and low interest rates in recent years: not only are we set to run out of labour, but our cumulative savings, and the income from them, seem disappointingly small. However, *for the economy as a whole*, stock markets and interest rates do not directly provide the real resources that fund society's pensions.

To understand why financial markets may not matter as much as we often think, forget for a moment something that you take for granted at the personal level – the idea that a pool of "savings" directly provides the real resources needed to pay for retirement. For society as a whole, this is not the case. There are no collective stockpiles of goods to be consumed in retirement – no warehouses full of tinned food, clothing or medicines. What pensioners need is made shortly before they consume it by those still in work. In other words, pensions collectively are resourced on what is termed a "pay as you go" basis: they are funded by the productive capacity of the economy, and that provision is part of business as usual. The economy's capacity to meet our needs is itself linked to past aggregate saving – and investment – decisions, but only indirectly and loosely. To see how loosely, imagine what would happen if we all tried at short order to double the portion of our incomes we save (or if you prefer, Google "The paradox of thrift"). The economy would shrink, because the immediate result of us all spending a lot less would be that business dried up, jobs would be lost and total incomes would fall – and with them, most likely, the flow of total savings from those incomes (hence the paradox).

The collective picture is thus a little more subtle than we often think. The financial assets that we each accumulate – whether in designated pension plans (state-run or private), or in general investment portfolios – offer notional security, but no guarantee of real benefit. If there is nothing to buy, our pension pots will be of no use. The most likely way in which this could happen would be if there were to be too much money chasing the available goods, in which case higher inflation would push many of them out of reach. The scariest would be a natural disaster or war that damaged the economic infrastructure.

I am of course not suggesting that we save less today because of this possibility. This book is arguing that in allocating our savings, choosing to hold a large portion in the form of financial assets that can benefit from economic growth will help maximise the size of our individual pension funds. These savings are available not just to buy shares in, and bonds issued by, existing businesses, but to fund new projects and businesses too: such investment will probably help boost future production and indirectly help ensure there is something to buy when we come to retire. But it is that investment and future production that ultimately provides the goods and services that we need from our pensions, not the financial assets themselves. A bigger personal pension pot gives us a prominent place in the queue for a share of that production, but for society as a whole it doesn't change the output available for distribution between those in work and those not. Individuals needn't concern themselves much with this, but society as a whole has to[11] – even where a state-organised pension plan has an explicit link between accumulated financial assets and nominal pensions disbursed.

There can be exceptions. Small countries enjoying an economic windfall can invest it overseas. The growth of their investment, and its ultimate purchasing power, then depends on the output of workers in the much bigger rest-of-the-world economy. Not every country can be Norway, however, and at the global level there is nobody to whom we can look to meet our needs when we're older.

How does recognising this help us tackle the demographic problem posed by more pensioners and fewer workers? Because it focuses the debate on what really matters – in contrast to most discussion of the "demographic timebomb". Economic growth matters most, and the obstacles to growth posed by an aging society are overstated. Those three reasons are:

(i) The scale of the additional burden posed by our aging population is exaggerated, because *demography* is not the only driver of *dependency.*

(ii) We are not using our available labour fully to begin with: if governments follow the right policies, labour supply could rise.

(iii) Even if labour supply does shrink, living standards need not follow suit, because economic growth is not driven by labour input alone.

The elderly are not the only dependants

Pessimists assume that the looming demographic changes are an accurate guide to changes in economic dependency, the burden carried by those in work, but they are not. The output of those in work has to support all those who are not working. Pensioners are not the only non-working-age group. Children are dependants too, and relative to the working-age population their numbers are much more stable. More importantly, not everyone of working age is in work.

Time-bombers routinely overlook both the unemployed (people of working age who are part of the workforce, but can't find a job), and the economically inactive (people of working age who are not looking for work, and so not participating in the workforce, for whatever reason). When we allow for the need to support the wider non-working population, the current level of dependency is of course higher than suggested by looking at pensioners only (Table 3.2) but society is coping and, importantly, the looming increase in total dependency is much smaller than the increase implied by the rising number of pensioners alone. The UK carried a higher burden back in the early 1980s: there were fewer pensioners then than there will be in 30 years' time, but unemployment rates were higher, and participation rates lower.

Labour utilisation can change

Time-bombers don't simply forget to place the older population in its wider context, they also forget that the context itself can change. They are effectively worrying about a shortage of labour without acknowledging that we're clearly not using fully what we've got to begin with. This is perverse – and bad analysis, because if labour utilisation were to change, prospective dependency ratios would change with it.

Most people who are unemployed would like a job if one were available. So too would many people who are economically inactive and not looking for a job, such as "discouraged" workers who've given up trying, early retirees, family carers and some students (circumstances permitting, of course). Lower unemployment and higher participation can make a big difference to the dependency arithmetic, as you can guess from Table 3.2. Compared to the naïve time-bomb analysis, the proportionate impact of more older workers in the numerator of the dependency ratio is diluted by the inclusion of the other dependents. Moving adults out of unemployment and non-participation, and into employment, further cuts the numerator and raises the denominator. Plausible changes in labour utilisation could even deliver lower dependency, suggesting that current pensioner living standards could be

Table 3.2   The elderly are not the only dependants: approximate composition of UK population, end-2013 (%)[a]

Group	%
Children (under 16 years)	18.8
Working age adults (16–65 years)	64.2
of which: employed	*46.3*
unemployed[a]	*3.7*
not in the workforce (economically inactive)	*14.2*
of which: looking after family	*3.6*
students	*3.6*
long-term sick	*3.2*
retired early	*2.1*
other (inc. discouraged)	*1.6*
of the above: would like a job	*3.6*
Elderly (65 years and above)	17.0
of which: in work	*1.6*
Total	100.0 (64 million)
Memo: elderly/working age adults	0.27
Memo: all dependants[b]/employed	1.16
Memo: adjusted for older workers[c]	1.09

[a] This unemployment rate is defined relative to the whole population: as conventionally measured, as a proportion of the workforce, the rate was 7.2%. [b] Children, elderly, unemployed and inactive working-age adults. [c] Numerator excludes the one million elderly (65 and older) who are in work; denominator includes them.

Source: ONS, author's estimates and calculations.

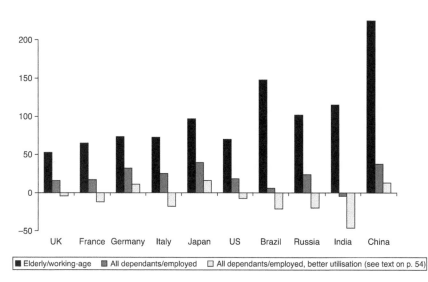

Figure 3.5   Prospective changes in three different dependency ratios, 2011–2041, %

Source: US Census Bureau international database; Datastream; author's calculations (see text).

financed at lower average taxes than today (Figure 3.5). For some countries, a prospective fall in total labour supply could become an increase.

All this assumes that pension ages and working hours stay the same, but of course they can change too, and increase a little if they need to (they may not, though many governments are already raising pension ages). Seemingly small changes could have a big impact: an hour added to the average working week would increase the supply of labour by around 3%; a year on the retirement age would eventually boost it by around 2%. For some, such changes would be an admission of economic failure, but it needn't be. A retirement age fixed when life expectancy was much shorter, and when physically demanding manual work was the norm, is arguably an expensive anachronism. Today's retirees have a quarter of their lives still ahead of them, in contrast to those (for example) in Victorian times for whom retirement amounted to a few insecure and unhealthy years after a lifetime of hard industrial effort. This assumes of course that older workers can play a productive role, but if the average person is living for longer, and more healthily, they may even relish being able to work an extra year or two. Similarly, the length of the working week has been falling steadily. Professor David Miles has noted that the proportion of a typical male's waking hours spent at work has fallen by more than a half in the last century and a half. Slightly longer working hours now may not be that contentious – particularly since so many jobs now are part-time in nature.

A final point on labour supply. Over a very long time period, even the birth rate may change. As noted, children can be seen as a form of pension provision, and the evidence for this is not limited to emerging economies: Professor Miles has also noted how, when state pension provision rose markedly in Italy in the second half of the twentieth century, the fertility rate there halved (helping explain why Italy's age mix is where it is now).[12] If the perception of a pensions crisis persists, we may yet find that demography itself begins to bend to the task at hand, and birth rates begin to rebound. It would likely take more than 30 years for such a trend to become established and have a material impact on labour supply, though – as we've noted here – it really isn't necessary.

Growth is not driven by labour alone

This is probably the most important reason for believing we can cope with an older population, but it requires something of a leap of faith, because it suggests we may get something for nothing. Even if the available supply of labour were to fall, it may not matter as much in practice as you might think.

It does sound a little odd to argue that growth might not be hurt much by a shortage of workers. More labour means more potential output: it is a basic input, one of the classical factors of production noted in Chapter 2. However, it is not the only factor of production. The other major input in most developed economies is capital, including both the stock of tangible fixed investment in infrastructure, buildings, equipment and machinery, and also the intangible, softer investment in human capital – for example, the programming that governs so many devices, and our growing stock of general knowledge.

The stock of capital rises as society sets aside enough production, from its current output, to more than compensate for the wearing out of existing assets. This is where those flows of savings mentioned earlier go: they free up resources, not to accumulate the things that we will be consuming when we retire, but to help ensure that we will have the productive capacity to make them when we need them.[13] You will not be surprised to read that convincing estimates of the size of the productive capital stock are difficult to compile. In fact, it has been a difficult thing for the economics profession to even *define* convincingly.[14]

More importantly, in practice, much economic growth comes not from using more labour (or more capital, or more anything) but from improved efficiency, what economists call "total factor productivity". In practice, and in plain words, much of this comes from learning by doing and from innovation. A couple of examples may help illustrate how such free lunches can exist. I think one of the unsung heroes of modern economic life is Mitch Kapor, who as the designer of a software package called Lotus 1–2–3, was arguably responsible for one of the biggest productivity surges in history: it made spreadsheets widely available. Computing technology generally has advanced sensationally. The laptop on which I'm typing this contains more computing power than the entire London School of Economics had at its disposal when I studied there many years back, and the amount of material, labour and capital that has gone into its construction is of course much smaller. The humble spreadsheet, which uses virtually no physical resources, is perhaps one of the best illustrations of how technology gives us more from less.

(Perversely, the conventional account of our current economic predicament sees new technology not as a way out of that economic hole but as part of the problem, because of what it might mean for jobs. In the context of the demographic debate, where labour is believed to be in short supply, this may not be such a concern. Generally, however, to decry innovation because it liberates labour for use elsewhere is mistaken, as we discuss below.)

More prosaically, think about a task you face for the first time – assembling a piece of flat-packed furniture, say. You're unfamiliar with the pieces, you don't know how carefully to tighten the screws, and so forth. It takes forever. Then you do it a second time (this does happen ...) and it's faster; a third time and it's faster still. You are "learning by doing", moving up the "learning curve": the same amount of effort is getting more done in any given time. This sort of thing is happening constantly across the economy, and when combined with new technology is capable of delivering more from less for as long as learning and invention is possible, which could be a long time. For the UK, a study some years back by the National Institute of Economic and Social Research estimated that this all-round productivity growth accounted for two-thirds of UK GDP growth in the second half of the twentieth century. At 2.4%, that GDP growth was of course firmly positive – even as the economy spent much of the period at less than full employment.[15]

What should governments do to help with all this? Above all, they should promote flexible labour markets and productive processes, and rather than attempt to pick winning technologies directly, create a climate in which science and innovation can prosper. Education might focus less on certification and more on the provision of core skills, with perhaps a renewed emphasis on the technical and vocational skills that will be in greater demand in a more automated, service dominated economy. A better-integrated tax and benefit system might reduce the disincentives to work an extra hour, or take an extra part-time job. The administration of pensions needs to be loosened up, so that the decision to start receiving a pension is not tied so tightly to the calendar. In countries where social norms still favour one-earner families, governments might foster debate. We may need more training courses for older workers, and those workers need to be adaptable. Employers need to be more flexible and open-minded too, and realise that the link between age and productivity is not a rigid one. What governments should *not* do to help fund our collective pensions is what so many of them *do* do currently – namely, exhort everyone to save more without doing anything to boost productive investment. Higher savings on their own can actually be counter-productive, as we've noted. Pensions in aggregate are not resourced from savings, but by production.

Finally, I have downplayed the role of financial markets in making available the real resources that fund pensions, but there are nonetheless some important investment implications for individual portfolios from the ongoing economic growth that will fund pensions – and some widely held notions that need to be debunked. Financial markets don't deliver growth – but growth affects those various markets in different ways. We will tackle the question of how best to allocate your savings in a growing economy, and how to view "thematic" investing, in Part II.

DECADENCE DENIED – THE WEST CAN COMPETE

And not by eastern windows only,
When daylight comes, comes in the light,
In front the sun climbs slow, how slowly,
But westward look, the land is bright.

– Arthur Hugh Clough

"We just don't make stuff in the UK any more" – how often do you hear that? The people who say it presumably don't travel often, because if they did they'd be aware that a UK company manufactures and maintains the engines that power around half of the global widebody airframe fleet; they'd know that another makes the wings for one of the two companies that dominate the civil airframe market; and that a third makes a large proportion of the scanning equipment they pass through at security control. Admittedly, they are not likely to ride to the airport in a car manufactured here – but that's partly because these days most cars made in the UK are exported: almost as many cars are made here as ever were, with the industry expecting the 1972 peak to be exceeded before 2020, and production is more efficient, though it is dominated by overseas-owned firms (the cluster of small, high-technology British companies focused on Formula 1 racing being the most visible exception). On their way to the airport, our pundit may have snacked or had a drink, forgetting that though not made of metal, processed food and drink are manufactured products nonetheless, as are the over-the-counter cold or headache remedies they might have taken, or the toothpaste, soap, deodorants and other personal goods they might have used as they got ready to leave – and UK companies are amongst the market leaders globally in processed food and drink, pharmaceuticals and household goods.

The UK *does* make stuff, and as profitably as it ever did: it has many world-class companies and workforces across the wider manufacturing sector (including, still, steelmakers, oil refiners and bulk chemical producers, basic industries that many assume have long since departed the UK). Many UK manufacturing companies invest abroad, and are as active and aggressive in pursuing foreign acquisitions as are foreign firms in the UK. In some specialist segments – for example, advanced automotive and aerospace engineering and design, and pharmaceutical research and production – UK manufacturing expertise is world-leading. As a proportion of the wider economy, the manufacturing sector has been shrinking, and at around 10% is smaller now than at any time for which we have data available – but almost every large economy sees the relative importance of its manufacturing sector decline (the trend in the share of manufacturing in French and US GDP is similar). It has been a recurrent source of concern for UK-based economists for the last half a century at least,[16] but viewed in a wider context it may not be troubling.

Our basic needs are mostly material. The list has lengthened over time – from food, shelter, clothing, tools and furniture, to include cookers, refrigerators, televisions, cars, computers, and mobile phones for example, and we'll come back to this shortly. Once these needs are met, however, our wants, and an increasing proportion of our income, are directed towards less tangible things, or services. Poorer economies have large agricultural or commodity-producing sectors, and gradually industrialise as they become better off. Wealthier economies tend to have bigger education, healthcare, distribution, travel, leisure, entertainment, media – and, yes, financial – sectors. A manufacturing sector whose relative importance is shrinking is not necessarily a sign of economic failure – it could even be the opposite, if it reflects a more prosperous economy's wish to spend more on the relative luxuries of services as it "deindustrialises".

There can be long periods in which the level of manufacturing output, not just its share in the wider economy, is flat or declining. In the UK, the most obvious instances in modern times were the 15 years or so after 1973, and now a similar period after 2000: both instances included severe recessions. In late-2014, the sector is expanding, and output has regained half the ground lost since its peak. Manufactured products are easily stockpiled, they are traded internationally, they include large items of capital equipment, and their technologies and production processes can change abruptly. This makes the sector very cyclical, sensitive to the immediate economic climate, and generally volatile. If such a decline lasts, it could become a more potent concern. There is no "right" level of manufacturing output, but having capability in the sector is important – manufacturing is where productivity growth is fastest, and the source of much exciting and wealth-creating innovation. Because they can be traded more easily than many services, manufactured exports help pay for the many imported products that we need or want. That does not mean that deindustrialisation is intrinsically bad.

Many politicians, and economists who should know better, like to talk of reversing this trend, and "rebalancing" the economy in favour of manufacturing. Proposals include a lower exchange rate, and/or measures to promote capital investment ahead of consumer spending (the idea being that fixed investment is more manufacturing-intensive). Such a rebalancing is not going to happen, however much we might want it to: as noted, a wealthier economy spends a smaller proportion on manufactured output. It is not clear that the politicians have thought very carefully about their reasons for wanting to reverse deindustrialisation: productivity in manufacturing is relatively high, meaning that it directly creates fewer jobs per unit of output than the lower productivity service sector.

Perhaps the most visible exception to the tendency for larger economies to become more service-oriented is China, which is currently the second largest economy in the world (on some measures, the largest). But this apparent exception proves the general rule: China's economy is big, but so is its population, and they are still relatively poor. China is still industrialising – providing its people with their more tangible needs. When this is done, and its markets liberalise further – China has been a laggard in the general trend towards financial liberalisation, with capital controls, a pegged exchange rate and interest rates and much credit expansion largely determined by dictat, not demand and supply – then China too will one day likely deindustrialise (and happily).

The casual assertion that "we don't make stuff" isn't confined to the UK, of course. And worries about decline are not confined to manufacturing, but to business generally. In the last decade or two, and particularly in the late 2000s with the commodity price and emerging market booms, the productive potential of the US, Europe and indeed the wider developed world has been called into question by fears of competition from the apparent juggernaut of emerging economies' industrialisation (most obviously, China's).

Roughly six billion people, or four-fifths of the world's population, live in the less developed or "emerging" world. Meanwhile, the global economy is increasingly open and integrated: the goods (and services) it produces are traded more freely than ever, and subject to fewer tariffs and controls; and the investment and technology used to make them is more mobile than ever, and can shift quickly to where it can be most productive. It seems obvious that eventually, most business, not just manufacturing, and most investment portfolios, will be located where most of those workers are – in the relatively low-wage emerging world. This is good news for mankind, but it has many developed world workers, politicians, and investors worried. And as with debt and demography, economists have not done as good a job as they might to reassure them. More often than not, by unthinkingly repeating those assertions, they have tended to play to those fears, and exaggerate the threat posed to Western living standards by the emerging world's development.

The possibility of relative and even absolute decline is hardly new. The Roman Empire, the Middle East and China after their early enlightenments, the Rennaissance powers and indeed the first industrialised nations, have all faded in influence and material status. The fading of economic and political empire is a sobering but at the same time fascinating process: the Schadenfreude it evokes speaks perhaps to some deep-seated need for personal reassurance that the big will be made small, that the mighty will be humbled. Influential and epic accounts, analyses, and allegories include Edward Gibbon's *The History of the Decline and Fall of the Roman Empire* (1776–1789), Paul Kennedy's *The Rise and Fall of the Great Powers* (1987), Niall Ferguson's polemic *The Great Degeneration* (2013) and of course Richard Wagner's 1876 Ring cycle (with its leading role for gold). The turmoil in capital markets, the failure of banks and the revealed limits to the potency of central bankers and governments has lent itself easily to talk of general decline and decadence, alongside the troubling debt and demography. Not only is the West bankrupt and old, but (we read) it is surely lazy and uncompetitive, and about to be supplanted by another more dynamic, youthful, cheaper and differently civilised world.

As with debt and demography, there is however a different, more nuanced perspective available – and hinted at already in our discussion of the manufacturing debate. It can be argued that one of the reasons for the faster progress being made by the emerging world is precisely its embracing of some of the assumptions and beliefs that underpin the Western worldview – the belief that the economic market can be less inefficient than the political one, and that free trade and democratic government are the least bad ways of organising things. This idea was articulated provocatively by Francis Fukuyama's thesis of "The End of History",[17] the idea being that history in the sense of an ongoing battle of ideologies has been ended by one of them – the economically liberal, democratic model – having won. Fukuyama's thesis was criticised for failing to take into account the rise of cultural and religion-based dissent from the model – notably by Samuel Huntington, and his notion of the *Clash of Civilizations*[18] – but how else to make sense of the subsequent exuberance in the emerging economies, particularly China's, if not to suggest that their governments have decided to play the same game? Why join the World Trade Organisation if free trade is bad or doomed? On this view the West may not be decadent, just early.[19]

Because it is not necessarily the case that the developed world cannot cope with a more integrated, quickly growing emerging world. The fact that more open global trade has been allowing emerging world living standards to narrow the gap with those in the developed world, and the probability that this process will continue for as long as world trade remains relatively free, tells us nothing about the level at which that convergence will happen. The extent of head-to-head competition[20] has been overstated: economic growth and international trade is not a "winner takes all" or "zero-sum" game, but a process that is often characterised by mutual gain. The emerging world is growing faster, but that does not mean living standards in the developed world have to go into reverse, or even mark time. Both developed and emerging blocs can become better off together. The latter may do so more quickly, but they are poorer to begin with.

The notion that international trade has the potential to raise total living standards – that it can make both sides to the transaction better off – is not as obvious as it should be, given the modern backdrop of a popular debate focused on the seemingly greater potential for economic exploitation and competitive threat. But as with individuals, countries trading with each other can specialise, and benefit from their different aptitudes and tastes: greater choice allows both parties a better chance of achieving an efficient outcome.[21] One country may do something more competitively than another; it may even do most things more competitively. Trade can nonetheless potentially raise total welfare enough to make both better off as long as they specialise in different things.

That specialisation is not only evident in the most obvious, classically competitive context. In practice, much international trade reflects the "vertical integration" of production: a company may have operations or suppliers in different countries, producing its own inputs (at the bottom of the production chain) where they are cheapest, and adding progressively more value to them as they are shipped from country to country (moving up the production chain, towards the final customer, in the process). In this case, the company may not see itself as competing directly with the supplying countries, though of course its other would-be suppliers might be. Another important complication is the existence of joint ventures: the two companies that make more cars than any others in China are General Motors and Volkswagen, which both have extensive cooperative ventures with local firms. Here the competitive dividing line is drawn more subtly still.

Moreover, where classical head-to-head competition between directly comparable products does matter, it is often – usually – shaped by many more considerations than a simplistic analysis of prices or wages, and of the exchange rates that allow them to be compared across countries. You wouldn't know this from the mainstream macroeconomic discussion of competitiveness, which focuses overwhelmingly on exactly those things (as has our discussion so far). This focus is understandable perhaps, because they are conceptually clear, easiest to measure, and their relativities can be tracked in real time as currencies move up and down, making them newsworthy. In practice, however, the extent of international competition that is driven straightforwardly by one country selling its products more cheaply than another, and thereby grabbing a bigger share of the global market – the sort of advantage that the lower-wage emerging economies are most likely to enjoy – is limited.

For things that are very similar, prices can matter a lot in determining how much business is done, and if prices do, then so too do costs, since they will shape the available supply of the product: lower cost suppliers will tend to drive out the rest. Commodities are the most obvious example – by definition, copper, corn or crude oil are largely the same whoever is producing and selling them, and prices converge towards a single global price (which may be quoted or denominated in a particular currency, usually dollars, but which is determined by the interaction of global demand and supply).[22] However, even in the case of commodities, a degree of differentiation can creep in. Oil is graded according to its "heaviness" (its volatility) and "sweetness" (low sulphur content), for example. Even if the commodity itself is more homogeneous, transport costs (for example) can fragment the market, as with iron ore and steel.

Most goods and (especially) services are differentiated in some way, making price only one of the factors shaping the decision to buy (or supply). The norm is not the "perfect competition" of the textbooks, in which for each individual supplier the price is effectively a given, and an attempt to set a higher one is punished by failing to sell anything. Instead, "imperfect competition" is the most common market structure: heterogeneous products compete with products that are not direct substitutes, and in which individual suppliers face not a given price but a trade-off between higher prices and lower sales, a downward sloping demand curve.

Clothing would be an obvious case: trade in mass-produced, commoditised cotton T-shirts is very price sensitive, but that in designer-branded items can be very price-*in*sensitive, so much so that at the very top end, some customers will view them as more desirable the more expensive they become, because the price is thought to signify quality, or the product itself is believed to signal something desirable about the buyer.[23] On a bigger scale, the continuing success of German engineering, for example, testifies to the fact that this price insensitivity – or inelasticity – can extend to entire industries, a point overlooked in many commentaries on the UK's post-war manufacturing prowess, which often concluded that the perceived problem would go away if only the exchange rate were lowered enough. Few people buy cars from Daimler or BMW, transportation systems from Siemens, or machine tools from the *Mittelstand*, because they are cheap – in fact they might distrust them if they were.

In the real world in which most products differ at least slightly from each other, the notion of competitiveness needs to be expanded beyond the simplistic comparison of prices and costs. Michael Porter at Harvard may have written more extensively and authoritatively on the topic than anyone else:[24] his influential categorisation of five competitive "forces" – direct rivalry amongst existing competitors; suppliers' bargaining power; customers' bargaining power; the threat of new entrants; the threat posed by substitute products – illustrates how broad that approach needs to be. Hence the room for all that vertical integration and those joint ventures.

Another consideration is that the pattern of economic output is changing all the time, in the developed as well as the emerging world. When we ran through the list of material needs above, some items viewed as essentials today – personal computers and mobile phones – did not exist half a century ago. The product cycle is impossible to predict, but demands from economically sophisticated developed world consumers may give the developed bloc an edge when it comes to the Next Big Thing, just as they have to date with biotechnology, mobile computing and digital media for example. Inventive product design and technological innovation are not the preserve of lower wage economies, and as new ideas and processes arrive there is as good a chance of them being utilised in the West as anywhere. Paul Markillies, technology editor at *The Economist* – with whom I was lucky enough to share a speaking platform on several occasions in 2012/2013 – has argued that the pace of technological change in manufacturing currently is such as to warrant talk of a "Third Industrial Revolution". He cites developments in software that are transforming product testing processes; a new generation of robots that are more intelligent, and capable of interacting more flexibly with humans; new materials and nanotechnologies that are expanding design possibilities; and additive manufacturing processes – 3D printing – that are making bespoke manufacturing more accessible, and have the potential to cut waste hugely. Meanwhile, the "internet of things", open sourcing, cloud data storage and virtual computers are delivering ongoing opportunities and efficiencies across businesses, not just in manufacturing. A greater emphasis on technology, generally, embodied in capital equipment and know-how, would reduce the relative importance of direct labour costs. Other things equal, this would improve the West's ability to compete, at least in some areas.[25] So too will cheaper US energy and higher wages in China.

The fact that new technology can reduce the demand for labour in developed economies too means that it is often resisted: job losses to robots (for example) are cited by some of the gloomier pundits as one of the reasons why "The Future Isn't What it Used to Be". This view is an old one: it can be traced back at least to the Luddites of the early nineteenth century who protested against the introduction of labour-saving machinery. It is mistaken, because the higher living standards and new products that technology fosters eventually create more employment. Immediate losses are painful, however, while future gains are uncertain, and a civilised society will ensure that re-training, and an adequate social security safety net, are available to help those displaced through no fault of their own.

Finally, remember that not all products and services can be traded internationally, and that there are practical limits to the extent of competition. Transport and management practicalities – such as how to ensure quality control at a distance – are causing many Western businesses to reconsider their use of overseas suppliers, particularly in respect of the "offshoring" of low-cost services. Many personal services are most naturally provided locally, by local suppliers: much retailing and leisure activity, for example.[26] Some utilities are effectively natural monopolies, and need to be regulated; in other instances the market mechanism fails completely, and government needs to step in to ensure that an important service is provided (defence or the arts, for example) or deterred (pollution or smoking perhaps). In each case there are limits to globalisation, and to the extent to which international competition can pose even a theoretical threat.[27]

In conclusion, then, a quickly growing emerging world is not necessarily the head-to-head threat to Western living standards that it is often made out to be. Again, this does not mean that there are no grounds for concern: low-skilled workers in labour-intensive industries that do compete directly with poorer countries will face a tough time as long as the global economy continues to open and integrate. Many jobs in the service sector however involve skills that have to be delivered locally, and which are not likely ever to be replaced by robots or other new technologies (catering, entertaining, nursing, plumbing and teaching being some obvious examples). Rather than throw up our hands in despair, we should concentrate on education and training, and on that ever-changing product cycle. Germany's success is a reminder that piling 'em high and selling 'em cheap is not the only business model available. The competitive ideal is to provide products and services that people want, not because they are cheap but because they are special.

If you keep all these points in mind you'll find plenty of sustainably successful Western businesses worth investing in. And in many cases, they will have rapidly growing sales, production and joint ventures in the emerging world.

DEPLETION – THE SUSTAINABILITY CHALLENGE

The stone age didn't end for lack of stone.

– Sheikh Yamani, Saudi Arabia's
Oil Minister, 1962–1986[28]

This is perhaps the investment topic that arouses the strongest feelings. The developed world's selfish failure to tackle climate change; China's grab for commodities, and its pollution; recurrent famine in Africa and India; nuclear risks illustrated at Three Mile Island, Chernobyl and Fukushima – the material threat to living standards seems real and urgent. We live insignificantly, spinning in space, on the smaller dry bits of a thin crust floating atop a ball of molten rock and metal, sustained by a life-maintaining but similarly thin blanket of oxygenated atmosphere beyond which lies the infinite and dimensionless void dotted with other moving, unfathomed but as yet largely inaccessible clusters of minerals, liquids and gases (some of which might be organised organically). What could be more natural than to worry that our physical resources are finite? They clearly are.

Nonetheless, we have been capable of underestimating them, and our potential to adapt, and of overestimating the impact of our actions. I have no geological or wider scientific expertise, but the key investment points here are general ones, and relate to frames of reference, not science. Our resources are limited, but that does not mean that we are able yet to estimate precisely the date at which we will run sufficiently short of them for our collective lifestyle to become unsustainable. It is not easy to gauge exactly how much there is left of even a single fossil fuel – in late 2014 the price of oil has fallen sharply, for example, partly because supply has been unexpectedly high – and when you allow for the likelihood that for many natural resources there are potential substitutes available, or synthetically produced supplies, it becomes more difficult again to estimate the point at which the earth's generosity will run short. In another context, its resilience in the face of environmental accidents to date has been impressive. This does not imply a lack of respect for, or a failed sense of stewardship towards, this wonderful planet. It does suggest that we should be circumspect in proclaiming an imminent end to economic growth on this account.

Economists have form here. Periodic supply scares have proclaimed prematurely that the world is about to run short of a key resource, and that living standards are about to fall as a result. One of the earliest examples, noted above, is Malthus' 1798 *An Essay on the Principle of Population*: he worried that a growing population would not be able to feed itself. For the Club of Rome, an international think tank which published *The Limits to Growth* in 1972, the worry was that we were about to run out of natural resources, such as oil. For Paul Ehrlich, a prominently pessimistic US commentator, it was both: having written an influential book *The Population Bomb* in 1968, in 1980 he publicly accepted a bet with a relatively obscure US economist Julian Simon, who'd argued that a basket of commodities would likely fall in price over the next ten years (he lost, Simon won: the price of all five commodities chosen by Ehrlich as likely to see their prices squeezed higher because of looming scarcity in fact fell, even as the global economy grew[29]). More recently, many writers have suggested that global oil production is peaking, and that surging demand from China in particular is almost guaranteed to push oil and other commodity prices up without limit, causing economic mayhem.[30]

It is natural to believe that with more and more people on the planet, the time at which we run out of food, metal, water, energy and a sustainable environment must be approaching. The logic is unavoidable: there must be some constraint on what the planet can sustain. Moreover, it is human nature to believe that the epoch in which you find yourself living is the watershed, the special time (and not just in matters of economics). To date, however, these supply shortages have not materialised, essentially because supplies of food, commodities and labour are not as fixed as we've thought, and because human needs and capabilities themselves evolve over time, and as circumstances change. This is not to say that there are no limits to growth, simply that our ability to identify and date those limits is poor – the result of a failure of imagination, an inability to guess at the technology that we are collectively capable of creating, and a failure perhaps to appreciate the sheer richness, diversity and resilience of our planet and its inhabitants.

The need to address climate change is probably the sustainability concern that understandably has most people worried. It is difficult to address for good reason: even if developed nations take more decisive action themselves, poorer countries see emission controls and higher taxes on fossil fuels as the rich world pulling up the development ladder after them, and will need to be compensated. But the issue may not be as urgent as feared.[31] A warmer climate is not without benefits, helping us to adapt to it: more people on the planet are vulnerable to the cold than to heat, and agricultural productivity in some areas may increase. Meanwhile, alternative energy sources will see their production costs fall as technology advances, including the cost of making nuclear supply, the most scalable source of non-carbon-based energy, still safer than it is. Technology will also improve energy efficiency across the board. In addition to their wider human significance, these ameliorative developments reduce the possibility of economic growth suddenly being braked on this account.

Pollution is a related concern, but one that is easier to tackle. Individual governments have successfully tackled air pollution caused by carbon-based fuel emissions in big cities without major economic disruption – in Los Angeles and London, for example. Economics can be directly useful here: pollution is a classic externality, a cost that arises because a key resource – in this case, the environment – is not priced, and the textbook solution is to try to bring it inside the market mechanism, using taxes or fines (or the sort of permits and offsets that are helping to address carbon emissions).

The point at which the scarcity of natural resources becomes a practical constraint is difficult to fix precisely, because so much of the earth's content is still unmapped. New supplies – perhaps beneath the seas – may initially be prohibitively expensive, but as extraction techniques improve, costs will fall. In the meantime, higher prices (if they occur – there is no guarantee even of that, as we're seeing with oil prices in late 2014) will encourage us to find substitutes, or to economise. In the case of food, better fertilisers and genetic engineering can boost supply. So too can better organisation. Reforming India's huge but fragmented agricultural sector, and reducing the massive waste that sees as much as a third of its output perish before it reaches the market, could have a global impact. Other developing economies see similar food wastage; and if the profligacy of richer consumers is taken into account, so too do developed economies.[32] Meanwhile, two-thirds of the earth's surface is covered with water, and desalination technology will surely improve further. A recent report reminds us that there may be water trapped within the earth's mantle.[33]

Remember also the earlier points made about population growth, and industrialisation. The world's population is already slowing, and in several large economies is already declining (and it may do so even in China from around 2030). As noted, a more productive population has less need of children to look after it as it ages (in developing countries especially, a large family often plays the role of a pension plan for the aging parents). And growth will not always be as resource intensive as it is currently: the emerging world too will at some stage shift towards more service-oriented spending and output, and as we've already seen, in developed economies rising living standards can be largely driven by productivity gains – by intangible inputs such as improved efficiency and technology that effectively give us more output without a corresponding increase in (tangible) inputs.

A final, subtler, reason for thinking that the sustainability challenge may be more manageable than feared is that some of the more pessimistic prognoses may have been analytically flawed. For example, the discount rates used in assessing the costs of climate change may have been inappropriately low.

The future is profoundly uncertain. The risk may not be that the world is one day "used up", but instead that it is destroyed outright in its economic prime by the sort of event portrayed in the film "Melancholia". However small the probability of this occurring might seem, it deserves somehow to be reflected in any cost/benefit analysis that extends into the future. The most obvious way to do that is to use a discount rate: to discount future costs and benefits simply because they are uncertain – the bigger the discount rate, the less important are the future values compared with today's. And this is where sentiment may have taken the upper hand in addressing the likely costs of climate change in particular. It is one thing to say that we are merely custodians of the planet on behalf of future unborn generations, but quite another to say that their welfare, in current value terms, is equally as valid as ours, that the costs and benefits they incur can be viewed with as much certainty as we view our own. Yet the studies that use an unusually low discount rate – most notably the UK government-sponsored Stern report – may be doing almost exactly that, and excessively inflating the estimated net costs to unborn generations of global warming. Discount rates are at the heart of investment analysis, and we shall talk about how interest rates more generally might be determined in Part II.

DANGER – GEOPOLITICAL TENSIONS

We are not enemies, but friends. We must not be enemies. Though passion may have strained, it must not break our bonds of affection. The mystic chords of memory will swell when again touched, as surely they will be, by the better angels of our nature.

– Lincoln

In late 2014, Europe has been facing potentially its most challenging political crisis since the Cold War, as Russia and the West face-off over Ukraine. A sharp fall in oil prices is adding to the pressure on Russia, perhaps increasing the risk that it will respond rashly. This is happening as destructive civil war continues to rage in Syria, Iraq is terrorised anew, the West tries to disengage itself from Afghanistan, and shortly after tumultuous regime changes in Egypt and Libya (and renewed conflict across Israel's borders). Tension around Iran's nuclear programme has yet to be definitively resolved. In Latin America, the Venezuelan regime has used violence to shore up its position in the aftermath of President Chavez's death in 2013, while Brazil experienced riots in the run-up to a World Cup competition that was resented by much of its still poor population. Nearly 300 schoolgirls have been abducted by a terrorist group in Nigeria; more than 100 schoolchildren have been killed in a terrorist attack in Pakistan. The world's newest nation state, South Sudan, has been experiencing civil war since its birth in 2011. There is unease at effective one-party rule in South Africa. An outbreak of the ebola virus has claimed several thousand victims in West Africa. In Asia, Thailand has experienced a military coup, China is confronting Japan and Vietnam respectively in the East and South China Seas, and the increasingly insecure North Korean regime continues to impoverish its population. A civil airliner carrying 239 people between Malaysia and China has vanished without trace, and a second carrying 298 people between Amsterdam and Kuala Lumpur was shot down over Ukraine. Meanwhile, the War on Terror still rumbles on, with the gruesome events in Iraq, and the killing of Osama bin Laden in 2011, perhaps the most visible recent reminders that the threat of violence of the sort that burst from a clear blue sky in New York on 11 September 2001 is still with us. And this is just a quickly drawn sketch: the world is clearly a dangerous place.

Or so it seems. The reality is that while these situations and events are unimaginably awful for the people involved, and distressing for the rest of us, and while terrorism is a very real threat, a careful look at the facts has to concede that the world is today less riven by conflict, and by random violence, than at any time in recorded history. What is certainly new is the immediacy with which we hear about and see these events: communications technology is so advanced that both organised and social media alert us to these events, and show them to us in horrifyingly graphic detail, as soon as they happen. Also new, perhaps, is the point touched upon earlier: more people on the planet these days subscribe to similar, individualistic values, and individual dangers perhaps resonate more loudly as a result. People *matter* more than when totalitarianism and religious faith governed more of the planet. These novelties, together with most generations' tendency to think that they live in "special times", or the "end of days", make us *feel* that this an especially dangerous time at which to be alive – even though it isn't.

I have perhaps an unusual perspective on the theme of international tension. When I was sixteen I was lucky enough to be given a Local Education Authority scholarship to study at Atlantic College in South Wales. The

College had been started by Kurt Hahn at the height of the Cold War. An international sixth-form, it was created explicitly to use education, outdoor pursuits and community service to foster greater understanding amongst its international students – most of whom were selected on merit, not ability to pay – at a time when it seemed as if renewed global conflict might indeed be just around the corner. The College took its first students in the autumn of 1962 – less than a year after the failed CIA-backed invasion of Cuba (the Bay of Pigs debacle) and just weeks ahead of the Cuban missile crisis.

Atlantic College became the founder member of the United World Colleges movement in 1967, which today has 14 members across the world, and it has students from more nationalities than ever (almost 90 in 2013). But in its 50th anniversary year, the College's governors[34] and the wider UWC movement were refocusing its mission – partly because the world had changed so much. There are of course still many challenges for concerned internationalists, including localised conflicts – particularly in the Middle East – and ongoing cultural and racial tensions and misunderstandings. Sustainability has become a major area of concern in the last two decades. And we still face the sort of domestic inequalities that can mean that a poorer student from a council estate in (say) Birmingham may as well have been living in a different country to a wealthier student from (say) Windsor. But the threat of globalised conflict has faded, both relatively and absolutely, and sufficiently so to need acknowledging by a College and movement founded to help reduce it. The issues raised by regional conflict and sustainability are now more central to the movement's mission as a result.

Involvement with the UWC movement may have made me particularly aware of the lowering of global tension in the last half-century, but I think most people, on reflection, will recognise the trend – particularly if they set aside the daily news feeds and actively seek out some longer-term perspective. There are many people still living who can remember first-hand the cataclysm of the Second World War and the holocaust. We often forget that a Third was narrowly avoided in Korea (and in Cuba, and arguably again in Vietnam, where war led to genocide in neighbouring Cambodia). China's "Great Leap Forward" led to tens of millions of avoidable deaths. While I was at university, the industrial-scale brutality of the First World War was being revived in the Iran-Iraq war. And shadowing daily lives through much of the 1960s, 1970s and early 1980s was that threat of nuclear holocaust, culminating in the doctrine of Mutual Assured Destruction as the USSR and US confronted each other with Inter-Continental Ballistic Missiles.[35] There is a different – lowered – degree of background risk now, particularly since the dismantling of the Berlin Wall and the reunification of Germany in 1989–1990 (and in late-2014, one of the last remaining Cold War faultlines is stabilising as the US and Cuba begin to normalise their relations). When Fukuyama published his essay on the end of history, he pointed to a steady long-term growth in the number of democratic governments, which tend to be less antagonistic, though this has not stopped the US from taking the lead in engaging in overseas conflicts from Vietnam to Iraq. He noted that there had been perhaps 3 in 1790; 13 in 1900; 36 in 1960; and 61 in 1990. Today the figure would be more than 100 (Freedom House suggests 118 in 2013).

Equating stability with a simple headcount of democratic regimes is a huge oversimplification, and peace and accountability have not broken out everywhere, or in a straight line fashion: the genocides in Bosnia and Rwanda were relatively recent, and as noted the Middle East and Afghanistan remain as troubled as ever. Nonetheless, agencies such as the Peace Research Institute Oslo have made it their business to collect and analyse the available data on violent conflicts, and – callous though it may seem to plot the loss of life on a chart – they confirm that the long-term tendency seems to have been towards fewer battlefield deaths.

The tendency towards geopolitical stability is echoed in a reduction in physical risk generally: violent crime and epidemics have been in similar retreat. Stephen Pinker's magisterial *The Better Angels of Our Nature*[36] makes the point compellingly, demonstrating that if our times are special, they are special in a good way. In his words: "Believe it or not – and I know that most people do not – violence has declined over long stretches of time, and today we may be living in the most peaceable era in our species' existence". I think he is right to suggest that much of this improvement stems from the empathy and knowledge that comes with shared experience and better communication. Coincidentally, contributing in a small way to the growth of such international understanding was one of the aspirations of the founders of the United World Colleges (UWC) movement.

Of course, things might yet change for the worse: the future is unknowable, remember. The most populous country in the world, China, is not yet democratic, though its economy and markets are increasingly open, and it is an unresolved question as to whether its "one country, two systems" approach is sustainable. More generally, who could have guessed in 1914 and 1939 how the fabric of civilised society was about to unravel? But there is no reason to default to pessimism.

The implications for investing are not completely one-sided. Economies, stock markets and commodity prices do often get a boost from crises and war-time demand: rearmament helped the US escape from Depression in the late 1930s; and the first time the British government used Keynesian demand-management principles was to suppress pent-up demand at the end of the Second World War lest it cause inflation. Rebuilding follows ruin. Generally, however, what's good for people is best for business – and investing.

4

SOURCES OF PERSPECTIVE – AND A TIGER'S TALE

We are all in the gutter, but some of us are looking at the stars.

– Oscar Wilde, "Lady Windermere's Fan"

In the previous chapter we addressed directly five major, commonly held concerns – debt, demography, decadence, depletion and danger – and showed why the threat that they pose to economic growth has been significantly overstated. The specific reasons varied, but in each case the less pessimistic conclusion was reached via a questioning of received wisdom and a deliberate search for a wider perspective. We saw that: people who worry excessively about borrowing overlook the position of lenders, and the distinction between real and financial wealth; demographic time-bombers ignore the labour currently going unused, and the potential for productivity-driven growth; declinists who see the West as decadent forget that it is a customer and partner as well as a competitor, and that the product cycle is constantly evolving; scarcity-mongers take too narrow a view of supply, and neglect the possibilities for substitution and for efficiency gains; and predictors of mass conflagration fail to place the new immediacy of local atrocities and conflicts in a global and historical context.

In this chapter we'll offer some further examples of how to take that wider perspective. There is no fixed route to doing so, other than being willing to question that received wisdom, and to look for "stuff we know that just ain't so", as Mark Twain puts it at the start of Chapter 1.[1] We will describe some tongue-in-cheek rules of thumb for raising the financial signal-to-noise ratio. Sometimes of course investors' collective views can be narrowly and excessively *optimistic*, as we've seen, and we'll revisit the Irish economy's "Celtic Tiger" boom and bust (and more recently, its rehabilitation), a label taken from a report I wrote in 1994. We will suggest however that excessive pessimism about the economic outlook is more commonly encountered than excessive optimism, and offer some brief thoughts on why this might be. Part II of the book will then discuss how the lessons in this chapter and in Part I as a whole can best be put into investment practice.

TAKING A WIDER VIEW

The uses and abuses of history

History is an obvious source of perspective, though a fallible and incomplete one. Even in the best of times we tend to think that our days are special, and this tendency increases in a downturn: our time horizons shrink, and we easily believe not only that times are tough, but that our generation is particularly challenged. An awareness of history can help reassure in this context (though it can't tell us what comes next, of course, as noted earlier).

The Great Recession of 2009 is a case in point. In the aftermath of Lehman's collapse, US GDP fell more sharply than since the demobilisation slump of 1945, while the stock market registered its largest nominal decline since the Crash of 1929 ushered in the Great Depression (again, we focus mostly on the US because it is by far still the most important economy to most businesses and investors). The freezing of the interbank market, and the attendant risk of monetary collapse, was still fresh in the mind, and comparisons had been quickly drawn with the Great Depression, the understandable fear being that banking collapse could perhaps trigger a repeat. In 2007 the UK had after all seen the first run on a bank in a 150 years, and Irish bank deposits had had to be guaranteed by the government.

Comparisons with the 1930s continued long after the immediate crisis had passed. But while the peak-to-trough shrinkage in the US economy was the biggest since the 1945–1947 episode, the magnitude of the drop in output, at just over 4%, was well short of the 13% decline seen then, and in the Great Depression itself the cumulative decline is estimated, in annual data, to have been at 26% between 1929 and 1933. The 2008/2009 fall was not much larger than the 3% decline seen in 1974–1975, and the pre-crisis peak was regained within three years (after both the 1945 downturn and the Great Depression it took seven years for the previous peaks to be regained). It is a moot point too as to whether a decline from today's much higher standard of living can be compared directly, even if it is of comparable proportions, with one that occurs at the much lower levels that prevailed in (for example) the 1930s and 1940s. As people get wealthier, the marginal value they attach to each extra dollar of income declines, and a loss of 4% of real income today represents a less significant loss of welfare than did a similar loss half a century or so ago.

The peak-to-trough fall in nominal closing stock prices from 9 October 2007 to 9 March 2009 was roughly 57%, which made it the largest nominal fall since the 85% decline between September 1929 and June 1932 (this sounds as if the decline ran the 1929 crash close, until you remember that falling from 43 (100 − 57) to 15 (100 − 85) is a further proportionate loss of almost two-thirds). But there had been nominal falls of almost 50% after the TMT debacle in 2000, and between January 1973 and October 1974. And in real terms, the peak-to-trough decline of roughly 59% compares with a peak-to-trough decline of around 52% after the TMT debacle in 2000; a fall of roughly 57% after January 1973; and a protracted (and interrupted) fall of 63% between December 1968 and July 1982. The real fall after the 1929 crash was easily the largest, at just over 80%, though this was a smaller decline than the nominal fall of 85% as a result of falling consumer prices (deflation). We shall discuss stock market returns and valuations more carefully in Part II.

As recovery continued, attention shifted towards the frustratingly slow decline in unemployment, but also towards the risk of inflation seemingly posed by central banks' unconventional monetary policy – specifically, the large-scale buying of bonds by the Federal Reserve and the Bank of England, the alleged "printing of money" noted earlier. Unemployment and inflation have represented the two most persistent economic concerns in the last half-century – notwithstanding the current interest in possible deflation, which we'll discuss next – and economists often add the two rates together to arrive at a "misery index". On both sides of the Atlantic, misery indices rose after 2007 – largely driven by unemployment, with inflation subdued in the recession and the Quantitative Easing thereafter. However, at no time did either the US or UK index come close to the highs seen as relatively recently as the 1970s and early 1980s, and more recently both inflation and unemployment have fallen back, and the indices have been running at historically low levels (Figure 4.1). How frequently do you hear it said that the economic climate is less miserable now than at almost any time in the last half-century?

As tax receipts fell, and public spending to alleviate the crisis rose, budget deficits yawned wide and US and UK government debt as a proportion of GDP surged. Again, however, government debt ratios have been higher within living memory – briefly in the US during the Second World War, and for half a century in the UK, through to the 1960s. As noted in Chapter 3, there is no "right" level of debt, and while the gross borrowings of governments must

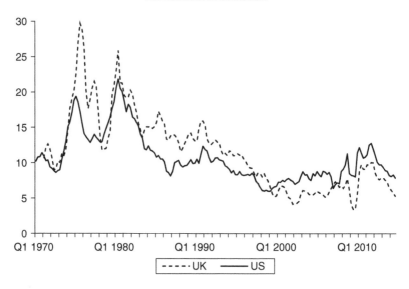

Figure 4.1 Misery indices (the sum of inflation and unemployment rates) for the UK and US, 1970–2014, %

Source: Datastream.

have some maximum level, there was little to indicate that that level was near in 2010, when deficits were at their highest and debt ratios increasing fastest. Rather, the opposite: even as the US saw its long-term sovereign credit rating cut for the first time by S&P from AAA to AA+ in August 2011, with the UK being similarly downgraded for the first time by Moody's and Fitch in February and April 2013 respectively, US and UK long-term borrowing costs had been tumbling to the lowest levels since the early 1950s, and the lowest inflation-adjusted levels since the early 1980s. These falls of course partly reflected investors' nerves, because even a downgraded government bond is still a relatively low-risk investment compared to most other assets. Thus the climate of gloom actually helped keep bond prices high and yields (the costs governments had to pay to borrow) low. Nonetheless, many mortgages and corporate bonds are priced with reference to government bonds, and to the extent that we worry about debt – again, remember Chapter 3's discussion – these historically low yields should be taken into account. More recently still, of course, deficits have been falling, and we may yet see the US and even UK government moving into surplus in the years ahead (which would not really be remarkable: it happened as relatively recently as 2001).

There *was* something special about the decline in US corporate profits in 2008/2009. It seems to have been the largest proportionate fall on record – bigger even than that seen during the Great Depression. Rolling "as reported" four-quarter earnings as compiled by S&P fell by roughly 92% in nominal and real terms between mid-2007 and early 2009: these were comfortably the largest declines on record. After 2000, real earnings fell by around 55%; and the decline(s) in the 1970s were smaller again. After the 1929 crash, data compiled by Professor Robert Shiller, and used extensively across the industry as the authoritative long-term source, show corporate earnings falling by around 66% in real terms and 75% in nominal terms (remember, the deflation of the time makes the real decline smaller). Figure 4.2 plots the data in logarithmic (proportionate)[2] form, as an index.

On closer inspection however the collapse in earnings was indeed attributable to something special, but that something was also very transient, namely the dramatic write-downs of financial assets at banks, insurers and at some large manufacturers with substantial financing departments. For the final quarter of 2008, the massive insurer American International Group reported a loss of roughly $60 billion, equivalent to one-tenth of the entire S&P 500's as-reported earnings in all of 2007. Together with large losses at other financial groups and at the credit-dependent auto sector, this helped push the aggregate index into a quarterly loss for the first time.

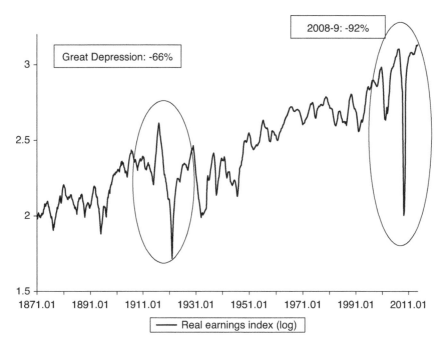

Figure 4.2 The largest fall in US stock market real earnings – and the biggest rebound (index, logged)

Source: Robert Shiller's home page; author's calculations.

Asset write-downs occur in every downturn. Even the modest economic recession or pause that accompanied the bursting of the TMT bubble after 2000 was accompanied by sharp reductions in the value of goodwill, an intangible asset that accumulates most visibly on the balance sheets of serial acquirers of other companies. This hit profits hard in both the US and European markets. The downturn of 2008/2009 however was exceptional in this respect: financial companies' balance sheets are particularly large relative to their profits, and the damage done by passing even a small proportion of them through the profit and loss account can be substantial. Bloomberg estimated the eventual total identified financial write-downs in the US at around $1.3 trillion, or more than twice as large as total S&P 500 earnings in 2007. Such a fall in profits was sensational, but always likely to be short-lived. It was clear – or should have been – that when the write-downs stopped, some very large negative items would disappear from income statements and earnings would rebound, and that they would do so of course proportionately faster than they'd fallen (simply as a matter of arithmetic: falling from 100 to 10 and then rebounding is a 90% loss followed by a 900% gain). And so it proved: the precise point at which the write-downs would start to fade was impossible to predict, but the scale of the very large rebound that would occur wasn't. Rolling four-quarter S&P earnings troughed in Q1 2009, and rose by more than 800% in the following year (their level recently is roughly fifteen times – that is, a gain of 1,400% – what it was at the low point). It nonetheless did come as a surprise to many professional investors who'd perhaps focused too much on the drama and too little on the data.

If anything, the historical perspective in this instance made the decline look worse. In fact, as suggested already, this aspect of the crisis serves to show the limitations of the historical approach by drawing our attention to the fact that aggregate four-quarter profits in the Great Depression seem to have fallen by *only* 75%, or just 67% in real terms, after allowing for the general decline in consumer prices at the time. This was a period, remember, when the economy shrank by more than two-fifths in nominal terms, and by more than a quarter in real terms. For operationally geared profits to have been so resilient in the face of such economic trauma is implausible. Accounting practices then were varied and dubious. Indeed, common standards were subsequently introduced largely because the 1929 crash and the Depression that followed it had made people realise just how arbitrary many published accounts had been.[3] Benjamin Graham and David Dodd's seminal "Security Analysis" published in 1934 contains some contemporary illustrations of the extent to which (for example) the treatment of depreciation could vary.

The questionable nature of very old data seems obvious. Yet many professional investors and pundits who are sceptical about today's accounts are often happy when valuing stocks to accept uncritically some 80-year-old profit and loss accounts or balance sheets that are effectively, by today's standards, unaudited.

National accounts for the economy as a whole are sometimes thought to sidestep this problem. Such data do at least have a conceptual continuity: the meaning of Gross Domestic Product has been consistent since its inception. This has encouraged some analysts to focus on aggregate US profit estimates from the Bureau of Economic Analysis's National Income and Product Accounts (in the UK, the Office of National Statistics constructs similar estimates). Again, however, the early data are not convincing: national income accounting itself only dates from the 1930s, as a tool designed to help monitor and tackle the Depression. Data for earlier periods had to be constructed retrospectively using whatever sources had existed at the time. And the national income-based measures of profits include non-quoted, or private, companies alongside the quoted (investable) sector. The early NIPA profits data may be official, but that doesn't make them convincing.

The latest corporate earnings cycle is thus best placed in context by looking more carefully at *why* profits fell this time, and by recognising that the credibility of historical data will vary inversely with how old it is (or, to be more precise, it will vary inversely according to how distant the period is to which it refers: much historic economic and financial data is not in fact "old", because it has been constructed retrospectively). Thus the balance sheet-driven nature of the profits collapse in 2008/2009 made it both more severe, but also more transient, than a more conventional downturn driven by falling operating margins and revenues.

Again, to repeat one of this book's key themes, there is no single, foolproof approach here – apart, that is, from the need to stay open-minded. When concepts are broad, and measurement and reporting processes vary over time, the valid historical perspective may be a relatively short one. It is difficult to say much with confidence about corporate profitability and balance sheets across even the developed world for periods earlier than the 1970s, and there have been some important changes to accounting standards even more recently. We can however take almost at face value a 100-year-old observation on interest rates.[4] Similarly, movements in stock prices are reasonably reliable, though we should be aware that the composition and liquidity of the big indices has changed considerably over time – and that there are right and wrong ways of viewing them.

Consider Figures 4.3 and 4.4 for example, which offer two views of the US
stock market since 1871. Figure 4.3 shows the price index rising at an apparently accelerating pace, to reach levels in 2014 that look vertiginously high.
Who in their right minds would want to buy at that exposed top-right point?
However, as we've already hinted in the earnings chart above, when looking
at a long historical run of data, a logarithmic scale – one in which each equal
vertical increment represents the same proportionate gain, as opposed to the
arithmetic scale in Figure 4.3, in which each incremental rise represents a
steadily smaller proportionate gain – is more appropriate. It also makes sense
to adjust for inflation, to see whether the gains are real or not; and to add in the
dividend income that represents a large part of the reason for wanting to own
stocks. When these three adjustments are made in Figure 4.4, the performance
of US stocks looks steadier, and far from being outlandishly stretched the market looks recently to have been more or less in line with a long-term trend.

Credible international economic data really only extend back perhaps
60–70 years, reflecting the efforts of such bodies as the OECD and IMF.
Much corporate data has an even shorter pedigree. This doesn't mean that
longer-term analyses should be discarded – or that the scholarship that has
gone into the collation of the data is not impressive – but it does mean that
we should be wary of drawing precise or confident conclusions from them.

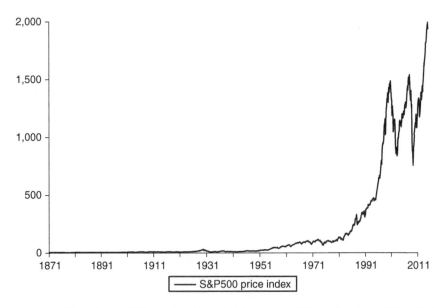

Figure 4.3 Two views of US stocks, 1871–2014: nominal US stock prices, 1871–2014,
arithmetic scale

Source: Robert Shiller's home page, author's calculations.

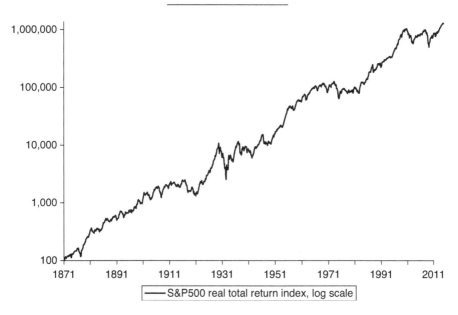

Figure 4.4 Two views of US stocks, 1871–2014: real US stock total return index, 1871–2014, logarithmic scale

Source: Robert Shiller's home page, author's calculations.

The British and American economic data are amongst the best established. In each case, economic performance over the last 60–70 years can be thought of, in hugely condensed and simplified terms, as following a rough V-shaped profile, in which the 1950s and 1960s represent the upper left arm; the late 1980s through to the early 2000s represent the upper right arms; and the 1970s and early 1980s represent the low point in between. The same is true of bottom-up corporate data, though it is decidedly patchy – even for the UK and US – before 1970. Thus the 1950s and 1960s saw (in broad terms) solid economic growth, low unemployment, modest inflation, and (patchily, given the data shortcomings) healthy profitability. The mix worsened, culminating in the high inflation, low growth – stagflation – and corporate losses of the 1970s and early 1980s, before improving again afterwards (Figures 4.5 and 4.6).

This stylised V-shaped trajectory is perhaps a disappointingly brief period for history buffs, but it has been a tremendously useful reminder (for example) that far from being unprecedentedly grim, the economic climate in recent years has not been as chronically bad as was the case in the early 1980s. It reminds me that while some measures of corporate profitability of late have been in the top half of the range seen in the last 40 years or so (setting aside the collapse in 2008/2009, which as noted was rapidly made

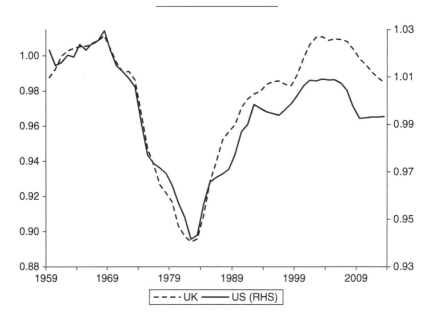

Figure 4.5　Proportionate growth/inflation ratios, UK and US, 1959–2013, ten-year moving averages

Source: Datastream, Measuring Worth, author's calculations. Ratios take the form $(1 + g)/(1 + i)$.

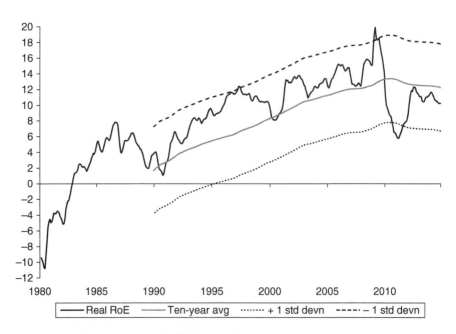

Figure 4.6　UK corporate profitability: real return on equity, 1980–2013, %

Source: Datastream, author's calculations.

good), arguably they should have been: if company performance even loosely reflects the wider economic climate, then the ascent has in reality been a bounce. With this in mind, it has not been surprising that many measures of stock market valuation, as we'll see in Part II, have been high by comparison with those seen in the 1970s – which were probably the worst times in living memory to be running a business (for reasons which are fascinating but beyond the scope of this book).

Peer pressure

History is not the only added dimension that can bring valuable investment perspective. Comparisons across countries can be useful; so too can an awareness of the institutional context. Again, however, we need to guard against taking simple comparisons at face value: the new dimension has to be relevant.

Consider for example the current experiments with Quantitative Easing, one of the "unconventional" monetary policies implemented in an attempt to support economies and banking systems after the 2008/2009 seizure. The idea behind QE is that central banks buy bonds, mostly from banks, in the market place, thus supporting their prices, keeping long-term interest rates (bond yields) low, and boosting bank liquidity. Financial markets are boosted directly, and the economy more indirectly as the lower yields and improved availability of bank credit make themselves felt on corporate and consumer confidence and spending power. Because QE has the potential to facilitate money creation, we have taken to referring to it as "printing money". And because when central banks have printed money in the past it has tended to end unhappily, this has worried many commentators and investors, as we saw earlier. "Too much money chasing too few goods" is a recipe for inflation, and the reckless use of the printing press was precisely what catapulted Germany's Weimar Republic into the catastrophic hyperinflation and monetary collapse of 1923.[5]

Today's QE is not however comparable to the actions of the Reichsbank. The rates of monetary growth it has delivered are modest: in the US and UK, narrow and broad measures of money supply growth are firmly in single digits, and have been there for most of the time since QE was introduced. In contrast, between the start of 1922 and late 1923, the German money supply exploded, multiplying more than 20 million-fold. As we saw earlier, much monetary growth in a modern economy is driven by borrowing from banks, and if people have no wish to borrow, the central bank may be "pushing on a string". Printing banknotes and dropping them from helicopters – the mistaken analogy drawn with QE in much discussion – would lead to anarchy, and for this reason it was never seriously proposed. This is not to suggest that QE poses no inflationary risk: if demand to borrow starts to accelerate meaningfully, spending power may yet need to be reined in quickly with higher interest rates (or Quantitative Tightening perhaps – the selling of some of the bonds bought). But the comparison with Weimar Germany has to date been counterproductive, and caused people to worry too much about inflation (and possibly to invest too heavily in gold, for example).

Japan is another country to which many pundits turn in search of a special angle on market issues, but as in the case of Weimar Germany, the lessons do not always translate well. The focus usually is on the prolonged attempt to get the Japanese economy and price level growing again following the bursting of a bubble in Japanese stock and real estate prices in 1990, a larger bubble than anything seen subsequently in the West, even in 2000.

In 1999 the Japanese economy had been stagnating and consumer prices gently falling, and a raft of fiscal and monetary policy initiatives had failed to spark it back into life. The government seemed to come close to experimenting with a more literal printing of money when it distributed shopping coupons to selected family groups in an attempt to boost spending. The parallel was not exact, because the coupons were not technically "money", but an alternative to tax cuts that the authorities hoped were more likely to be spent. The amount involved was small, and in practice the impact on overall spending was difficult to identify (many households used the coupons instead of, not as well as, cash).

Also in 1999, however, the Bank of Japan had introduced a "zero interest rate policy", and then followed through in 2001 with a local version of the Quantitative Easing that would eventually be adopted, in another context, by the Fed and the Bank of England.[6] The results were mixed: growth eventually picked up a little, but deflation continued. The Fed and the Bank of England seem to have concluded from Japan's experience that to have an impact, their own QE from 2008 needed to be large. Investors who concluded that Western QE would be associated with poor stock market performance – as it was in Japan, where stock prices continued to fall – would have made a costly mistake if they'd used that as a reason not to buy US stocks in early 2009.

More general inferences have been drawn by many observers from Japan's deflation, which began in the late 1990s and is only tentatively ended as I write, despite the latest and most aggressive experiments with Quantitative and Qualitative Easing, part of the package of measures labelled "Abenomics" (after Prime Minister Shinzo Abe). Most topically, US and UK inflation rates have recently been running below 2%, a level that may not be significantly different from zero when allowance is made for possible measurement error.

As a result, even as the gold bugs fret about the potential hyperinflation that could follow QE, many economists are worrying about the proximity of falling consumer prices – and if the West tips into deflation, the argument goes, it runs the risk of "turning Japanese", of "Japanification", and of seeing its GDP stagnate for a "lost decade" (or two).

It is not obvious however that the economic world need stop turning the instant measured inflation turns negative. Nor is it obvious that Japan's malaise reflects its deflation, which has in fact been little more than a measurement error itself, with the CPI falling by just 8% over more than 14 years, an average deflation rate of just 0.6% (of which half has now been reversed).

Deflation's falling prices can raise real borrowing costs sharply, and are thought likely to encourage businesses and consumers to defer spending in the expectation of buying more cheaply at a later date. In the Great Depression, deflation meant that real interest rates soared, but the Depression caused the deflation, not vice versa: if we're faced with another, we'll have plenty to worry about without adding deflation to the list. In the meantime, Figure 4.7 shows that it would take a major fall in consumer prices for real interest rates to approach Depression levels: the odd percentage point or two is inconsequential in this context.

In an emergency too central banks now recognise that there is no reason why nominal interest rates can't turn negative for a while.[8] Received wisdom

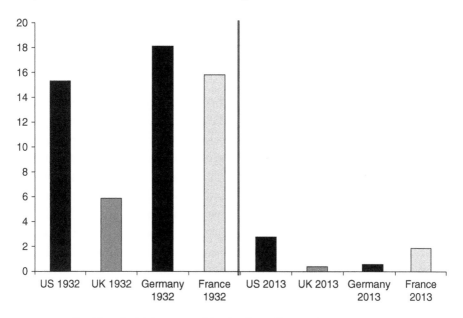

Figure 4.7   Real bond yields now and in the Great Depression, %

Source: Crafts & Fearon, Homer, Measuring Worth, Datastream, author's calculations.[7]

used to say that such an event would lead to cash hoarding, but in practice a charge on deposits could be viewed as the cost of storing money, much in the same way that we pay to store furniture (the economic point has been conceded as soon as you recognise that negative *real* interest rates do not always trigger major reallocations of balances into notes and coins). Remember too the points made in Chapter 3 about the likely scale of the aggregate debt burden for the economy as a whole: at the very least, higher real rates for borrowers will be boosting lenders' income, whether they spend it or not. Similarly, the notion that a little deflation will defer spending is unconvincing. Wages and profits might fall as part of the deflationary process, and there might be little point in waiting to buy something if you think your pay may fall just as much as its price.

They say that hard cases make bad law, and economically Japan is a hard case. The motivation of Japanese workers, businesses and policymakers has been different from that of their Western peers. Japan's post-war economic development was shaped by several key factors: the influential Ministry of International Trade and Industry (or MITI, now subsumed in the Ministry of Economy, Trade and Industry) and the *keiretsu*, influential business conglomerates; a tightly regulated domestic economy, with foreign investment and labour flexibility held at low levels; and a cultural emphasis on market share and stability.[9] Japan's failure to grow more robustly since 1990 is more likely to reflect this lack of dynamism than the modest deflation it has experienced. Meanwhile, as we saw in Chapter 3, Japan faces a particularly pronounced demographic imbalance, and has relatively little slack in its labour market: it will find it more difficult than most countries to deal with its older population.

Rather than expecting the West to become more like Japan, we should expect Japan to become more like the West, and more conventionally capitalist.[10] The government currently is trying to promote structural reform as the "third arrow" of Abenomics, and the market for corporate control is slowly becoming more active, but convincing liberalisation is still not at hand. Japan is a classic illustration of the way in which the popular economic debate fails carefully to distinguish between correlation and causation. Its deflation is just as likely to be a consequence of its economic predicament as a cause, and may have little relevance to the West. In the meantime, we should try to avoid the rather patronising tone that often creeps into the Western discussion of Japan's problems. If Japan does continue to grow only slowly it is doing so at a level of prosperity, social stability and cultural sophistication that many would envy.

Changing the metaphor

Fears of deflation currently are most widespread, and receiving some unexpected academic and central banking support, in the eurozone, where economic growth at the best of times is lacklustre and the ongoing sovereign debt crisis is believed to render the economic outlook particularly fragile. We have shown already how debt in aggregate can be placed in perspective – we used the US as an example, but the same points broadly apply to any large, self-sufficient economy. Viewed as a whole, the euro area is just such a region. Its smaller peripheral countries are anything but, however, and the threat that their predicament potentially posed (and may yet pose again) to the viability of the single currency itself meant that the region's wider solvency was of little reassurance at the height of the crisis in 2011 and 2012.

Trying to place the Greek situation into some sort of historic or peer perspective in 2011 was difficult. The euro itself was little more than a decade old, and the modern world offers few comparable examples of monetary union between a large group of sovereign states. The media and market discussion focused closely on the political dynamics in Greece and at the European Union – dynamics that were obviously unpredictable even to the key protagonists. Many commentators argued that collapse was inevitable, because the euro's design was fundamentally flawed (just as many had argued that the global economy was flawed, albeit for different reasons, in 2008/2009).

Arguably, however, the narrowly partisan nature of the discussion, and the sense of urgency engendered by tumbling peripheral bond markets – and eventual Greek default in 2012 – caused many participants to overlook the institutional context, and in particular the potential role that could be played by the European Central Bank if the two key supporters of the single currency – Germany and France – kept their nerve, as they seemed to be doing. Much of the media discussion also failed to distinguish between the peripheral economies, which differed qualitatively. Even amongst the smallest, Ireland's supply-driven economy, with foreign direct investment responsible for much of its growth and dynamism, was very different to those of Greece and Portugal, while the strengths of the Spanish economy – in 2013 it produced more cars than France or the UK – were overlooked amidst the focus on its construction boom and bust, and its high unemployment rate (which is largely structural, rarely dipping into single digits even in normal circumstances). Meanwhile, the euro's architecture had always been known to be incomplete – to be credible a single monetary policy needs to be buttressed by similarly coordinated banking supervision and fiscal policy at least – but this had not prevented it surviving its first decade.

This suggested an alternative metaphor to the "make or break" view fostered by a market debate that was lurching from one EU summit and Greek (and Italian, and Spanish) political flashpoint to the next. The metaphor was borrowed from Greek mythology, with the tale of Sisyphus and his arduous and never-ending task. The investment conclusion, as in most of the examples provided so far, was to resist the temptation to bet on a more dramatic outcome.

These further examples, after those in Chapter 3, show some ways in which we can question the unthinking assertions that often characterise the investment debate: there is almost always another point of view (if not several) in investing, even if there is no easy rule as to how exactly you go about finding it. This is not the worst economic climate since the 1930s – it's not even the worst in my working lifetime. The huge fall in corporate profits in 2008/2009 was always going to be temporary. Quantitative Easing is not printing money, and the risk of hyperinflation has been overstated. So too, arguably, has the risk posed by deflation. Japan is more likely to become like the West than vice versa. A "muddle through" for the euro is just as tenable as the make or break view.

RAISING THE SIGNAL-TO-NOISE RATIO

There are hundreds of economic data releases every month, just for the major economies. There are even more corporate announcements, particularly during results seasons; and financial and commodity markets themselves are constantly in motion, being shaped by, and having the potential to shape in turn, the economic climate. Then we have the ongoing rounds of various global, EU and other regional policymaker summits, the proceedings of the international think tanks, and of course the regular meetings and pronouncements of the central banks, and the workings of the government budgetary and electoral processes. The research teams at the investment banks, the consultancies and the media are constantly generating ideas and opinions that claim our attention. How can anyone stay on top of all this information?

Some people are simply capable of processing and storing more information than others. A Manhattan-based hedge fund manager springs to mind who really has heard everything, and holds all the news and opinions effortlessly in mind – or at least, if he doesn't, I am unable to tell. The good news for the rest of us, however, is that much of the data and many of the views are not that important, even in the short term. It is the job of the financial adviser to help investors see past the superfluous information and focus on the things that might matter most. Of course even the wisest adviser cannot predict the future, or successfully call the short-term twists and turns of the business cycle, and an improved signal-to-noise ratio should not tempt you into market timing.

Because no two business, interest rate or stock market cycles are exactly alike – it's different every time, remember – there are few economic indicators or policy levers that matter always, and in the same way. The importance of expectations in economic and financial behaviour, and the behavioural traits hard-wired into our supposedly rational minds, mean that a deterministic model of the economy and markets does not and can not exist (and there is little point in searching for one). That said, if I were able to access only a few selected data points and policy parameters each month to decide which phases of the business cycle and investment cycles we might be in, my list would include:

- The new orders component of the monthly US ISM survey for manufacturing, which has been around for half a century and is a good – but not infallible – guide to industrial trends in the most important and direction-setting economy for capital markets.
- The monthly data on US personal spending, which tell us quickly what Global Inc.'s most important customer has been doing with their money.
- US three-month money rates, the ten-year Treasury note yield, and the latest Federal Open Markets Committee minutes, which will illustrate current liquidity, the consensual view on expected long-term growth and inflation, and the Fed's thinking on policy.
- The German IFO survey, which does for the most important economy in Europe what the ISM survey does for the US (the Purchasing Managers' Indices for Europe are promising alternatives, but do not yet have the IFO's track record).
- An account of the latest ECB press conference, which conveys the second most important – and *the* most underestimated – central bank's views of current and projected liquidity conditions in its area.
- The monthly UK retail sales and balance of payments data, and China's monthly "data dump" of retail sales, industrial production and capital spending data (though see the caveat below).
- The Brent crude oil price, and the CRB index of spot commodity prices; inflation-adjusted trade-weighted exchange rate indices

for the dollar and the euro; a forward PE ratio for the S&P 500 index, and the consensus earnings level underpinning it.

Lower priority items would include: direct inflation and labour market indicators, because they tend to lag, and the outlook for them can usually be inferred from the other data, bond yields and the big central banks' views; surveys of consumer confidence, because what consumers feel is much less important to markets than what they do; comments from the Bank of England, which are more detailed but carry less weight than the other two central banks', even in the local UK stock and bond markets (which are largely shaped by wider, global trends); data from Japan, which tends to follow its own very idiosyncratic course, and usually has a small effect only on global portfolios nowadays; and data from emerging markets other than China, because the bloc is so fragmented and is again rarely a prime mover of global markets.

Looking beyond the various data releases and key market indices, there are a few filters that can be applied to financial commentaries, to avoid spending time on some of the redundant points being made. Some of the following somewhat tongue-in-cheek rules of thumb touch on issues to be tackled in Part II:

- Views based on macroeconomic identities – statements that are true by definition, and which merely rearrange existing information – are mostly timewasters. Perhaps the most commonly encountered one is the "quantity theory" of money, which states that the amount of money in circulation, multiplied by the number of times it is used, equals the number of transactions in the economy, multiplied by their prices. This insight never seems to deliver a useful investment conclusion: look for the expression "MV = PT", and avoid. Equally frustrating is the identity-driven observation that the share of profits in GDP cannot rise forever: it's not helpful, because nobody thinks it can.

- Obscure theories are obscure for a reason. When someone describes themselves as a follower of the Austrian "school", they are telling you more about their need to belong than about the drivers of interest rates. The reason that a lot of high economic theory has required so much elucidation, and inspired so much disagreement, is that it is poorly presented. Ideas in economics and finance are not especially complicated, and you don't need to spend time watching others fail to fathom this out.

- Comparisons with other business cycles, and with other countries, can be counter-productive, as we have seen: precedents and peers are not always relevant. You have one investment portfolio, here and now, and how it might have performed in other circumstances, or in another country where the investment culture might be different, is an interesting hypothetical question but not a profitable one.

- "Thematic" investment ideas are usually a bad idea, unless the theme is a not-for-profit one (such as the wish to avoid armament or tobacco manufacturing for ethical reasons, and implementation can be difficult even there). There are so many moving parts in the investment world that a one-dimensional view is unlikely to do consistently well for long – as we will note in Part II. The only investment theme you need to consider, subject to your personal financial needs and appetites, is the preservation and growth of your real wealth.

- Esoteric valuation measures are a waste of time. Again we will revisit this more carefully in Part II, but if only a small group of people have access to a special ratio or database, then it is not likely to move markets, even if it looks "as if" it does. There is no holy grail of valuation, and "as if" theories of knowledge are specious.

- Economic growth is a key reason for wanting to invest in stocks to begin with, but it does not matter equally at all times and in all places. Articles suggesting that emerging markets must do best because they grow fastest should be set to one side. And the fact that economists' forecasts for China's booming retail sales and industrial production data (for example) are routinely within a few tenths of a percentage point of the out-turn, while they miss much smaller growth rates in the US and Europe by bigger amounts, is telling us more about news management than about the nuances of China's business cycle. Disregard articles suggesting that Europe must be a bad investment because its GDP grows relatively slowly (or because the euro is relatively strong).

- Cost-cutting does not drive the profit cycle. In the case of oil and other commodities, commentators routinely confuse revenues and costs: in the major stock markets there are more big producers of commodities than there are big users of them (banks, pharmaceutical, telecom and technology companies don't buy much oil, for example). More generally, the big movements in aggregate profits are driven arithmetically by the business cycle and what it does to revenues, pricing power, productivity and (as we saw above) asset write-downs. It is extremely unlikely that an across the board cut in employment would boost aggregate profits, simply because such a cut would hit total revenues. Henry Ford noted that it is the customer who pays the wage bill, and it can't be good business for industry in aggregate to sack its customers.

- Much time spent on short-term security selection in an attempt to beat the market benchmarks is wasted. You do not need to research the entire global market, or sift through managements' waste bins, to find companies whose securities offer attractive long-term returns. Alternatively, a wider mix of stocks and bonds can be put together quickly and inexpensively using the increasing range of "passive" or tracking funds that are available, and those funds tend to do at least as well as the average "active" fund that plays the short-term benchmark game.[11] It is often said that the existence of star investment managers confirms the existence of stock-picking skill, but it doesn't. The laws of probability suggest that someone has to outperform, and distinguishing between skill and luck is not easy: if it were just about smartness, there would be a lot more stars than there are. It is difficult to pick stocks to beat the indices because in a narrow, technical sense, markets are relatively efficient when it comes to pricing-in all that is known about the companies concerned. Stock selection is engrossing, but diminishing returns kick in quickly, and many investors are effectively paying to indulge their fund managers' hobby. The giveaway is often the number of stocks managers choose to hold. A fund holding 50 stocks is more or less a tracker, and should be priced accordingly.

Why is there so much financial noise? Partly because we confuse detail and information with knowledge, and there are just so many moving parts in today's interconnected but still diverse global capital markets. Partly because many pundits and policymakers do believe that a "true" model, or data generation process, does exist, and that it is sending important messages (such as the five big concerns discussed in Chapter 3). But also partly because much financial commentary is not intended as practical advice, or to inform: it exists to express opinion, to advertise, to show-off, and even to entertain. More on this in Part II.

AVOID CLICHÉS LIKE THE PLAGUE: THE CELTIC TIGER

When we collectively fail to take a broader view, expectations can become self-fulfilling and reinforcing. Ireland's Celtic Tiger episode was just such an emotional roller coaster ride, and a fascinating – and unnerving – illustration of the way in which media and markets together can leave all perspective behind.

I wrote the short "Celtic Tiger" note 20 years ago in late August 1994 as part of a Morgan Stanley report that focused on the prospects for the Irish Stock Market, which had recently been upgraded to "developed market" status. The Exchange Rate Mechanism had in 1993 undergone what was to be the last of its periodic crises; in 1992 the UK had been unceremoniously ejected from it. A single currency was a distant and very uncertain prospect on the horizon, and it was far from clear that Ireland would be included in it were it to happen.

An exchange of views began at dinner with Irish CEOs and officials in Kildare – graced by Jack Yeats' "Harvest Moon" – and we followed up with a lengthier visit to meet Dublin-based economists, fund managers and executives. Having drafted the economy-focused part of the report, we found ourselves struggling for a title. Even an economist could see that "Ireland: Growing Quickly Without Much Inflation" left something to be desired, and at almost the last minute, the phrase "Celtic Tiger" sprang to mind. I quickly sounded-out our (Irish) in-house editor, and the rest as they say is history (or at least a small footnote to it). Nothing I have written – or will write – has resonated so loudly. A friendly Irish economist once wished me boiled in my own spit for coining the phrase, and I have apologised many times in Ireland in print, on radio and on TV for my unwitting cultural vandalism. We never actively promoted it: the phrase quickly developed a life of its own. Amongst other things, it eventually provided the title for a West End show.

There was less to the report than you might think: it aimed simply to give international investors some idea of the macroeconomic landscape. As often happens, the underlying picture took a while to settle clearly. As it did so, the most visible feature was that Ireland's emerging growth story was largely a supply-side success. The eventual surge in house prices followed as a much later consequence, though one that was given added momentum by the low euro interest rates (unexpected back in 1994) and misguided policy.

The "Tiger" report was always an outside view: we did not pretend to offer an informed local analysis. But as an external commentator, maybe, one has a broader perspective, and perhaps a greater awareness of relativities. Local analysis can focus too much on that detail. Economists seem often inclined to be most pessimistic about the economies with which they are most familiar.

As noted, there was substance behind the initial boom: growth between 1993 and 2000 was not driven by reckless borrowing and lending. The foundations of the "Tiger" have largely been forgotten, but included: the deliberate courting of foreign direct investment (FDI); very low and stable business taxes; membership of the single European market, and the opportunities it posed for multinationals looking to establish a local export base; a relatively young, educated, flexible, competitive and English-speaking workforce; and the beginnings of several sectoral "clusters". More prosaically, Ireland's small size also had an arithmetic significance. A new plant based in Ireland then had a proportionate impact on the local economy some 30 times larger than if the same plant had located in Germany, for example. For American-owned companies in particular, the cultural overlap was also attractive.

The forecasts in the Celtic Tiger report were in fact wrong. Growth was stronger, and lasted longer, than we'd expected. Between 1993 and 2000, growth averaged 9%. The pace of growth slowed somewhat, and its character changed as house prices and bank lending then gathered momentum (when my career took me elsewhere, saving me from having to make some difficult calls). Nonetheless, it still averaged a far from sluggish 5% through to 2007.

Predictions of imminent disaster were commonplace throughout the 13-year period. When the collapse did ultimately arrive, however, it did so not because the supply-side export-driven model had failed. Arguably, it worked so well that it engendered over-confidence, an erosion of competitiveness, and a willingness to try to bank too much of tomorrow's growth today. The supply-side drivers of the initial success were forgotten, growth became more domestically driven, the balance of payments went into deficit, and bank lending and Georgian house prices went into orbit. Nemesis eventually followed hubris.

Not that it was Ireland's alone. The local collapse coincided with the global trauma outlined in Chapter 1. But Ireland's fall was dramatic even in this wider context, culminating in the government's brave emergency decision in 2008 to guarantee Irish bank deposits in the face of the implosion in the value of local banks' assets as house prices went sharply into reverse. The decision was arguably not the government's to make, inasmuch as the currency of denomination was the euro, not a local creation, and it illustrates again how closely banking supervision and monetary policy are linked in practice.

Banks played a big role in Ireland's crisis, just as they did globally, and there too a vigorous and rapidly growing bank sector may not be needed for recovery. Much FDI is self-financed, in any case. The failure of the Irish banks was at least a straightforward one: reckless property lending, a failure of what we might term "utility" banking as opposed to the opaque complexities noted in Chapter 1. The exposures concerned were visible, easily disentangled and mostly lodged firmly on specific balance sheets.

It is not often that one moves on to new pastures before one's investment idea does, and I feel privileged to have been able to spot, and to be in a small way associated with, such a supply-side success. I do however have mixed feelings about the way in which the phrase took on that independent life, which is the reason for including this account of it here. As a descriptive term it worked well, but I wonder whether in a small way it may have fostered some of the eventual over-confidence that marked the 2001–2006 period in particular.

The symbiotic interaction of media, markets and the public mood in Ireland is a classic illustration of a loss of perspective, and an illustration of just how economically potent that can be – as Keynes recognised with his notion of "animal spirits" (particularly appropriate here), and as we've noted already in Chapter 1. To the extent that clichés and headlines substitute for thought, offering a collective "making sense" of markets that is based on easy repetition as opposed to objective analysis, they can contribute towards the unthinking, momentum-driven borrowing and lending decisions that fuel booms and busts, decisions that might not be made after a less colourful, lower-case debate.

The later excesses and euphoria were very visible, as was the collapse. But it seemed in late November 2010, when the "troika" of the IMF, EU and ECB arrived in Dublin to negotiate the support package needed, that the mood had perhaps become as excessively pessimistic as it had been optimistic in 2006/2007.[12] The economy has been slowly recovering since, partly because it does still enjoy (and is visibly demonstrating) some of the structural supply-side advantages that underpinned the initial "Celtic Tiger" period – not least, more than its fair share of inward investment, and one of the most flexible developed-world labour markets that this economist has seen. Even after the decline, per capita GDP in Ireland in 2014 stands some 85% higher than in 1993, which represents an impressive annual compound growth rate of 3%. But in future I will avoid clichés like the plague.

ANCHORING DOWNWARDS: WHY GLOOM GETS A GRIP

In December 1996, Alan Greenspan, the Fed Chairman, famously remarked that the US stock market seemed "irrationally exuberant". The market subsequently more than doubled before peaking in 2000, and only briefly revisited the level at which Greenspan made his comment at the very low point of the 2008/2009 collapse (since when it has trebled, as of late 2014). Whether the Fed Chairman was premature or not, investment exuberance and despondency alike are based on overly narrow worldviews. In my experience, the latter emotion is encountered more frequently, and mistakenly – which is a big reason for writing this book. Over-optimistic episodes such as the euphoria of the latter stages of the Celtic Tiger craziness, the TMT mania of 2000, and the complacency that marked the Great Moderation in 2006, have been less common, and less intense, than the more pessimistic emotional spasms that punctuate our recent financial history. Crises – or embarrassments, or accidents – of one sort or another are encountered more frequently than booms or blessings, even though the steady ascent of GDP per capita over most of the last half-century – a prolonged "muddle through", perhaps – should have made people aware that something out there has gone much more right than wrong.[13]

It is too easy to blame the media. There is a close, symbiotic and largely overlooked relationship between journalists and the spokesmen working at financial institutions. Many journalists don't have the time or statistical resources to do as much of their own research as they'd like, while the big banks and investment management firms employing the economists and analysts want the free advertising that comes from seeing employees being quoted or broadcast – and will often pay a prominent economist more, whether their analysis is accurate or not. Journalists will tell you that bad news certainly sells: a headline suggesting that the world may end tomorrow has to be bought; whereas a headline suggesting that tomorrow will be pretty much like today... well, it wouldn't be a headline. And sales do matter: not just for the immediate income, but for attracting advertising revenue. So the easiest way to be quoted as a City economist is to be quick on the draw with a gloomy assessment of the latest data release when the papers and TV companies call.[14]

Most of the City economists and financial journalists you will be able to picture are pessimistic. One pundit has been professionally and prominently sceptical about the US stock market for 30 years: his reputation has grown steadily, but not as fast as the S&P 500. Many are effectively and validly employed as public relations officers, not analysts or advisers. But you can't easily make people buy something they don't want to, and the media-market circus does not explain why there is that public appetite for bad news to begin with.

The closeness of this relationship is itself one of the reasons that extrapolative expectations can take hold. City economists themselves are more likely to believe something if they see it on the front page of the *Wall Street Journal* or the *Financial Times*, even if it's a comment that they have supplied themselves. Tail-chasing can extend to the markets: traders and investors are quite capable of reacting to newspaper headlines that are reporting yesterday's market news; prices of stocks and bonds have been known to respond (for example) to a movement in the US leading indicator that is attributable to the stock and bond prices included amongst its components. It is always easier to repeat received wisdom than it is to think for yourself, and if groupthink gathers pace, market momentum can follow.

Many journalists and economists do see their mission as one of providing objective and accurate advice and information; many are genuinely pessimistic. It is often argued that optimism is synonymous with product-pushing, and naïvely inductive, even though bond-related financial products do well in bad times, and *anybody* taking a view about the future is being inductive – gloomy forecasts can go wrong too. Also, frankly, being a pundit can be enjoyable and good for our self-esteem, and the temptation to entertain or show-off is difficult to resist. The easiest points to score are usually critical of the authorities and the status quo: the naïve, unthinking optimist with a vested interest in life going on is a much easier target than the world-weary wit who just knows that disaster is around the corner. In some contexts, satire is a force for good – it is nice to think that dictators are done for when they become the butt of jokes – but when it comes to futurology, it has been a costly default setting.

But again, why is that receptive audience out there – why are we so quick to applaud the pundits who tell us that there is only bad stuff ahead? Some concepts taken from the intersection of psychology and economics are useful here. The insights from behavioural finance, and a lot of experimental evidence, suggest that we worry more about losses than we covet similar-sized gains; that our views are further shaped by our frames of reference, where we're starting from, the road we travelled to get there, and by regret over missed opportunities; and that our intuitive appraisal of a situation can be influenced by evidence that is not directly relevant but which has somehow stuck in our minds and anchored our views.[15]

To be human is to face the most one-sided of outcomes, the biggest loss imaginable, and as we get older and less patient we read about it happening to others more and more. Our experienced lives sometimes take second place to our remembered lives in shaping how satisfied we are, and intense recent events tend to matter most in those remembered lives. In thinking about macro matters most people are taken outside their usual field of expertise, and forced to rely more on intuition. They may be inclined to pessimism because for each of us at some stage the world will indeed end. It has not however been a good investment philosophy – so far. Keynes famously wrote that "In the long run, we are all dead". His preceding sentence, however, is often overlooked: "But this long run is a misleading guide to current affairs".[16]

Part II

WHAT TO DO ABOUT IT

5

KNOW THE GAME, KNOW YOURSELF

another dangerous enemy to a trader is his susceptibility to the urgings of a magnetic personality when plausibly expressed by a brilliant mind.

– Edwin Lefèvre, "Reminiscences of a Stock Operator", 1923

the best is the enemy of the good.

– Voltaire

Part I presented an alternative account of recent financial history and our current economic predicament. It suggested that rather than being faced with aggregate insolvency and an economy holed below the waterline, we live in a world of financial accidents and embarrassments in which liquidity occasionally dries up – sometimes drastically – but in which the underlying drivers of prosperity can be resilient. This less gloomy assessment lends itself to a "muddle through" approach, not an apocalyptic one, and suggests that it may still be worth investing – even, or especially, in the big developed economies of the West.

Now we have to think more carefully about the investment process itself. In this chapter we'll discuss the importance of having a personal investment policy that takes into account your financial needs and personality, and how to go about framing one; but first we need to be frank about what investing may *not* be about.

SATISFICED? YOU SHOULD BE. WHAT INVESTMENT IS NOT ABOUT; AND THE IMPORTANCE OF SHOWING UP

The shelves of the financial services industry are overflowing with products, and the media are bulging with financial news. The front page macroeconomic stories may read pessimistically more often than not – and excessively so, we've argued above – but when it comes to choosing specific investments, whether bonds, stocks or funds, our industry's advertising, and the financial pages and supplements, make it seem as if investing is about a continuous hunt for big profits and high performance, and that someone somewhere is ahead of the game and getting it right. By the law of averages, of course, someone has to be ahead, just as someone has to be behind. That someone is not always the same person, however; they are not always right for their stated reasons, or indeed any; and as we shall argue later, there may be nothing wrong with not being ahead of the pack – everything depends on what your investment goal is. Practical investment is not about *optimising*, seeking the best possible outcome, even though that word features extensively in much textbook and practical discussion of portfolio construction (see Chapter 7). Rather, it is about *satisficing*, finding a simple solution that is acceptable – that is, one that will preserve and augment real wealth over the longer term.

Institutional money managers and sales teams who are held to account for their performance on a quarterly basis can't easily relax: they are committed to trying to be that person, the one who is ahead of a very specific and competitive game. They obviously can't all be, and you need to think carefully about what you are effectively asking them to do when you give them your money to invest. Performance is uncertain, and few active managers consistently deliver it on a scale worth paying for, simply because "beating the market" in the way that secures public success is very difficult without a crystal ball. Where individual companies and currencies are concerned, the larger stock, bond and foreign exchange markets in particular are very efficient, in the narrow technical sense of pricing-in all the available public information (this does *not* mean that they are always rational, or stable).

Over the longer term, economic growth may be more resilient than feared, but it rarely proceeds at a dramatic pace (though it is still surprisingly difficult to second-guess its short-term gyrations). Globally, growth rates are usually firmly in single digits, even when inflation is added, and this should be a starting point when considering the order of magnitude of likely investment returns (but a starting point only). A very active and lucky fund manager might double or treble your funds in a short space of time, but you may not be able to spot which one in advance, and you may not be able to do much better than average yourself should you decide to manage your own portfolio – our relatively optimistic outlook notwithstanding. A do-it-yourself approach, possibly using "passive" or "tracking" funds that simply match the composition of the wider stock and bond markets, can be attractive, but investing in constant pursuit of dramatic gains is a bad strategy however you choose to implement it. The first step in framing a personal investment policy is therefore to be realistic: investing is not usually about getting rich quickly.

From time to time, opportunities to double or treble your money in a short space of time do come along, even in today's economic climate, and of course I'm not suggesting you deliberately avoid them. Investors who had the nerve to buy the US stock market at its post-Lehman Brothers low point in March 2009 have seen the S&P 500 index treble: taking dividends into account, the total pre-tax return to a dollar-based investor as of late 2014 has been more than 200% (equally, if you'd been unlucky enough to buy US stocks at their pre-crisis high in October 2007, and then sold at the bottom in March 2009, you'd have lost more than half your investment in less than two years). Such large moves are relatively rare, however, and if you see them as the norm, you may be tempted to invest too much, or too recklessly, at times when the possibility of such returns is small and the chances of a setback are higher. Even when potentially large returns are available, and you agree with the points made in Part I, it is not easy putting opportunistic plans into practice in the middle of a public panic: psychologically, buying a falling market is very difficult. An institutional investor in Boston told me that he bought stocks only when he felt physically sick with worry, but not everybody has that fortitude.

One seemingly seductive short-cut to bigger returns in particular should be avoided by almost all private investors, namely: leverage. There are only two rules to remember here: rule one, do not use borrowed money to buy stocks; rule two, remember rule one. The importance of debt as a constraint on the wider economy is routinely overstated, as we saw in Part I, but at the individual level its impact can be, as we also noted, life changing. Adding borrowed funds of £9,000 to a personal stake of £1,000 can turn a potential 10% gain (£100 on that stake of £1,000) into one of 100% (£1,000, the 10% gain on a total investment of your £1,000 and the £9,000 borrowed funds, as a proportion of your £1,000 stake), more than enough to pay likely interest charges. If that potential gain turns out to be a loss of 10%, however, your stake is wiped out, with interest still to pay; and a bigger loss could leave you in debt or even bankrupt.

Institutional investors, who are investing other people's money and not personally liable for losses or debts incurred, often use borrowed funds to amplify potential returns, as do some private investors who follow markets closely and trade carefully. Companies and homebuyers of course use borrowed money to invest all the time, though the investments they are making are (usually) more tangible and less volatile than financial assets. Some readers may therefore think I'm being overly conservative (particularly, again, since Part I explained so carefully why, at the whole economy level, debt needn't matter as much as is commonly feared). Using borrowed money to invest in securities markets is dangerous, however, and best avoided if you value your peace of mind. If you want leverage to work for you in the investment markets, you can always own shares in a bank or another leveraged company, or invest in a private equity partnership: that way, your returns are less directly geared, as the effects of the company's borrowing on its investment performance can be mixed, but your potential losses are capped at the level of your stake.

Rather than being delivered speedily by big or leveraged market moves, then, you should view investment returns as most likely to accumulate over a lengthy period, and to reflect the cumulative compounding of the effects of economic growth, corporate dividends and interest rates. Einstein dubbed compound interest the eighth wonder of the world; Woody Allen reportedly said that most success in life comes from simply showing up;[1] and Greg B. Davies, an ex-colleague and behavioural finance specialist, says the most useful advice for private investors often is "don't just do something, stand there" (in particular, don't be panicked into selling at times of crisis). For most private investors, investment is best viewed as an ongoing, largely passive participation in markets – a taking part, a showing up – as opposed to an active in-out trading process.

As noted, this is not the approach usually described. Financial reporting, and the research produced by the financial sector, is devoted to short-term news, and to unearthing new and exotic opportunities for profit (and loss). Investment is presented as a continuous, proactive, anticipatory and perfectible (or "optimisable") process. Forecasts are made, and game-changing events predicted. In practice, however, anyone who has ever had to produce economic and financial forecasts and prognoses will be aware that they are useful only inasmuch as they help us gauge the scale of the unpredictable surprises that are about to unfold instead. A realistic investment process will recognise that we are simply unable to forecast well: despite the consensual tendency to gloom described in Part I, the timing of most US recessions is not predicted in advance, and those that are predicted tend not to occur on schedule (or at all). In reality, often the key is not forecasting shocks, but responding to them – or not – when they occur.

This view more readily lends itself to a "buy and hold" strategy with some periodic rebalancing than to a more aggressively tactical, market timing approach that tries to play the short-term fluctuations in the business cycle. Many pundits – and active fund managers – portray a buy-and-hold strategy as naïve; and for a while amidst the depths of the 2008/2009 collapse, global stock markets had given back a decade's worth of returns in dollar terms. At the same time, bonds were hitting new highs: in the US and UK, stocks' relative performance briefly unravelled more than two decades of gains, seemingly undermining even the long-term case for growth-related investing (to say nothing of the notion of an equity "risk premium").

There are of course no guarantees that a particular asset will perform well on even a long-term view. That said, the worldview outlined in Part I suggests that you need a good reason for betting strongly against growth, and pundits forget that for most private clients the alternative to ongoing engagement in the markets through a long-term buy-and-hold strategy is not an active, tactical approach but instead a more complete disengagement. Most private investors hold a large proportion of their investable wealth in cash or bank deposits, where at recent and prospective levels of interest rates and taxes its real value is being slowly eroded by inflation.

YOU DON'T GET PAID FOR TAKING RISK, AND THERE ARE NO RISKLESS ASSETS

If get-rich-quick returns are not usually on offer, investors should also be on their guard against overly detailed analysis and predictions. In my lifetime, UK short-term interest rates have moved between 0.5% and 17%; the monthly year-on-year inflation rate has moved between −1.6% and 27%; and quarterly year-on-year real GDP growth has ranged from −6.8% to 10.2%. Corporate earnings and profitability can be defined and measured in many different ways, and all of them display even more volatility than the economic data – as of course do stock markets themselves. Thoroughness is important, but so too is an awareness that, having given an investment outlook your best shot, and knowing the scale of potential volatility, you should then present it in a rounded, approximate fashion. First decimal places have little practical use when talking about growth rates and investment returns; and outside the institutional bond markets, second decimal places arguably have none. Similarly, the predictions of a company's profit based on a modelled income account that has hundreds of line items in it are not necessarily more accurate than those based on a more streamlined model. Precision can be spurious, lead to overconfidence, and make us think that we know more, whether optimistically or pessimistically, than we really do. Real-world investment analysis is unavoidably inexact and incomplete: again, it is about satisficing, not optimising.

Perhaps more contentiously, you should also guard against taking too seriously one of the most influential components of investment analysis, a body of academic work that has come to be known as "modern portfolio theory". This work is built on very some very shaky foundations. For one thing, it assumes – as does most conventional economic analysis – that investors are rational, that they act objectively and deliberately with carefully calculated returns in mind: that is, that they are systematic profit-maximisers. This assumption has been challenged successfully by the experimental approach of the behavioural finance school cited earlier, who have shown just how much decision-making is subconscious and subjective, resulting in inconsistent and irrational outcomes. A second flaw in modern portfolio theory has been less directly challenged,[2] but is just as important for asset allocation: the theory assumes that there is a necessary relationship between the riskiness of an investment and its likely return. Specifically, the theory says that the riskier the investment, the greater the likely return. This notion that investors will therefore be rewarded for taking risk is widespread, and intuitively appealing – but it is misleading, and like leverage, potentially dangerous to your financial health.

It is intuitive, because if investors are collectively faced with a safe asset and a risky one, you would expect the latter to be somehow cheaper (we discuss valuation in Chapter 7), and so carry a higher yield, or a seemingly greater chance of capital gain. If likely returns looked the same, investors would choose to hold only the safe asset: to do otherwise would mean taking risk for no reason. The extra return theoretically carried by risky assets has become known as their "risk premium", the amount investors require to compensate them for taking on that risk, and the incorporation of such risk premia into theories of portfolio construction has shaped not just the impressive intellectual investment infrastructure represented by that modern portfolio theory, but countless real-world investment decisions and products. But it has also explicitly promoted the notion of investment as an optimising process.

The idea is fine; and the main message in this book is that it is worth investing, and in particular that it is worth investing in some risky assets. But the idea does not easily translate into practice, and you should not invest in assets simply because they are risky. If we could be sure of being paid for taking it, it wouldn't be risk. In the real world, many risky assets are cheaper, but they do not reliably deliver better returns, and some of them can deliver catastrophic losses. Risk premia do not exist, and to view the investment world as functioning "as if" they do is a mistake.[3]

The risk that we worry about as investors is rather different in practice to the risk that features in most of the investment literature. The temptation there is to equate risk with the historical volatility of returns, something that can be measured and manipulated mathematically with some precision, and used as an input in calculating "risk-adjusted" outcomes that allow us to rank assets according to how seemingly safely their returns have been generated. Other things equal, a long-term return of 10% generated by an asset whose monthly returns show an annualised standard deviation of 20% is less attractive than the same return generated with volatility of just 10%: stability is obviously something to be valued. In practice, however, things are more complicated.

Firstly, the risk we worry about in investing lies in the future, and in measuring volatility – and everything else for that matter – the information we have lies in the past: volatility itself can be unpredictable. Even measuring the past is not as straightforward as we'd like it to be: data on investment returns and volatility can of course only be compiled for assets that existed, and so are subject to "survivorship bias" – they exclude those companies and markets that failed, whose returns were (very) negative. Volatility itself is not necessarily the best measure of discomfort: we are of course not indifferent to whether an asset we own rises or falls in price. Upward volatility is not risk, but a pleasant surprise.

Most importantly, however, meaningful risk is simply not measurable and computable in the neat, probabilistic sense assumed by financial theory. Financial economists often use the analogy of flipping a coin to illustrate risk, and how it might be taken into account; but the unpredictability attaching to coin-flipping is not really risk at all, since most of us would be happy to assume that a large number of flips will deliver an approximately 50:50 heads:tails result. As investors, we are worried about wider uncertainty – and uncertainty is simply not computable. Moreover, it affects all assets, not just the ones whose prices move most under normal circumstances.

The best-known illustration of the alleged "equity risk premium" is the historical observation that stocks have outperformed bonds in most countries for which long historical records are available, and that because they have been the most volatile asset historically this can be viewed as a payment to compensate for that volatility. In fact, the scale of the outperformance seems larger than the relative volatility of stocks alone would suggest;

within stock and bond markets the most volatile countries, sectors and securities often underperform their less volatile peers (the US stock market has been a long-term outperformer, but is one of the least volatile, for example); and a moment's reflection tells us of course that few investors who bought (say) US and UK stocks in the early twentieth century seriously expected economic growth, inflation and interest rates to evolve as they did. To give two obvious examples, the "cult of the equity" that followed UK life assurance and pension funds' reappraisal of stocks as growth assets in the late 1950s, and the surge in inflation that hit bonds so hard in the 1970s, were not predicted. Historical investment returns were arguably not a payment for bearing equity volatility or even uncertainty, but were instead simply a happy accident for stockholders. That does not mean that similarly rewarding out-turns cannot occur in the future, but it does suggest that it will be the financial and economic context that drives whatever happens, not the relative "riskiness" of stocks.

The distinction between probabilistic risk and uncertainty is not new: modern portfolio theorists chose to overlook it in their desire to make investment analysis more objective and rigorous. Keynes published an influential book on the topic before he tackled the business cycle.[4] Once you accept that the future is profoundly uncertain, and that potential outcomes do not have probabilities and expected values that can be meaningfully computed in advance, you accept that there are limits to what we can usefully say about how to construct investment portfolios. This is only a problem if you expected there to be a lot to be said to begin with, or if you are existentially uncomfortable with uncertainty. In my experience, private investors are much less troubled by this than are many more academic analysts – possibly because many private investors have day jobs and businesses that confront them more directly with the coarse unpredictability of life. Again, this does not mean that there is nothing to be said, or that risky assets shouldn't be a core holding for long-term investors.

As noted, uncertainty applies to all assets, not just those that are most obviously volatile. The idea that there is a "riskless" asset that defines the "safe" return against which to gauge all the others is mistaken. There are some risks that apply to all assets – the asteroid strike noted in Chapter 1, for example, or a nuclear or biological holocaust perhaps that would destroy businesses, governments, and fiat money, and render even gold worthless. Other risks apply more to some assets than others. We are perhaps most aware of cyclical risks – the danger of recession, unemployment and bank failures, and the attendant falls in corporate profits and corporate credit-worthinesss – and these risks typically hit stocks hardest. Inflation risk,

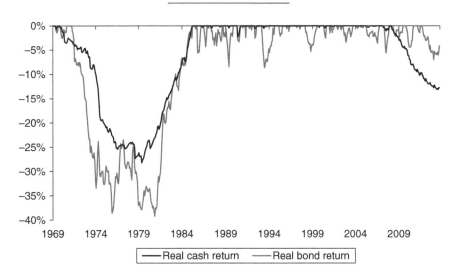

Figure 5.1   Real drawdowns – cumulative declines – in the value of UK cash and bonds, 1969–2014, %

Source: Datastream, Bloomberg, author's calculations.

however, is less visible but arguably just as potent, and can hit conventional bonds and cash particularly hard. If you view the returns from these assets in real, inflation-adjusted terms, it is much more difficult to see them, as does much portfolio theory, as "riskless" – even before recognising that government creditworthiness is not always stable, or of the highest quality, and that the banking system as a whole, and our cash with it, is also potentially vulnerable to collapse (as the events of 2008/2009 reminded us). Figure 5.1 shows episodes when the real worth of UK cash and government bonds has fallen, with the inflationary 1970s resulting in significant losses as short- and long-term interest rates failed to keep pace with inflation.

KNOW YOUR PUNDITS – AND THE ONLY "THEME" WORTH INVESTING IN

The previous section discussed some elements of the "modern portfolio theory" that underpins much conventional financial analysis. The approach presented in this book can arguably be viewed as "postmodern portfolio theory". It is trying to allow for some of the questionable impressions conveyed by the conventional view, and to replace the notion of an optimal (ideal) process with that of a satisficing (good enough) one; but also, like postmodern critiques elsewhere, it is aware of the context within which that view has developed and is typically presented,[5] and of how that context has shaped market commentaries, advice and outcomes. The contextualisation of investment commentary is particularly important for the private investor because their engagement with the markets is not continuous, and occurs at arm's length. That said, professional investors often overlook some of the points that follow.

As we've already seen, the public debate on macroeconomics and finance often takes on a life of its own, and a pessimistic one at that. This partly reflects lazy thinking (a less productive part perhaps of the "fast" or intuitive thinking described by Daniel Kahneman),[6] the hunger for a clear narrative, the sense that we live in special times, and an awareness of mortality, that are all part of human nature. Much of the noise is also attributable, though, to the varying aims of the participants in that debate. The motives behind economic and financial commentaries are not always straightforward, and may even be hidden to their authors – or at least to their conscious minds.

Many journalists see their primary role as an objective informational one, and this is probably the default setting for what most of us expect when we read or watch the news. The first function of the media is to inform and communicate, and the best journalists go beyond this, and have a mission to explain and educate. Readers and audiences are left with more information at their disposal, and with some idea as to what it might mean, as a result.

The dividing line between objective fact and subjective analysis or opinion is however a very blurred one in economics and finance, as can be seen from our assessment of the topical concerns addressed in Part I. As noted, not all journalists have the data resources to do their own research and interpretation, and even those that do may feel compelled to reach a conclusion. Few journalists and City economists reporting and commenting on (say) an unexpected rise in unemployment will be able to resist suggesting that it tells us something about what has been happening to GDP growth, and that this in turn may tell us something about the government's budgetary objectives and the outlook for interest rates. Fiscal and monetary policies in turn are by definition normatively and politically loaded, and few commentators do not have their own opinion on whether (for example) unemployment is a better gauge of falling inflationary pressure than are (say) money supply data, or what the rights and wrongs of (say) fiscal austerity and monetary hawkishness might be.

Some people go into City economics or the media because they have strong views about these things to start with. I studied economics partly to find out more about the way society was organised, and in particular why unemployment was high in some places and times but not others (this was South Wales, in the late 1970s). For a while I was fascinated by what seemed to me to be the overly ambitious claims made for the then popular policy of monetarism, and even after starting work found it difficult not to take a swipe at what seemed to be the shortcomings of one or other monetary aggregate as an economic indicator. Whatever the rights and wrongs of that thankfully forgotten debate, the point is that it is particularly difficult to separate information from opinion in an inexact field like economics – and that the more interested you are in the subject matter, the more likely you are to hold an opinion.

Thus the line between informing and educating on the one hand, and proselytising and advocating on the other, is blurred, and more so in the realm of economics than in other, more scientific, disciplines whose subject matter is not human behaviour and in which controlled experiments are possible. This is not an accusation, but an observation, and being aware of that blurred line can help in placing financial advice in context.

Another function performed by economic commentary is perhaps more unexpected: some pundits are successful not because they are right, but because they are entertaining. This is most apparent in broadcast media and on the conference platform, but it can be the case with written reports too, as those of us who remember the outlandishly colourful and inventively illustrated stockbrokers' booklets that used to be a feature of UK budget coverage will remember. Some of the best-attended investment conferences are packed not because their speakers are necessarily right, or important, but because they are engaging, clear, provocative, and (intentionally) funny. I have heard it suggested that economics and finance can be rather dull, and for jaded institutional investors in particular, whose inboxes are jammed with research reports from dozens of earnest sell-side analysts, something that is easy to watch, read or listen to, and brings a smile, is going to get more attention. In the TV studios, as a pundit you know that the worst thing – if you want to be invited back to secure the free advertising that such appearances bring – is to be dull, or worse still, to dry. The presenter's producer is constantly in their earpiece urging them to keep the show moving and animated: content is often secondary to excitement. We may be talking heads only, but the more animated, the better.

Presentation skills matter hugely in all walks of life of course: as a parent and school governor, the time allotted to developing them (and the other so-called soft skills) in the formal curriculum seems to me to be too little. In the realm of big picture economics, however, the subjective nature of the content perhaps makes delivery style particularly important, and to be entertaining and persuasive there is somehow more justifiable than in (say) physics or geology. If you make many presentations yourself, you may be familiar with the way in which artistic licence can take over, transforming nuanced reality (and a carefully detailed powerpoint pack) into a gaudy spray painting.

You don't have to set out to be entertaining: audiences can tolerate and digest an unadorned presentation if the speaker has credibility. Ideally you will be right and interesting. Audiences will be happy with right but boring, or wrong but interesting. What you must not be is wrong and boring. So keep in mind the entertainment motive: next time you see a pundit or after dinner speaker being scarily plausible, or plausibly scary, ask yourself what they're trying to do. It's a legitimate tactic in an arena as overpopulated as macroeconomic commentary, but the message may not be intended to be taken completely at face value.

Some participants in the macro debate may have less wholesome reasons for being there. We hinted at this earlier: put bluntly, it can be enjoyable being on the public stage – enjoyable and gratifying. If we want public acknowledgement, a way of marking our passage through the world in the formal records of the day, then being a City pundit is perhaps a relatively easy way of grabbing a little existential reassurance.[7] It also offers the opportunity to publicly rubbish the competition – which can help further reduce our intellectual insecurities. So we have to acknowledge that some economic commentary probably exists as a form of self-expression: it is there to convince you that its author exists, is a pretty clever chap,[8] and the only person on the planet to have spotted that a quirk in Japanese accounting means that the global economy is doomed.

Finally, but perhaps most importantly, remember that much media and industry comment is there to help promote something more tangible than the authors' reputation – that is, advertising revenue. We noted in Part I that advertising may be most easily sold in a pessimistic wrapper: ironically, broadsheets proclaiming imminent economic disaster may do a better job for their sponsors than would more balanced accounts that sold fewer copies. The bulk of the goods and services advertised – savings products in particular – rely of course on the world continuing to turn on its axis.

Pundits pushing a particular market view may believe in it, but that doesn't mean that their companies do not have financial products or proprietary investments aligned accordingly. Cynics like to assert that such pundits are always optimistic about (say) growth in general, or the emerging economies in particular, because their companies need investors to be buying stocks through them, or derive a lot of their banking income from the emerging regions, but this need not be the case. The tendency to macro pessimism means that much commentary can act as a booster for sales of investment products that do best in tough times – namely, bonds. And the firms promoting the products may be doing so because they sincerely believe them to be the most appropriate investments at the time.

As noted, few participants acknowledge these varying motives behind financial commentary, and many perhaps may not even be aware of them: not everyone is alert to a postmodern perspective, and able (or willing) to see the debate in its wider setting. Private investors however need to be aware that not all of the public information and advice on offer is necessarily framed with an eye on its likely accuracy. Apocalypse and revelation are much less likely than muddle through, but pundits need their pet causes to be taken seriously and their egos stroked; media companies need readers and viewers; financial companies need revenue. You don't have to meet these needs – but if you do, be aware that you are. And if you find the arguments in this book entertaining, you probably need to get out more.

A final point on what investment is not about. From time to time, hot topics take on a life of their own, and investment products are created and marketed around them. Sales teams in both the institutional and private investor marketplaces are constantly on the lookout for the opportunities to boost revenue (as of course are sales teams everywhere). Many investors too can relish the engagement with current affairs that active, thematic investing brings, and feel that if their adviser is not showing them such opportunities they are not doing their job properly.

If that sort of engagement is important to you, then there is nothing to worry about. Similarly, if you have specific ethical or financial considerations that you want to be reflected directly in your portfolio – a wish to avoid arms manufacturers or tobacco companies, say, or a need for income yielding investments – then it would be wrong if these themes were not in there, and it would be part of your adviser's job to make sure that they were. Generally, however, most investors are not seeking topicality, or specific ethical characteristics, but have a wider goal in mind. In the modern portfolio theory world, their goal is to maximise risk-adjusted returns (or minimise return-adjusted risk), and in our postmodern world they are seeking less ambitiously but more realistically to maintain and grow their real wealth. For such investors, "thematic" investing may be an expensive diversion, and should be kept at arm's length – and to be fair, many salespeople are not aware of the complications here, but genuinely believe that the themes they are promoting do likely have wider, and longer-lived, relevance.

There are several reasons for not taking thematic investing too seriously. Such themes are only a few of the many drivers of the capital markets; they can be much more difficult to implement properly than they sound; and by the time they have become familiar enough to warrant their label, their useful practical impact is largely in the past – they are, as we say, already "in the price". An excessive focus on a specific theme can lead to poor performance, because it is highly unlikely that the theme singled out for attention will be the dominant influence on portfolios, sometimes even in the short term, when the topic is hottest.

By far the most important influences on markets are the evolving business cycle – the evolution and interplay of growth, inflation, corporate profitability and interest rates – and geopolitical and policy contexts. It is unusual for a specific topic to have an impact that surfaces visibly for long above these constantly swirling influences. Perhaps the most obvious instances that spring to mind are the "new economy" mania of late 1999/early 2000, or the credit boom of the early 2000s, but these were themselves largely shaped by the business cycle and policy, and of course both ended unhappily. There is some evidence that broader investing *styles* can be successful, such as small company and "value" investing, but even here the evidence is patchy and unconvincing.

Even if a particular idea or sector were to be popular, and the broader macro backdrop were somehow put on hold, there would still be no guarantee that the theme would work, and deliver strong investment performance. Other, overlooked, themes might be making themselves felt, and offsetting or outpacing the effects of ours; it can be surprisingly difficult to identify and isolate the key practical attributes that best reflect a specific theme. And as noted, if it is a prominent enough theme to be topical, then to some extent at least it may already be reflected in current asset prices.

The demographic time bomb discussed in Chapter 3 is a good example of the limited usefulness of even the most obvious (and long-term) investment theme. As we saw, a greyer population can be predicted (unusually) with confidence, but the macroeconomic implications of that theme are far from straightforward. In particular, it tells us very little about prospective growth: an older population is not necessarily going to suffer from a shortfall in labour actually supplied, and growth is in any case not driven by labour input alone. It also tells us very little about real interest rates: an older population might be thought likely to be less patient, and so demand higher returns on its investments, but those returns are not driven by investors alone.

The same uncertainty applies to the valuation of securities, independently of the macroeconomic backdrop. Some economists, for example, have plotted stock market price-to-earnings ratios (the most commonly used equity valuation tool – see Chapter 7) alongside historic demographic data. They conclude that a large younger cohort, the baby boomers, caused higher valuations in the 1980s and 1990s, and they infer that the increase now in the elderly cohort (as those boomers retire) will therefore have the opposite effect. The notion makes some sense – retirees do hold more bonds and fewer stocks, though whether they should is a moot point (Chapter 7 again) – but it ignores all the other drivers of stock market performance, and the charts are almost certainly an example of mistaking correlation for causation.

In fact, on a 30-year view, pretty much everything that can affect security prices is up for grabs. A confident handle on one projected trend – demography – is therefore of much less use than you might think, simply because there are so many other moving parts that can move unpredictably and markedly, and *independently of demography*, to offset that trend. And this is before we consider the starting level of valuations: even if the thesis is right, if it is already reflected in low stock prices, future returns can still be respectable.

The same considerations apply even at the sector level. A larger elderly population will of course favour healthcare products and services, and leisure and entertainment too. Companies able to profit from labour market flexibility will likely benefit from the changes in participation rates and retirement ages as society begins to adapt to the altered pattern of labour supply. However, some of these points are so obvious that they may be partly priced-in to company valuations already, while labour market flexibility is such a broad theme that it would be very hard to be sure of incorporating it clearly in portfolio construction.

Moreover, the winning sectors' relative performance could be undermined by the unknown new industries that will almost certainly emerge on this timescale. If you doubt this, go back and take a look at how many pundits were recommending mobile telephony and digital media in 1984.

This particular point is an instance of what I think of as the "denominator" problem encountered throughout the investment process. All investing involves selecting something and expecting it to perform better than the alternatives – a relative appraisal that compares the investment (the numerator) with the alternatives (the denominator). And no matter how much research you undertake into a particular investment – whether a theme, an asset class or a single stock – diminishing returns set in quickly, because so many things in addition to the characteristics of the investment itself will shape its performance in practice. You may get the numerator right, but be blind-sided by the myriad overlooked uncertainties in the denominator.

The best way to build the demographic theme into your investment portfolio is probably simply to keep an open mind. At the very least, an aging population does not mean that stocks are necessarily a bad long-term investment, but that is hardly an idea that justifies paying extra charges for a "themed" investment product.

Similar issues are encountered with other topical themes. Investments aimed at capitalising on society's response to climate change, for example, have predictably fallen prey to the business cycle, and to changing supply prospects for shale oil and gas, and really became widely popular only when the prices of alternative energy sources, and of products using them (such as electric cars) had already soared. A possible "hard landing" for the Chinese economy is a current theme that has many followers, but in addition to the obvious cyclical uncertainties – a buoyant US economy might support China's exports for longer than feared, for example – there are serious implementation difficulties that its purveyors don't always make clear. China's capital markets are still developing, and for overseas investors their liquidity, particularly when it comes to short-selling (that is, betting on a falling market) stocks and the currency, is poor. Implementing a gloomy view on China often involves taking positions in other, more liquid markets (such as commodities, or the Australian dollar) which have been correlated with China, but which of course may not remain so.

Even straightforward ethical themes can be difficult to implement. Avoiding arms manufacturers seems fairly easy – but how big a proportion of a conglomerate's revenue needs to come from that source for them to be classified as an armaments company? Should the line be drawn at the finished goods level, or do components count too? If the latter, how far back down the value chain do we go? Do we count the companies making the metals and other materials from which the arms are made? The more potential investments you exclude, the greater the chance that you will lose some of the diversification that makes a broad stock market investment attractive to begin with. Moreover, many ethically-driven investors can little afford to own poorly performing or narrowly focused investments, most obviously charities (whose long-term time horizons make them obvious investors in the wider equity markets). At UWC Atlantic College our Board of Governors is, we hope, ethically aware, being committed amongst other things to helping foster international understanding and sustainability, but in framing our investment policy we have so far decided not to have an explicit ethical guideline. We took the view that it would be difficult to define one without unduly restricting our investment managers' ability to deliver the returns needed to achieve our more immediate charitable goals – and those goals are our most important responsibility.

Keep these points in mind when offered the opportunity to invest in any theme other than that of meeting your primary investment objective.

You may enjoy the sense of having skin in a particular topical game, or "fund management by fairy tale", but if so, again, perhaps you should get out more.

A PERSONAL INVESTMENT POLICY

Investment, then, is unlikely to be about getting rich quickly, or being necessarily rewarded for taking risk. It can be a more passive, inexact and less urgent discipline, and perhaps a less directly competitive one, than it often appears. The public advice and commentary surrounding it needs to be viewed sceptically; and it should not be approached thematically. It is possible to try too hard, and many institutional investors in particular do exactly that, because they feel that they need to be seen to be acting to justify their fees.

The main message in this book nonetheless is that excessive pessimism does often lead to opportunities for patient, long-term investors who are willing to question and disregard received wisdom, and who have realistic expectations: it can be worthwhile getting involved in markets, particularly those that offer exposure to ongoing economic growth. The starting point is to decide the basic principles that will shape your engagement, the formulation of a personal investment policy, and this is what the rest of this chapter will cover. In Chapter 6 we look at the key investable assets available for most private investors, and in Chapter 7 we look at their valuation and likely returns, and how best to combine them in portfolios.

Many people can benefit from investing in markets – particularly as the costs of getting involved are falling steadily, one of the more positive side effects of the cumulative richness of embarrassments noted in Part I. That does not mean that it is suitable for everyone. Financial markets are volatile and uncertain, and as we've seen, in practice there is no such thing as a completely "riskless" asset. You need to be as sure as you can be that you do not invest more than your financial circumstances and personality can bear, and that you do not place all your investable funds into just one asset. This sounds obvious, but risking money in the capital markets that you have held aside for a new car, a family wedding or the mortgage payment, is not a good idea. Having *any* significant savings invested in risky assets if you are particularly nervous by nature can be a bad idea. But so too is having all your potentially investable funds concentrated in cash – or in the same business upon which you depend for your livelihood.

There are perhaps three main reasons for holding a pool of savings – if you're lucky enough to have one, or to be able to build one, of course. First, to make sure that you have sufficient resources available to meet an unexpected emergency, what we might call the rainy day motive; second, to boost your current spending power by using investment income and possibly the capital too to supplement your main source of income; and third, to support the future living standards of your family and any future generations.

The overriding requirements of rainy day assets are predictability and liquidity: you have to be reasonably sure of what you have, and that you can turn it into cash quickly. An income generating fund can tolerate a little more volatility, and is less likely to need to be liquidated quickly, but it will have to focus on investments that offer relatively high and predictable yields (which is not easy at present). The long-term endowment-oriented fund faces fewest constraints. It can invest in long-term assets whose value can't be quickly realised, or indeed may be formally locked-up for several years; it needn't worry about short-term fluctuations in market values; and it is likely to be indifferent, tax considerations aside, between capital appreciation and yield – it can hold investments with no income at all if it expects their value to grow over time.

That doesn't mean that a long-term fund faces no constraints. Even individuals and trustees who have the luxury of investing to endow their family or charity's long-term future will have varying appetites for volatility, uncertainty and illiquidity, and their financial personalities still need to be taken into account. Levels of investor knowledge and sophistication will vary tremendously, and it is important that even long-term investors understand, and are happy with, the nature of the investments that they are making – or at least that they are comfortable giving a trusted adviser discretion over those decisions.

Broadly speaking, however, the closer the main investment goal is to the endowment approach – the aim of conserving and ideally growing the real value of wealth for you and your dependents' futures – then the easier it will be to become involved with those parts of the capital markets that can benefit from the ongoing, muddling through of the global economy. Again, that does not mean that long-term investing will necessarily be rewarded for taking on uncertainty and illiquidity, or that the best long-term investments necessarily have those characteristics. Some of the best investments historically have been those backed by large, well-known global franchises, and there are few investments more liquid than a blue chip stock. The long-term investor simply faces more opportunities for capitalising on economic growth.

Your personal investment policy will take into account your large, committed expenditures; it will estimate what you might need for a rainy day, or for supplementing current spending; and it will identify any balance remaining that can be used for taking advantage of those wider opportunities.

Implicitly, and for reasons noted earlier, this means that you should not consider borrowing to acquire an investment portfolio, particularly a relatively uncertain and illiquid one: as the saying goes, you should invest only what you can afford to lose, and most of us cannot afford to lose borrowed money.

You need to expect a degree of volatility even in a portfolio containing a mix of assets. A typical diversified portfolio might display an annual standard deviation in returns of around 10%: if returns follow what is called a "normal" statistical distribution around their average, this means that you might expect returns to be within ±10% of that average roughly two-thirds of the time.[9] Given the expected returns outlined in Chapter 7 below, this means that you should expect the portfolio to be down noticeably roughly one year in six. A stock-only portfolio can easily be twice as volatile as this (in 2014 the big stock markets have been much less volatile than usual, but it would be safest to expect this not to last). Exposing your hard-earned savings to such volatility can seem frightening. If it is, then you should invest correspondingly less, or tilt the portfolio accordingly away from the most volatile assets (rather than buy the expensive derivative insurance favoured by many advisers).

The sort of illiquidity you might expect in a long-term portfolio will depend on the assets chosen – see Chapter 6 – but for some investments in private equity or real estate it can extend for years, and in a crisis even some usually liquid securities can be difficult to sell. At those times, being relatively liquid can perversely count against an asset, because as another saying goes, in a crisis you don't sell what you should, you sell what you can. If the only markets open for business are those in blue chip equities, then those are the assets that will be sold, and their prices depressed, by investors needing urgently to raise cash.

Your personal investment policy will also take into account the way in which your broad objectives are to be implemented. Once you have established the extent to which your investments should be allotted to rainy day, income or growth strategies, you may feel happy delegating completely the selection of investments to a trusted, discretionary fund manager who knows your objectives. Access to a full service wealth manager who will offer a custom-made portfolio constructed to try to meet your stated objectives is increasingly difficult to obtain from the traditional private banking groups unless you are lucky enough to have around half a million pounds (more than three quarters of a million dollars) to invest and are willing to pay an annual charge of roughly 1% of that amount. As technology improves and dealing costs fall, however, there are an increasing number of specialised firms and online platforms available that offer more accessible and cheaper services.

You may however have specific views on the asset mix, funds and securities you want to invest in. You may want to instruct your manager to take those views on board, or even to build, monitor and periodically rebalance the portfolio yourself – and the cost of the do-it-yourself approach is also falling steadily. The choice will depend largely on whether you believe in investment skill, and can identify who has it, and at what level it is best exercised. You may be able to do as good a job of portfolio construction as a professional wealth manager, but it takes time, and your time may be better spent elsewhere. Moreover, the active, discretionary management of assets is not the only service that your wealth manager offers – or at least, it shouldn't be (see Chapter 8).

As we noted in Part I, it is very hard for even professional investors consistently to pick individual bonds, stocks and commodities that will outperform their wider market indices (or "benchmarks"), and if anything I am understating the case: many writers would put it more strongly than this. Index-tracking or "passive" funds that simply match the composition of those wider indices, and do so more and more cheaply, are an increasingly popular way of populating portfolios for investors who recognise that "active" management is tough (and expensive). Passive investing effectively delegates portfolio construction to the markets – or at least, to the people who compile the various market indices.

In principle, this approach could even be extended to the asset allocation part of portfolio construction, the higher-level decision as to what broad asset mix to use (for example, how many liquid assets, bonds, stocks, commodity futures and so forth to hold – see Chapter 6). What we call "tactical" asset allocation, the short-term tweaking of the mix to reflect the evolving business cycle, is bedevilled by the difficulties of market timing and the clumsiness of asset allocation committees, and there are a lot of superfluous and inflated claims made even for the various models of long-term "strategic" asset allocation on offer.

Some markets are more efficient – in the sense of being harder to beat– than others, however; and some investors enjoy the greater sense of engagement that comes with owning an active fund, or from having a regular update with a discretionary manager. Moreover, there are unresolved governance issues with passive investing: shareholders in particular, as the owners of a business, are empowered to scrutinise, and if necessary take action to improve, the performance of its management, and a purely passive investor is not going to fulfil this role – which could become a problem if the market were to become dominated by such funds. As far as asset allocation is concerned, there is some important portfolio maintenance that will be neglected by a completely passive and automatic asset mix – even when we have decided what that might be (again, see Chapter 7). As a result, there is still room for reasonable disagreement about the extent to which a purely passive approach should be adopted.

Your attitude to these and other implementation issues, alongside your broad investment aims and your tolerance of volatility, uncertainty and illiquidity, are all part of your wider financial personality, and should be reflected in your personal investment policy.

Finally, in an ideal world, your personal investment policy might also contain some rules to guard against overtrading. The temptation to invest reactively, in line with recent dramatic news and market moves, can be high. Bad news is followed by selling, good news by buying – yet by the time the news is reported, much if not all of the market adjustment has occurred (much financial news is of course simply the reporting of *yesterday's* stock prices). And as we have seen, there is a lot of news. The result is that rather than buying low and selling high, many investors end up selling close to lows and buying close to highs, and the cost in terms of forgone long-term returns can be significant.

The dangers are reduced if you use a completely passive approach, or a discretionary manager who is able to show more composure (which is not always the case for many professional wealth managers, even though we might hope that they would know better). They are not eliminated, though, because at the end of the day it is the private investor who can decide to take money away from the wealth manager, or from passive funds, or to put new money in. Finance professionals are not immune from this temptation. I had a sobering but, in retrospect, illuminating conversation in early March 2009, at the very low point of the 2008/2009 stock market rout, with a chief economist and an asset allocator who were both experienced, and adamant that clients should be advised to sell. There was certainly no arguing with the market mood on the day, but the decision to follow it, as they suggested doing, would have been a costly one. Rules to guard against this sort of emotional reactivity are difficult to design, however, and the emotions inspired by falling markets in particular are strong. Perhaps the most practical way of avoiding excessive trading is simply to promise yourself that you will not look at the financial news very often.

In selecting a discretionary manager, or an actively managed mutual fund, you can use portfolio holdings and turnover as a guide to whether the manager might be overly active: a large number (50, say) of holdings that are replaced every year (say) would be on the high side, but the context matters here. Such a large number of holdings statistically usually would be highly likely to make the vehicle a virtual tracking fund, as we noted in Part I; but if all those holdings and that activity have in fact been delivering stellar performance, then arguably the manager has simply been doing what you're going to be paying them for. Finally, a personal investment policy needs to say something about the importance of diversification. As with much else in finance, in putting this simple but extremely important idea into practice the savings industry has over-engineered many solutions.

The key ideas are simple: do not place all your eggs in one basket, and try to ensure that the various baskets you end up using will not all get dropped at the same time, particularly at times of stress. We may believe that one investment has a good chance of doing better than others, but we can never be sure, and spreading our savings across several different assets should mean that if we are wrong, and our favoured asset performs more poorly than we expect, then one of the other assets may perform unexpectedly well, and offer some partial compensation at least for the disappointment. With hindsight, it is easy to look back and wish that we'd had all our savings in the markets that did best, but diversification ideally plays the role of providing some portfolio insurance, and should be viewed similarly. Just as you ought not to regret insuring your house because it didn't burn down, you ought not to regret owning some assets that performed poorly, because in different circumstances they could have saved your portfolio from damage.

There is both more and less to diversification than meets the eye. More, because you need to consider your wider financial circumstances, not just your investment portfolio. You also need to recognise that in practice, assets don't always move in relation to other assets quite in the way that you might expect them to. Less, because there is already a lot of diversification built into some straightforward and inexpensive financial products, and you don't need to pay for much of the financial service industry's statistical ingenuity and financial engineering expertise to get it.

In practice, it is all too easy to end up with dangerously concentrated resources. For private investors, mindful perhaps of Warren Buffett's advice to invest only in businesses you understand, the temptation to invest in the company that pays your wages, in the industry in which your family business is active, or in the style in which you manage your daily affairs, can be hard to resist.

Our employers and the taxman often encourage us to hold shares in the companies we work for, for understandable reasons, and those proprietary and tax advantages can be substantial, and worthwhile. Nonetheless, if we are not careful, we can end up with the bulk of our savings – as well as our salaries and careers – riding on the fortunes of one company. The risks are most visible perhaps in financial services, and it wasn't just the well-paid executives and investment bankers at Bear Stearns and Lehman Brothers who lost much of their wealth, along with their jobs, when their firms went under during the crisis. Thousands of less well-off employees were also hit when the share prices of other financial firms collapsed, including companies in the UK such as Northern Rock, HBOS, Lloyds and the Royal Bank of Scotland, for example. But employees at some non-financial companies caught up in the crisis also suffered big losses, for example those at General Motors, which filed for bankruptcy in 2009.

Similarly, I meet many investors who are the owners and managers of successful businesses, and their first questions often refer to the prospects for investing in their industry. Knowing its leading companies and strategies as they do, they naturally expect their industry knowledge and expertise to be reflected in their investment portfolio. In practice, the best advice can be to suggest the opposite, namely, that they invest in almost any industry but their own – simply because they already have so much at stake in that industry in their own business.

A typical instance was a South American family whose wealth had been generated in a commodities business, and which was looking to invest its accumulated cash in a multi-asset portfolio. Expecting a lively debate on the relative merits of agricultural, industrial and energy commodities, they were surprised to find that the customised portfolio we recommended for them had less commodity exposure than usual, not more (we will discuss the general merits of investing in commodities, or more accurately commodity futures, in Chapter 6).

More generally, people who work in volatile, cyclical industries such as construction and property development, or resource extraction, successful entrepreneurs, venture capitalists and private equity managers, for example, all take risk in their day jobs, and to advise them to invest their personal savings in particularly uncertain and illiquid assets could be effectively to recommend doubling up on risk, not diversifying it. Also, many nest eggs are grown steadily over long periods by individuals who are simply too busy to get around to sorting out their finances. Their wealth is often held as accumulated bank balances, and their largest single investment is cash, not as a result of a carefully considered appraisal of the economic outlook but simply because they have not had time to think carefully about the potential risks posed by inflation, and the opportunity costs of not being invested in other assets.

Similarly, it is not as easy as it sounds to ensure that the different assets across which you diversify your savings will in practice perform differently when you need them to. During the 2008/2009 panic, several asset classes that were supposed to move in different directions, or at different speeds – and that had done so, in the past – turned out to be closely correlated, and all fell together. At times of stress, investors collectively may not be capable of discriminating between the extent of various assets' underlying exposures to the factors driving the crisis, or of recognising that no asset is truly risk free, but instead tend to consolidate the various asset classes into two perceived groups only – relatively safe ones and relatively risky ones. As we shall see in Chapter 6, there can be good reasons to do so. Your personal investment policy should focus, as a result, not on the number of different assets you hold, but on ensuring that these two big groups have a significant presence in your portfolio, however they are labelled.

More positively, you don't need to invest exotically or expensively to get some of the benefits of diversification. Funds focused on the major developed stock markets – the US, Continental Europe, the UK – are spread across a wide range of industries, and their component companies generate an increasing proportion of their revenues and profits not just in their respective regions, but globally, with the emerging regions increasingly important. Amongst other things, this means that while their stock prices are denominated in their local currencies, they implicitly offer a degree of foreign exchange diversification too. For example, the sterling value of BP's revenues will tend to vary with the level of the pound: a fall in the exchange rate will boost the sterling value of oil, which is priced on global markets, and vice versa. Moreover, there is often more dispersion of returns, and so greater potential diversification, across companies within a single large developed stock market index such as the FTSE 100 or the S&P 500, than across individual countries or industries, and the large companies in these indices are if anything more liquid than many individual emerging markets.

It is in fact impossible to know for sure exactly what underlying geographical and currency exposure you have once you start investing in companies that produce, trade and compete internationally, because they do not have to report the regional breakdown of their profits. This means amongst other things that it is not possible ever to perfectly "hedge" the underlying assets in an equity portfolio, and by extension, any wider multi-asset portfolio containing equities. This point has been largely overlooked by much portfolio theory and industry practice, which proceeds as if it is (and so arguably incurs unnecessary costs).

The lack of detailed knowledge about where companies ultimately make their money is only a problem if you believe that investment is about optimising, not satisficing. Knowing that perhaps around three-fifths of the earnings generated by your blue chip UK index fund are derived from outside the UK (smaller company funds, and the Continental European and US markets, are less internationally exposed – but the portions are rising there too) should be enough to allow you to worry less about UK-focused risk at least. The FTSE100 in particular is to other stock markets a little like Manchester City or Chelsea are to the rest of the football league – most of the big players are not really local.[10]

We shall discuss diversification again in Chapters 6 and 7. At this stage, your personal investment policy needs simply to register that some diversification is important, but to guard against over-engineered and expensive solutions.

6

BACK TO BASICS: WHAT YOU NEED TO OWN – IT'S ABOUT TIME

If wrecked upon the Shoal of Thought
How is it with the Sea?
The only Vessel that is shunned
Is safe – Simplicity –

– Emily Dickinson

If you accept the case for investing outlined in Part I, if you are happy with the idea of investing as a long-term, imperfect satisficing process, and if you have framed your personal investment policy, then the next step is to consider more carefully what investments you should own. Readers familiar with investments may want to skip this chapter, which contains an introduction to the main asset classes. That said, it is an unconventional introduction, and reaches a rather unfashionable conclusion about what really belongs in a private portfolio.

The conventional approach to portfolio construction starts with asset allocation: it considers the various asset classes available (for example, bonds, stocks, real estate); selects those that might be appropriate; and then decides in what proportion they should be mixed, and whether that mix should be fixed strategically (on say a five-year horizon) or tweaked tactically to second-guess the business cycle (on say a three–six month horizon). It finishes by deciding the practical implementation of the chosen asset allocation, that is, the selection of the individual securities and pooled funds,

whether actively managed or passive, that is to be held. Both the asset allocation and the implementation that you choose should reflect your personal
investment policy.

In this chapter we discuss the main asset classes, what their differentiat-
ing characteristics are, and which of them are "must-haves" for private investor portfolios. In Chapter 7 we will consider how best to combine them. Our
approach will differ from the conventional one, however, in that it will focus
a little more on what the various assets can be expected to deliver in steward-
ing your wealth, and a little less on the formal labels attached to them.

To be considered an eligible investment, an asset should do three things.
Firstly, and at the risk of stating the obvious, it needs to offer an attractive
return, or at least the possibility of one: there is little point in holding an
asset that you think cannot perform.[1] Second, it needs to offer a return that
is uncorrelated with those available on other assets, otherwise there would
be little point in owning it alongside them. Third, it should be easily accessible – another obvious point but one that is often overlooked (for example,
by advisers keen to promote the investment merits of commodities, of which
more below). Typically, advisers point to around a dozen asset classes that
are commonly thought to meet these requirements. We discuss these below,
before arguing that some of them do not really meet the requirements, and/
or do not count as a distinct group. Most private investors probably need to
own perhaps three or four genuinely different asset classes only.

HERE FOR THE DURATION: THE KEY
INVESTMENT CHARACTERISTICS

Just as an object can be described in terms of its location in three spatial
dimensions – quantum mechanics aside – a financial asset can be described
in terms of its position in several key investment dimensions. The most
important are perhaps *duration*, *title* and *liquidity*, and these characteristics
determine the role played by the asset in your portfolio.

Investing is inextricably linked to the passage of time. An investor
expects to be rewarded for waiting, for not consuming their savings: they
expect their patience to bring a measurable return, whether in the form of
a regular payment of income *on* their capital, the eventual return *of* that
capital, or both. Investment *duration* is linked to the lifetime of an asset,
but is usually shorter than it: an investment might last a long time, but its
duration can be relatively short. Instead, it is a measure of how long it will
take for the investor's patience to be rewarded, a measure of where, in time,
the effective centre of gravity of its returns are located – close to hand, or a

long way into the future. To be comparable, the projected cash flows have to be translated into present values by using a discount rate, and the further into the future they lie, the lower is their current value and their effective weight in the total cash flow generated by the investment. Longer duration investments are particularly important for investors driven mostly by the endowment motive, and because their cash flow can last a long time, they involve less reinvestment risk: you don't have to replace them often. That said, because their value derives from cash flows that stretch a long way into the future, they can be amongst the most uncertain and volatile investments that there are.

The duration of the investment depends on the interest rates used to discount the future cash flow generated by the asset, but also, importantly, on the profile of the cash flow itself, which is why growth is so important in investing. If an asset has a long life and also delivers a regular and growing payout, it can have very long duration. It is most common to talk about duration in relation to bonds, where it can take on some very specific and technical meanings according to the exact context, but all investments can be placed somewhere on the duration scale, and bonds are not usually the longest duration investments in portfolios.

It is usually real growth that matters most in long-term investing, because one of the main goals is to maintain and augment our living standards. This means that in estimating the duration of an investment, we should deduct any general inflation, or add back any deflation, to the projected growth in its cash flow. But we should also do the same to the interest rates that we use to discount that growth, and duration itself is measured in years. The drivers of real growth and of inflation are of course often the same, but they can move in different directions, and historically have occasionally done so.

Investment *title* is used here in an ownership sense, and refers to the nature of your entitlement to the cash flow produced by an investment. It is a key determinant of the qualitative investment risk that you are taking on. You can either lend, in exchange for a specified return, which usually, but not always, includes the scheduled repayment of the principal; or you can decide to own specified assets outright. Admittedly, there are also contingent assets whose title changes according to specified circumstances, but such investments are relatively few in number, and illiquid.

A loan investment offers a greater title to specified future payment – the likelihood of being paid is more secure – than does ownership. Loans can be direct, or take the form of bonds; for most private investors, the latter are the most common, though savings certificates are a direct loan to the government, and bank deposits and cash of course are direct loans to the commercial banking system and to the central bank issuing the currency respectively. In practice, not all loans are equal in title: corporate loans and bonds in particular, often referred to as the "credit market", have varying degrees of "seniority", according to where the lender ranks in the event of default on the loan. The most senior bondholders' claims are met first, and because of their lower risk they carry lower interest payments. The least senior bondholders rank last, and they are paid more interest as a result – though as we noted earlier, that does not mean that they necessarily deliver better returns for the added risk, because in the event of a default, principal losses can be high. Alongside varying degrees of seniority, there can be other ways of structuring lending risk, including the use of some of the borrower's designated assets as collateral (as in "asset-backed securities"); the existence of covenants governing the management of the company's business; and in some cases the possibility of the loan converting into an outright equity or ownership asset in certain specified circumstances.

Ownership is the riskiest way of investing. It sounds secure, but owning something is no guarantee that it will produce a return in the form of income, or capital gain (or even capital repayment or realisation). It is most commonly found in private investors' portfolios in the form of equities or stocks quoted on the public exchanges, or in the form of unquoted private businesses; but real estate, commodity futures and some hedge fund and private equity vehicles offer this form of engagement too. There are usually no specified interest payments: while most companies pay shareholders a regular dividend, they do not have to, and the amount paid is at the managers' discretion. There are usually no formal arrangements for the return of capital, as this would involve winding-up the business; and the owners of a business rank below its creditors and employees in the event of it having to be wound up: shareholders get what is left, if anything. Another company might want to buy the residual assets from the owners, but that can't be planned for in advance. More positively, of course, owners are entitled to the profits and capital gains made by successful businesses: potential returns, once the specified payments to debt holders have been paid, are unlimited.

The distinction between investments that are essentially loans and those that represent ownership is not always made as clearly as it should be. Generally speaking, the safeguards and market customs attaching to loan arrangements are usually tighter and more clearly defined than those attaching to ownership assets, perhaps because, as we saw in Part I, loans are closely entwined with the notion of money, and the money supply needs protection from systemic risk. In practice, too, most investable loans are the bonds issued by governments, and because they control taxes and enjoy a monopoly over the legal use of violence, their creditworthiness is usually the best that there is.

The third key dimension in investing is *liquidity*, the ease with which you can buy and sell an investment asset. For private investors, this is not just determined by whether a recognised exchange exists for the asset, but also by more prosaic concerns such as the size of the transaction. For example, many of the most appealing commercial properties available for investment are so large that they can really only be bought by big institutional investors, or by syndicates of smaller investors that can be difficult to arrange. Until recently, the same was true of many corporate bonds.

Other characteristics of investments matter too, such as the nature of the uncertainties that they face, but duration, title and liquidity are the three that matter most. The notion of duration in particular incorporates much of the economic and financial uncertainty facing an investment. The longevity and predictability of the cash flow it generates, and the interest rate to be used in discounting that cash flow, have to be gauged before you can take a view on its likely duration. Long duration ownership assets can be very risky, but many of them can be highly liquid nonetheless, and some of them are amongst the most attractive to invest in if you subscribe to the positive views outlined in Part I. The bulk of a portfolio's returns over time will come from its long duration assets, with the rest effectively providing diversification – portfolio insurance, perhaps, or investment ballast.

THE USUAL SUSPECTS: THE MAIN ASSET CLASSES

These are the groups of assets usually identified by investment advisers as being the main asset classes suitable for private investors.

Cash is the most obvious asset with which to start. In the investment context, "cash" usually means not physical banknotes – it is not practical or safe to hold a significant portion of your wealth in this form – but accessible bank deposits, and other highly liquid assets that can be turned into deposits quite quickly, such as short-dated (up to a year perhaps) high-quality bonds like government bills, and possibly some corporate certificates of deposit (CDs). These liquid assets are effectively circulating loans – to the banking system in the case of deposits; and to the named issuer of the liquid bonds, bills or CDs (banknotes too are loans of a sort, to the central bank).

The return on these money-market instruments is linked to the general level of short-term interest rates. After allowing for tax and inflation, returns have recently been negative (fixed-term deposits have carried a better return, but are not cash in the investment context because they are not liquid). The real post-tax returns may improve if, as seems likely, interest rates normal-ise from their current historically low levels, and inflation remains subdued (more on this in Chapter 7). They would have to rise a long way, and/or we'd need to see significant deflation, however, for the yield to become positively attractive, and for now the main reason for holding deposits and near-cash in an investment portfolio is their relative stability, and their usefulness as a source of finance for the more attractive opportunistic investments that will crop up from time to time.

Cash (or near-cash in this context) is probably the closest thing to a nominally risk-free asset, since its face value is only at risk if banks and the various forms of deposit insurance fail (and in such circumstances it is a safe bet that most other investment assets would be even more vulnerable, at least in the short term). As we have seen, however, those risks are not always negligible. In real terms, an unexpected surge in inflation could hit cash hard if interest rates fail to keep pace with it. Notes and coin, and many sight deposits currently, have no duration: they may be around for a long time, but carry no interest and their nominal value is fixed. Some money-market instruments have duration, but it is very short.

Government bonds are tradable securities representing a loan to the gov-ernment. They usually carry an interest payment or coupon fixed in nomi-nal terms for the life of the bond: if the relevant interest rates were 3% at the time of issue, each £100 holding would carry a £3 interest coupon. When bonds were held and traded in physical form, the interest coupons were just that – detachable pieces of paper attached to the bond certificate that the holder could "clip" and present for payment. This "fixed income" character-istic means that if interest rates change during the life of the bond, the price of the bond in the market will adjust accordingly to bring the total prospec-tive return on the bond, allowing for its eventual repayment at face value, into line with the new level of interest rates. If our bond matures after one year, and one-year interest rates were to rise unexpectedly to 4% just after it is issued, then its price would drop to £99, so that when it matures and the principal is repaid at its par value of £100, an investor buying the bond at £99 will receive a 4% "yield to redemption" over the year – the £3 coupon, plus the £1 difference between the buying price and the principal repayment.

An investment in government bonds can have long duration. The cash flow profile is dominated by the very large principal repayment at the end of the investment, and this can easily be 30 or more years into the future. There are some bonds outstanding that have no fixed redemption date: the dura-tion of such "perpetual" bonds is long but not infinite, however, and varies inversely with their yield. There are also "zero coupon" bonds that pay no interest, but deliver instead a single payment to investors at the end of the bond's life that combines the capital repayment and an implicit, rolled-up interest payment: such bonds have a duration that matches their time to maturity. If you are ever offered the opportunity to invest in a zero-coupon perpetual bond, politely decline.

The average duration of the most important government bond markets varies over time and across regions. It is currently around five years in the US, seven years in the euro area and ten years in the UK. Government bonds are liquid, and their nominal returns are pretty secure: government credit-worthiness is generally the best (UK government bond certificates were literally gilt-edged to indicate their special nature), and the cash flow attaching to even a downgraded sovereign bond will generally be viewed as much more predictable than that generated by (for example) a stock.

Most investors should own some government bonds. Their fixed income means that their prices move in the opposite direction to interest rates, and since rates tend to fall at times of economic stress, bonds can actively protect a portfolio against cyclical risk: in a recession or crisis they don't simply hold their value, like cash, but actually rise in price, helping to compensate for the losses being taken on more economically exposed parts of the portfolio. When most assets were falling in value in the 2008/2009 panic, those of government bonds were rising strongly. They can also protect against deflation, since their fixed nominal coupons and principal are worth more in real terms if consumer prices fall. Currently, interest rates are historically low, and seem much more likely to rise over the next few years than fall: after a 30-year bull market driven by falling nominal and real interest rates, the prospective returns on government bonds now look unappealing (see Chapter 7), and bond duration may actually work against you. Nonetheless, it would be foolhardy not to own any: they would provide some valuable portfolio insurance in the event that our economic outlook is too positive.

Alongside conventional government bonds, inflation-linked bond markets have been growing steadily in recent years (after a very slow start in the UK gilt market in 1981). Inflation-linked bonds (in the UK, "index-linked" gilts) formally peg the principal value and coupon payment to a retail or consumer price index, and they can be viewed as "real" or inflation-adjusted bonds: their yields offer a direct indication of forward-looking real interest rates (and currently are mostly negative). The gap between their calculated real yield and the yield on conventional bonds of comparable maturity is a measure of the expected "breakeven" inflation rate priced into the market. If you believe actual inflation will turn out lower, you should favour the conventional bond, and vice versa. Indexed bonds tend to be more volatile than conventional bonds, partly because they are less liquid, but their duration, title and liquidity relative to most other non-bond investments can be attractive. In the UK, the inflation-linked uplift to principal is exempt from tax, which for private (tax-paying) investors has strengthened the investment case for owning them.

Inflation-indexed bonds are not however always the exact "hedge" against inflation that many assume them to be. The inflation for which investors are compensated is that which occurs over the lifetime of the bond (more or less – there can be some small discrepancies in administration towards the end of the investment), and this may not be the period during which you happen to be holding it. Investors' expectations of inflation can change sharply, and if you are unlucky enough to buy an already issued indexed bond after an inflation scare, when inflation expectations have overshot and are about to fall, you can find yourself holding a bond whose value tumbles even while inflation itself remains positive. Also, in the event of deflation, the inflation adjustment to your coupon and principal will of course be negative (at least with UK index-linked gilts: US Treasury Inflation-Protected Securities include some protection against the impact of deflation on the principal, though not the coupon). Nonetheless, most portfolios should contain some index-linked bonds as part of their government bond allocation.

Also to be considered as part of the government bond markets are the high quality bonds issued by the US government-backed mortgage agencies, and those issued by supranational organisations such as the European Bank for Reconstruction and Development.

Investment grade corporate bonds are mostly fixed income securities, and behave quite similarly in portfolios to government bonds. "Investment grade" indicates the ratings allotted to the bonds by the various rating agencies (for Moodys and S&P it corresponds to BBB and higher), but because they are issued by companies, their creditworthiness is ultimately not as convincing as that of the bigger governments, and tends also to move in line with the business cycle. As a result, corporate bonds usually have higher yields than government bonds, and the gap between the two – the spread – is variable. (An exception to this rule currently is the case of Italy, where the government's creditworthiness is viewed less positively than that of many Italian companies, and many corporate bonds trade at a lower yield than comparable maturity Italian government bonds.)

The spread reflects the weaker title attached to corporate bonds' cash flow – but there is of course no guarantee that you will be paid more in total for taking that risk, as the higher yield could be more than offset by a default and loss on the principal. That said, typical investment grade yield spreads to government bonds of comparable maturities have been around 1–1.5 percentage points, spiking to around 4 percentage points in the crisis, while historical default rates have been around 0.2% and realised losses less than 0.1%.

Generally, corporate bonds tend to perform less strongly than government bonds in a recession, when the risk of default rises, but much less poorly than stocks (of which more below); similarly, in good economic times, they are less vulnerable to rising interest rates than government bonds, but unlikely to perform as well as stocks. In the US, the biggest and oldest corporate bond market, the returns on high grade corporate bonds have usually – 33 times in the last 50 years – ranked between those on stocks and government bonds. Over that period, their extra return over government bonds has been less than a percentage point.

Corporate bonds are considerably less liquid than government bonds, and usually offer a little less duration. They do traditionally offer a good source of income for investors seeking a decent yield, but currently, with interest rates and bond yields generally so low, they are not an obvious "must-have" for most private investors.

Speculative grade corporate bonds, also known as "high yield" and "junk" bonds, are rated below investment grade bonds, and are correspondingly the least secure and liquid part of the "credit" market. They are much more exposed to the wider economy and trends in corporate creditworthiness than are investment grade and government bonds, and trade more pro-cyclically as a result, performing relatively well when the economy grows and poorly in recessions. Their maturities tend to be shorter than investment grade bonds, and their interest coupons are markedly bigger, and their duration is significantly lower as a result (at around four years). This does not make them completely immune to interest rate risk, however: when interest rate expectations change sharply, speculative grade bonds can sell-off along with the purer interest rate plays. Spreads have averaged around 5 percentage points compared to government bonds of comparable maturity, and briefly surged to 20 points in the crisis. Loss rates have however been substantial too, at around 2.5–3 percentage points (spiking to around 8% in crisis-hit 2009).

The asset class has not always been viewed as a distinct investment category: it became popular amongst institutional investors only in the 1980s. Speculative grade bonds are more likely than investment grade corporate bonds to have a chance of outperforming both government bonds and stocks, and a notable instance occurred in the initial recovery from the 2008/2009 panic, as the monetary nature of the crisis encouraged policymakers to introduce some specific measures that favoured bonds generally over stocks, and high-yielding bonds had sold off sharply as the credit crisis first erupted. The sharp rally that followed has subsequently made the asset class very popular with wealth advisers. However, such an event is relatively unusual, and speculative grade bonds currently are offering such historically low yields that they also may not be a "must-have" for private investors (though they are still of course the highest-yielding of the various fixed income asset classes). Their riskiness and lack of liquidity means that private investors should not consider picking individual securities, and only consider owning speculative bonds as part of a specialist fund – whose charges can significantly reduce the apparent yield on offer still further.

Other bonds that can offer attractive returns for private investors include the various forms of securitised assets encountered in Chapter 1 – mortgage-backed and asset-backed securities (MBS and ABS) – and floating rate bonds whose interest payments are linked to money-market rates. Where exactly they sit in the credit markets depends on their issuer and credit rating. Again, they are not necessarily "must-haves" in private portfolios, and in the case of MBS in particular, when interest rates are moving and the number of mortgagors refinancing is changing, they carry some specific risks – independently of the parcelling problems noted in Chapter 1 – that can make them more like a "why bother?".

Developed equities (or stocks, or shares) are the most volatile of all the major asset classes, but also the most important driver of long-term returns: the investment case for holding them is all about time. Their dividend payments are not certain, and there is no promise of eventual capital repayment or even of capital realisation: an ex-colleague used to note that the St Petersburg index fell to zero in 1917, and did not bounce back. Nonetheless, if you believe that the global economy will continue to muddle through for all the reasons set out in Part I, then owning outright a small but diversified portion of Global Inc. is the best way of having a chance of benefiting from its growth.

You are not guaranteed to share in that growth, not least because governments often get in the way, driving wedges between economic growth and corporate cash flow in the shape of taxation, bureaucracy and administrative controls and sometimes even confiscation. Moreover, you might be unlucky with the timing of your entry point, and buy your stocks just ahead of a correction: even in a growing world, that could still leave you having to wait a long time for the investment to be made good. Nonetheless, a basket of stocks is likely to generate a stream of rising dividends into the indefinite future. The title to cash flow is low, because dividends are discretionary, and stocks are very volatile ownership assets, but analytically that cash flow resembles that of a perpetual bond with a growing coupon, making it the longest duration asset class, and one of the most liquid to boot.

It is not generally appreciated that stock markets offer much greater liquidity and transparency, and are much easier for private investors to access directly, than bond markets – even those for government bonds. As noted, this can occasionally be a curse as well as a blessing, for example when high-frequency traders trigger "flash crashes" with their automated trading models, or when stocks are dumped into the market to generate cash needed by investors unable to sell their other, less liquid assets. On the whole, though, it means that you can usually buy and sell quickly, and at prices that are widely visible and competitive.[2]

Figures 6.1 and 6.2 show how the stylised cash flow profiles of conventional bonds and stocks, each with a present value of 100, differ. The bond's cash flow, shown in Figure 6.1, is the most secure, remember, but it might last for just ten years, with a weighted centre of gravity – duration – at perhaps eight to nine years: there is a stream of constant coupon payments followed by the repayment of capital on maturity, and then the investment is over, and the investor has to find another one. The stock's cash flow is less predictable, but the dividend coupons received will likely follow the sort of path shown in Figure 6.2: they continue into the indefinite future, and while their individual

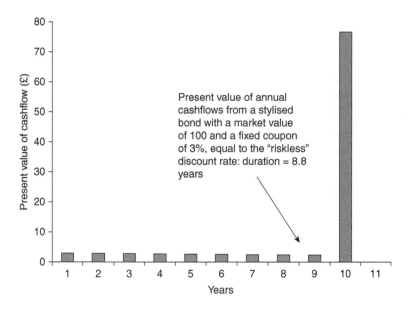

Figure 6.1   Stylised bond cash flow
Source: Author's calculations.

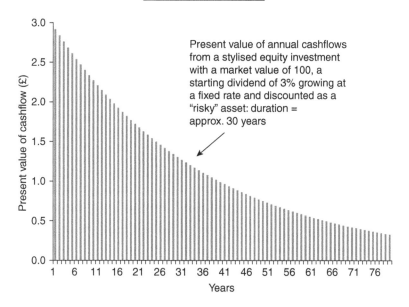

Present value of annual cashflows from a stylised equity investment with a market value of 100, a starting dividend of 3% growing at a fixed rate and discounted as a "risky" asset: duration = approx. 30 years

Figure 6.2   Stylised equity cash flow
Source: Author's calculations.

present values become diminishingly small, their total worth mounts incrementally, and can more than compensate for the absence of a capital repayment, delivering a duration that might be measured in decades.[3]

It is this growing stream of income that makes stocks such an important investment asset. It took professional investors a long time to realise its significance. The "cult of the equity" gathered momentum in the 1950s and early 1960s, as institutional investors at pension funds and life assurance companies realised the importance of dividend growth:[4] previously, stocks had been valued for the level of their yield, and for the possibility of capital gain, with little careful thought given to the long-term implications of dividend growth. Having learned the lesson, the investment community then became too complacent about it, overlooking the potential attractiveness of bonds at a time of falling inflation as it did so. The demise of the UK cult of the equity effectively began in the 1990s with the more conservative pension accounting noted in Chapter 2, and it was firmly interred by the financial debris that accompanied the richness of embarrassments noted in Part I. Of these, the dotcom bubble in 1999/2000, and the collapse in UK bank dividends after 2007, did the most damage to the income-driven case for equity investing.

The attractions of higher dividends are not limited to the income they represent. On a long-term view, growth in dividends is likely to be reflected in share prices. If it were not, the yield on stocks would otherwise rise without limit. Suppose, for example, that the level of dividends doubles: if share prices didn't keep pace, the yield would double too. Of course, if the general level of interest rates, which can shape the return available on many other investments, was also rising, or if a recession seemed likely to make that rise in dividends a short-lived affair, then a higher yield on stocks might be appropriate. Other things being equal, however, a doubled yield on stocks might stick out like a sore thumb. The natural response of investors would be to bid-up stock prices until the yield represented by the higher dividend (the dividend as a percentage of the stock price) fell back to more appropriate levels. On a long-term view, then, share prices can be expected to move in line with dividends, and the prospective total return that can be reasonably expected on an investment in stocks is the dividend yield you start with plus the likely dividend growth.

Again, this is not guaranteed to come to pass. Sometimes dividend yields rise and stay high for no reason – sometimes because stock prices actually fall, even as dividends continue to grow. Sometimes dividends don't grow, or even fall for a while. Generally, however, dividends are less volatile than stock prices, and at current low levels of interest rates and bond yields you might be happy with the income stream that they represent, and able perhaps to view any eventual rise in share prices as icing on the cake. For investors seeking income, most stocks currently offer more of it than do most bonds, though at the cost of course of much higher volatility and uncertainty.

We will revisit the issue of prospective returns, and valuation, more carefully in Chapter 7. Briefly, at current dividend yields, and with unremarkable long-term growth rates in mind, the prospective total return on stocks can seem implausibly high. Opinion pieces in the financial broadsheets, and even some professional investors, often suggest that because it is higher than the likely nominal growth rate (output growth and inflation together) of the wider economy, it is somehow unsustainable, and evidence of a rose-tinted view of stock markets. This is mistaken: the growth of dividends is unlikely to exceed the economy's growth rate for long, but that decides only the capital gain portion of the total return on stocks. It is perfectly feasible for the total return on stocks to exceed nominal GDP growth indefinitely.[5]

As I hope I've made clear, as the part owner of a business, even a business with limited liability (as quoted businesses are), a shareholder faces a very insecure immediate outlook by comparison with someone holding cash or bonds. Day-to-day volatility in the big stock market indices can be daunting, as noted earlier, and individual stocks can move more dramatically again (hence the importance of diversification). Stocks are not appropriate for all investors. That said, the further into the future we try to see, the greater the general uncertainty that threatens all assets, and the fewer the number of things that we can (almost) take for granted. If you share the views in Part I, then an approximately capitalist, growing world economy might be one of those things. If it isn't, it is not clear what other assets will offer better long-term insulation from the unfathomable storms that otherwise lie ahead.

Indeed, there is at least one storm that stocks are usually better placed to weather than are some other financial assets, namely: inflation. They are also much less exposed to some modest deflation than is popularly assumed. This is because they represent shares in the productive assets of the corporate sector, and so have some "real" characteristics. They are similar in this respect to index-linked bonds, though the inflation compensation that they offer is informal: it is approximate only, and not guaranteed. If inflation lifts all prices and costs similarly, it can leave corporate profit margins unaltered – and the same is true of deflation. Exceptions would be if the inflation were instead the "cost-push" kind, resulting from an autonomous surge in input costs, which would hit margins hard; or if the inflation or deflation were encountered as a result of – or were to trigger – a wider economic upheaval that affected output significantly. Stocks often suffered along with other financial assets during much of the stagflationary and strife-torn cost-push trauma of the 1970s, though taking the decade as a whole they fared less grimly than bonds in particular.

All this assumes that stocks really do enjoy in practice the sort of duration appeal suggested earlier. But their cash flow does indeed last a long time. The top-down evidence on wider stock market (index-level) returns is well established and documented carefully, for example (subject to survivorship bias) in the yearbooks co-authored by the London Business School.[6] The bottom-up evidence from the United States is also powerful, however – and less unrepresentative than you might think if, as seems likely, the world is slowly gravitating towards the American model.

In the late 1960s, a group of large US companies believed capable of delivering long-term growth became known as the "Nifty Fifty", and investment advisers tipped their stocks as a one-stop, buy-and-hold solution to long-term investing. As with many investment "themes" – see Chapter 5 – this one did well for a while and then seemingly crashed and burned: the growth stocks, always pricey, became even more expensive, and fell back to earth. They didn't disappear, however, and in late 2008 I found that two-thirds of the stocks still existed as separate companies, and that an even larger proportion of the original franchises was still generating cash once allowance was made for their acquisition by, and merger with, other companies.[7] Their fortunes have varied – some had seen their original business models overtaken by new technology, most visibly perhaps Eastman Kodak, Polaroid and Rank Xerox – but almost all the of the "fifty" seemed still to be operating at some level. Very few government bonds that were trading in the late 1960s were still with us in 2008.

At first sight you might think that this perhaps contradicts my earlier advice to ignore "thematic" investment ideas. It does not. The idea that a core holding of large, well-enfranchised businesses can deliver attractive returns over a long period is not really a "theme" at all, but the central case for holding stocks, which should be a core component of most private investment portfolios aiming at long-term wealth preservation and growth.

Emerging market bonds and *emerging market stocks* can offer added dimensions of uncertainty not encountered in other fixed income or stock markets. Most obviously in the case of bonds, they can offer more significant sovereign (government) credit risk, and exchange rate risk, and they are less liquid: they carry correspondingly higher yields as a result (not all emerging market bonds are issued by governments of course, and many are denominated in "hard", developed currencies). Emerging market stocks also offer that exchange rate risk, and reduced liquidity, but rather than receiving materially higher yields, investors hope to be rewarded by benefiting from the more direct exposure to the rapid domestic growth rates of the emerging economies.

It is a moot point as to whether the differences between emerging and developed markets these days are still large enough to warrant them being described as distinct asset classes (the so-called frontier markets are much less liquid, and more volatile, but too small to count as an asset class). Greece was classified as a developed country when it defaulted on its debt in 2012, and if it is exchange rate volatility that you seek, then the big developed currencies can be pretty volatile – in both directions.[8] South Korea and Taiwan's stock markets, which are still classified as emerging, offer better liquidity and diversification than some developed markets. Meanwhile, many developed world companies are active globally, and offer some emerging market exposure at developed levels of market liquidity and governance. At current levels of bond yields, it is not obvious that private investors need to have some emerging market bonds (or bond funds) in their portfolios. Emerging economy *growth* is however still a must-have characteristic, but it may best be captured in portfolios by viewing global equities as the relevant asset class, not "developed" and "emerging" markets separately. As with small company stocks, or speculative grade bonds, if you want to tilt your global equity implementation in the direction of direct exposure to emerging growth, it makes sense to rely more on pooled funds than on individual stock selection.

Private equity funds use loans and their members' subscriptions to buy businesses, typically using borrowed funds alongside their members' funds. The businesses they acquire may be start-ups or established businesses, quoted or private. Often the targets have been struggling, and the management (selected by the private equity group) is charged with restructuring them, usually by focusing single-mindedly on profitability or cash flow (as opposed to the family or employee focus, or perhaps general lack of skill or luck, of the outgoing management). Once the business has grown, or been rebuilt, the typical exit is for it to be floated on the stock market, or sold to another firm, allowing the private equity fund to realise its profit and either return the cash to its members or look for another target.

Private equity investments are usually large, and can be very illiquid, since several years are required to allow for acquisition, restructuring and divestment (typically, five to seven years). They are also high risk, since the target is often in difficulties and the title you are taking as an investor is one of leveraged ownership (though the risk is not open-ended: exposure is limited to the capital subscribed). Duration is hard to gauge: there may be no regular dividend payments, and the timing and scale of the final pay-out is highly uncertain. The private equity group itself will be paid well for its efforts in collating and managing the fund. The performance of private equity groups can vary significantly, and poor data makes it difficult to generalise, but returns generally seem to be broadly similar to those that an individual could synthesise for themselves by borrowing to buy a straightforward quoted equity fund, albeit without the unlimited exposure to loss that a personal loan would usually involve. Private equity can thus be viewed as a compound asset: a short position in cash combined with a long position in illiquid equity. It is best viewed as an implementation technique, not as an asset class in its own right.

Commodities performed strongly after the millennium, and have become a popular "alternative" asset. Their gains have been associated with the growing prominence of the Chinese economy. It is consuming energy and industrial commodities rapidly as it builds its power, transport, manufacturing and housing infrastructure, and it promises to consume more soft, agricultural commodities as its increasingly prosperous consumers demand more of the foods typically demanded by higher-income societies (such as meat and dairy produce, which requires animal feed). The investment demand for commodities is an attempt to ride on the back of the perceived "super cycle" driven by the imbalance between this growing emerging demand, and supply prospects that are believed to be static or shrinking. Other emerging economies are also growing rapidly and adding to commodity demand as they industrialise, but many of them are also large suppliers of commodities too – most notably, Brazil, Russia and South Africa. China is larger, and has understandably excited most attention.

Fostered by the success enjoyed by some pioneering managers of "alternative" assets, notably the endowment funds at Yale and Harvard universities, and by academic research demonstrating their lack of correlation with other assets alongside their stronger recent returns,[9] the popularity of commodities with investment advisers and their customers has grown, and so too has the accessibility and liquidity of funds designed to allow private investors to own them. However, whether the investment case is a solid one or not – and we saw in Part I that resource depletion may not be quite as urgent an issue as is popularly believed, and the very long-term trend in most commodity prices has sloped downwards – there are some important practical considerations that suggest commodities should not be a core holding for private investors.

Most importantly, because commodities are bulky, it is usually prohibitively expensive to invest in them directly. In practice, most investments are made not in physical commodities, but in the futures markets, and the prices of commodity futures can behave very differently to the prices in the physical or spot markets. In particular, futures prices can be much more difficult to relate to the demand and supply narrative, the evolving interaction of users and producers, that has fired the popular interest in commodities, and a financial future is not the tangible, "real" asset that most investors imagine a commodities investment to be.

Moreover, commodities generate no cash flow. They have no yield or dividend, and the various "roll" and "collateral" yields that the futures markets deliver are not reliable or efficient ways of obtaining income. The investment is an ownership title, and the ultimate worth of the principal at stake is impossible to gauge: the absence of a direct yield makes an investment in the commodity markets even more difficult to value than investments in more conventional assets, and there is no natural compounding of returns. Commodities have no meaningful duration – after all, most of them are first and foremost consumables.

One commodity in particular is often singled out for special attention. As we saw in Part I, gold's traditional role as a monetary asset has given it near-mystical status in many advisers' minds, and it is popularly believed that if the modern financial world were about to end, gold would offer one of the few reliable stores of value. Gold has been valued by humans for perhaps 3,000 years or so, an esteem achieved largely without institutional support. Three millennia of monetary credibility delivered without the assistance of an independent central bank is not to be sniffed at – or so the argument goes.

However, this is likely a longer investment horizon than even the most far-sighted private investor is willing to consider, and the value of gold is anything but stable in the shorter term (which in this context can extend for decades). In late 2014, an ounce of gold is trading at roughly $1,200. In early September 2011, shortly after the US sovereign debt rating was downgraded from AAA for the first time, the price briefly hit $1,900. In early 2001 it was roughly $250; in early 1980 it had briefly touched $850. This sort of volatility gives the lie to the notion that gold is a precise store of wealth, or an exact hedge against inflation. In real terms, the gold price has varied tenfold since 1971 (when the dollar decoupled from it): it is currently in the top half of that range, but has already fallen by a third from its recent high, and after its all-time high in real terms, touched in early 1980, it lost four-fifths of its value before stabilising in 2001 and eventually rallying.

Admittedly, gold is easier to hold in physical form, whether directly or in the form of certificates testifying to ownership of bullion kept secure in vaults somewhere on your behalf. As with other commodities, however, it has no duration, and the notion of "fair value" is elusive. Finally, while gold does often perform strongly at times of monetary crisis, the notion that this makes a small position in gold a useful hedge or insurance policy for the rest of your portfolio is mistaken. If gold is to stand a chance of hedging a portfolio it needs to be a big portion of it, but holding perhaps a quarter of an investment portfolio in a volatile ownership asset with no duration would hardly be a low-risk strategy.

Hedge funds and similar vehicles are another increasingly popular "alternative" asset class of late, and can arouse strong emotions. Hedge funds can follow various strategies – second-guessing the business cycle or merger and acquisition situations, for example, or picking stocks, or playing the currency, commodities and other futures markets – but what they have in common is that they have been lightly regulated, often offshore, and have been able to use implementation techniques that are not always available to other collective vehicles such as mutual funds. Traditionally, hedge funds have been accessible mostly to very wealthy investors, and have been relatively opaque and illiquid, often with formal constraints on investors' ability to withdraw funds at short notice. This illiquidity caused a problem for many investors in the panic of 2008/2009, but subsequent industry rethinks, and the introduction of more liquid and less loosely regulated vehicles compliant with the European Union's UCITS[10] Directive, have allowed more investors to access the various strategies offered and to be reasonably sure of being able to take money out in a hurry. Many UCITS vehicles offer daily liquidity, for example. Their illiquidity apart, traditional hedge funds had a less bad crisis than they might have done: returns were poor, with little collective evidence of the eponymous "hedging" of risk activity, but there were few big failures, and the funds posed little systemic threat.

Hedge funds have high annual charges: commonly 2% of the assets invested with them, plus a share of perhaps 20% of any profits they make for you. Collectively, their performance after allowing for these fees has been mixed – so much so that it has been calculated that they have added no value for their investors, who allegedly would have been significantly better off holding safe, liquid assets such as treasury bills.[11] The hedge fund managers themselves, of course, have been extremely well rewarded by virtue of those high fees, suggesting that the best way of making money from a hedge fund is to run one, not to invest in it. Added to this, many of the managers are super-confident men-in-a-hurry (again) who in some cases have benefited from being close to a pool of slow capital in the form of wealthy relatives and friends. They are often capable of flip-flopping their views and positions on a whim, making an investment with them in some ways resemble "an undertaking of great advantage, but no-one to know what it is". Recently some high-profile US hedge fund managers have been convicted of insider trading. Hence those strong emotions.

The poor performance and high pay of hedge fund managers may simply be an extreme illustration of the shortcomings of the wider fund management industry, however. Some of the cleverest, hardest-working and most serious professional investors I have met have been at hedge funds, and the idea that the collectively mediocre results of the sector are deliberate is mistaken. My misgivings about the sector are more practical.

Despite their name – derived from the relatively conservative approach of the first fund, opened in 1949, which aimed to carefully "hedge" its market exposures – an investment in a hedge fund can involve a considerable degree of risk. Liquidity is still relatively low compared to stocks and bonds, and few hedge funds pay dividends: with no formal yield, their explicit duration is short (the duration of the assets they hold may not be, of course, but hedge funds' relative lack of transparency makes this difficult to gauge). More importantly, in a more tightly supervised world in which borrowing is unfashionable, the traditional implementation advantages enjoyed by hedge funds – the ability to sell short, and to use leverage – have faded somewhat. Arguably, they are not really a distinct asset class at all, but merely a way of implementing positions in already existing assets, which they will do as well or as badly as their skill and luck permit. Selecting hedge funds is not easy: it can be just as difficult as trying to decide which stocks are likely to outperform the wider market, for example. Some advisers recommend holding a "fund of funds", a separately managed fund that chooses the funds for you, but this of course simply layers an extra fee on top of the already-high charges of the underlying funds, and almost guarantees mediocre performance.

Collectibles – classic cars, musical instruments, art, jewellery and so forth – are often tipped as good investments, but if they have performed well that has been a happy accident. The golden rule here is easy: if the things that you are collecting bring you pleasure, and/or you value the status that they may bring, that is an end in itself. For every Stradivarius and Vermeer whose value has soared and whose sale can be easily arranged (albeit through an auction house whose fees would make a hedge fund manager blush) there is a long list of forgotten makers and painters whose works languish in cheap, unsellable obscurity. This is a classic instance of an old asset potentially having little duration: collectibles do not have a yield – other than the emotional return you get from looking at them, or charging others to do so – and their ultimate worth is highly uncertain and largely influenced by collective tastes, not economic growth. Even if you are lucky, or able to afford the very best established names, storage, insurance and maintenance costs can be high. Collect these things because you like them and can afford to, not primarily because you expect them to further your investment objectives. The same is true of *fine wine*, which is much less liquid than it seems, and whose quality can only be decided definitively by changing it from an investment to a consumable. Its promoters often suggest that wine offers the best of both worlds – that you can enjoy its financial appreciation and relish its taste – but it is no different to cake in this respect.

Real estate is a distinct investment category: it offers ownership title to a long-lasting income-generating tangible ("real") asset that is often uncorrelated with other investment assets. Its duration alone would make it worthy of consideration, but its tangibility is also distinctive inasmuch as it offers some loose insulation from the ravages of inflation or financial crises generally (other than crises driven by overvalued real estate, that is). It belongs in most private investors' portfolios to some extent. The difficulty lies in establishing its liquidity, and in deciding how to incorporate in our investment policy the largest single real estate – or any – asset that most of us will own, namely our homes.

As noted earlier, many commercial real estate investments (offices, malls, factories, for example) are too large for most private investors to consider buying outright, and most of us need to pool our investments with others' if we are to get access to them. There is not always as plentiful a supply of such collective funds available, and participation often requires tying-up the funds for years at a time. Open-ended funds, where the fund managers use new inflows to acquire new properties, are more liquid, but the "lumpy" nature of their investment profile means that inflows of new cash are often piling up on the sidelines while critical mass – or appropriate investment opportunity – is built up, which can dilute returns.

Some advisers recommend the use of real estate vehicles quoted on the stock exchanges as a way of building more liquid exposure. However, the price to be paid for adding liquidity in this way is that the asset you are acquiring can have more in common with stocks than with property. Quoted property companies mostly take the form of Real Estate Investment Trusts, or REITs, which have to pay out most of their income as dividends, but even so their value can be influenced not just by the value of their underlying assets but also by the company's management and balance sheet leverage, and by the wider stock market. REITs are best viewed as part of your stock holdings, not real estate.

From a portfolio construction perspective, the difficulties of dealing with your main residence are more subtle but important, and represent another reason for viewing the investment process overall as an approximate, satis-ficing one rather than as a precise, optimising one. If you are lucky enough to own your own home, it likely represents to you an asset that yields both a consumable service – accommodation and emotional satisfaction – and a long-duration investment return. Not knowing how to apportion those two components, the consumption and investment elements, of an asset that for most of us would represent a material portion of our total wealth, means we cannot easily view our investment portfolio in the holistic way that the finance textbooks might suggest. Even if we could, the indivisibility of the residential asset makes the neatly fungible optimisations in the textbooks irrelevant: switching, say, 10% of your portfolio from real estate into stocks, when your house is the only real estate asset you own, is not a meaningful option. Of course, you could borrow against the house, and invest the new mortgage in stocks. In doing so, however, you are not reducing your expo-sure to property as such, but effectively reducing your position – and maybe even going short – in cash.[12]

In late-2014, house prices in the UK have again been rising relatively rapidly – at a double digit rate – and from a starting point that was histori-cally elevated to begin with. Many first-time buyers are effectively locked out of the market. This ongoing strength in UK house prices generally, and of those in London in particular, like most of the other housing cycles in the last 50 years, was *not* predicted in advance by most economists or the media, despite the obvious hints provided by (1) a very visibly growing population, (2) shrinking household sizes, (3) controls on new housing supply and (4) fall-ing real mortgage rates. Low interest rates have of course helped keep prices high, and may be unsustainable. The same is true of current government policies aimed at boosting the availability of mortgages. In the meantime, however, the population is still growing steadily, the supply of new homes remains tightly controlled by planners and housebuilders, and the UK is still an attractive destination for much footloose international capital. Real estate may not be liquid, but UK real estate is less illiquid than many other countries' real estate. Net of purchase taxes, and in some foreign currencies, London house prices have looked less obviously crazy to overseas buyers than they may have done to us. The absence of capital gains tax on a domestic buyer's principal residence is also an overlooked source of resilience.

With current rental yields low and mortgage rates likely to rise, this is not an obvious time to be building a buy-to-let empire. If, however, you do own your main residence, if you view it as representing a significant part of your investable wealth, and if your mortgage is manageable even at significantly higher rates, it may be worth keeping it. There are few one-way bets in investing – in either direction.

Finally, while there is a long-established tradition of both institutional and private investors owning property, some special categories of real estate have recently become popular as "alternative" assets – *forestry and farmland*, for example. Their distinctiveness is the greater unpredictability of returns, and the lower liquidity, that they offer: this does not necessarily make them unattractive, but they can be difficult for most private investors to access.

Which of the above asset classes are essential holdings for most private investors? As noted, it is debatable whether the differences between developed and emerging stock markets are still large enough to warrant viewing them as separate asset classes, and private equity and hedge funds arguably represent simply a particular way of implementing positions in other, already existing assets. Setting these concerns aside for the time being, Table 6.1 provides a subjective rating of each of these popular asset classes according to how they might be positioned under each of the three key investment dimensions noted above – namely, duration, title or security, and liquidity. Five stars is the highest score under each heading, one is the lowest.

I have given five asset classes a total score of ten or more, consistent with an average subjective ranking across all three dimensions of at least three stars: cash, government bonds, developed stocks, emerging market stocks and real estate.

The illiquidity and insecurity of private equity, and the illiquidity, insecurity and lack of obvious duration of hedge funds, suggests that whether they are genuinely distinct assets in their own right or not, they are not obvious "must-haves" for private portfolios. Commodity futures' lack of duration,

Table 6.1   Commonly identified asset classes and their key characteristics

Investment	Duration	Title/security of payment	Liquidity
Cash and near-cash	*	*****	*****
Government bonds	***	*****	*****
Corporate bonds: investment grade	**	****	***
Corporate bonds: speculative grade	**	***	**
Emerging market bonds	**	**	**
Developed equities	*****	***	*****
Emerging market equities	*****	*	****
Private equity	****	*	**
Commodity futures	*	**	**
Gold	*	***	***
Hedge funds	**	**	**
Collectibles	*	*	*
Fine wine	*	*	*
Real estate	*****	****	**
Forestry and farmland	***	***	*

Note: Asterisks denote author's subjective assessment of the extent to which each asset class has the characteristic: highest = *****, lowest = *.

Source: Author.

weak title and relative inaccessibility make them unappealing. And collectibles and fine wine are best viewed for what they are – sources of enjoyment, not investment return. The credit markets can be attractive, but investment grade is not currently distinct enough, and speculative bonds are too illiquid, for them to be must-haves. Forestry and farmland can be difficult to sell, with unclear income streams. Cash, government bonds, developed and emerging stock markets, and real estate are the best-scoring asset classes in the table, and these should provide the bulk of your investment portfolio. If we view global stocks as a single-asset class, we will be focusing on just four key assets.

Excluded from the table above, and the discussion so far, has been any mention of the "hybrid" assets that combine elements of two or more asset classes, such as convertible bonds (corporate bonds that can be converted into stocks, to the bondholder's advantage, if the stock price rises far enough) or structured products (combinations of zero-coupon bonds with derivatives that can create bespoke combinations of equity and bond risk). They can be useful for private investors, but are illiquid, expensive, and by definition are not distinct asset classes: they are not "must-haves".

Similarly, little attention has been paid here to foreign exchange. The currency in which an asset is denominated is a characteristic of that asset, not a separate asset in its own right: you can only invest in foreign exchange by holding another asset (such as money-market instruments, bonds or stocks) denominated in that currency. Moreover, exchange rates are even more difficult to predict accurately than other market prices, and investment advice that focuses primarily on trying to second-guess currency movements carries low conviction – or at least, it should do.

The absence of "alternative" assets from our short list of "must-haves" may come as a surprise, and our list is certainly unfashionable in current investment circles. Of course, while they may not be essential holdings, that does not make them "must-*not*-haves". But put bluntly, the main investment options you face are staying liquid (the equivalent of keeping cash under the mattress), lending to the government, owning a small portion of global business, and owning some property. Realistically, what significant "alternatives" to these can there be?

Most personal investment policies will suggest having at least a little of each of these core assets, and a lot of some. In Chapter 7 we look at how an appropriate mix might be determined.

7

PUTTING IT ALL TOGETHER –
WEIGHTING IN VAIN?

The will to a system is a lack of integrity.

– Nietzsche

Received wisdom mistakenly assumes that the developed west is incapable of offering attractive investment opportunities in a debt-burdened, demographically challenged, decadent, depleted and dangerous world. Meanwhile, much specialist investment analysis and advice is spuriously precise, treating the investment process as a continuous, fiercely-competitive search for the best possible "risk-adjusted" returns.

This book has argued that the constraints on growth are much looser than we think; that the investment process needs to be viewed in a firmly "postmodern" setting, and is largely about showing up and satisficing, not seeking perfection or being necessarily paid for taking "risk"; and that private investors need only hold a small number of simple asset classes offering duration, title and liquidity.

In this chapter we discuss how a long-term investor seeking to maintain and augment their real wealth might blend these assets together in a portfolio that can capitalise on ongoing economic growth, but without betting the ranch on it. In order to decide how much of each asset to hold, however, we need to discuss a little more carefully what we might reasonably expect each asset to offer by way of an investment return. The answers are closely related to the vexed issue of valuation, that is, what the right price to pay for an investment might be – independently of any fund management charges and dealing costs – because the prospective return on an investment is a combination of its intrinsic returns together with any change in its valuation during the holding period. If an asset is particularly expensive (or cheap) to begin with, part of the expected return from holding it will reflect the fall (or rise) in valuation as it returns to a more reasonable level: such prospective changes in valuation can easily be large enough to offset or even outweigh the likely cash flow generated by the asset.

REASONABLE EXPECTATIONS AND FAIR VALUES

As we noted in Part I, the future is profoundly uncertain. This does not stop pundits making detailed predictions regarding likely investment returns, or confidently proclaiming an asset – or interest rate, or exchange rate – to be mispriced. The detail and confidence is misplaced: the estimation of likely returns, and the valuation of financial assets, is unavoidably subjective and imprecise.

There can be a huge gap between sophisticated theory and harsh reality when it comes to valuations in particular. In theory, the value of an asset is driven by largely objective factors such as its prospective cash flow and a relevant discount rate. In practice, few financial factors are genuinely objective, because the future is so uncertain and because textbook definitions of cash flow and discount rates do not always have neat real-world counterparts, or are ambiguous. Moreover, realisable value depends on there being somebody willing to buy the asset from you: if assets cannot be exchanged they have no practical worth as stores of wealth. If there are no immediate buyers on the day that you want to sell your shares or bonds, the prices of those assets might need to fall a long way to entice buyers into the market; and in the extreme case in which no buyers can be found, your assets could have no realisable value that day. For the large, developed government bond and stock markets this is an extremely unlikely event; but in a crisis, when potential buyers are wary, valuations can fall a very long way indeed, as we saw in 2008/2009. Some assets – for example, speculative grade corporate bonds, secondary quality commercial property – can be difficult to sell at the best of times.

Nonetheless, there are some useful rules of thumb that can help us gauge the order of magnitude at least of a reasonable expected long-term return, and whether an asset might be obviously expensive or cheap. Prospective cash-flows on investments are mostly derived from three immediate sources: interest rates, corporate profits and rental income. The first two are by far the most important: broadly speaking, expectations for them move together, but because lower interest rates boost the prices of bonds, at times of crisis their value can rise while those of business-related assets falls – and vice-versa when recovery begins. This is why much theoretical diversification across the wider range of assets discussed in Chapter 6 counts for little when times are especially uncertain: investors' fears and hopes polarise around those underlying sources, and group assets according to whether their returns are predominantly driven by interest rates or the health of corporate business. The former are seen as safer, or "risk-off" assets, whose valuation rises as the creditworthiness, cash flows and valuations of the corporate sector fall, while the latter are lumped together as more dangerous, "risk-on" assets – whether they be commodity futures, emerging market stocks and bonds, speculative grade bonds, or developed stocks.

In the short-term, interest rates can change independently of the prospects for business, as central bank policy rates – or investors' collective nervousness – can move in the opposite direction to the business cycle, and shift rates and bond yields accordingly. Similarly, there can be short-term fluctuations in the business climate that are not reflected in altered interest rates. On a longer-term view, however, expectations for both interest rates and corporate profits, whether in nominal or real terms, are themselves largely driven by a single, unifying driver: economic growth. Expected long-term returns on investment portfolios thus effectively boil down into a single issue: what do we assume about growth, and is that assumption already priced-in to current market values? Hence the focus in Part I. The links between GDP, interest rates, corporate profits, and the valuation of securities, are loose and variable, and anything but guaranteed; but in gauging likely investment returns, one thing matters more than anything else – and to borrow a phrase, "It's the economy, stupid".[1] It doesn't matter quite in the deterministic, continuous way suggested by econometric models: sometimes there is no discernible link at all between the markets' moves and that month or quarter's economic news. Instead it matters more in a stage-setting, regime-creating way: it shapes the wider investment climate, not the daily weather.

INTEREST RATES

Interest is perhaps the most visible source of investment return, and interest rates are the prices that directly affect more financial variables than any others. They vary according to maturity, currency, whether payment is in the form of a fixed coupon or a floating rate, how it accrues, the creditworthiness of the borrower and so forth. Some long-term interest rates are only easily accessible to private investors in the shape of fixed-coupon government bond yields; some short-term rates can only be accessed through institutional funds. We mostly have in mind here short-term rates such as three-month interbank rates, but the discussion of expected returns applies to most rates and bond yields.

Short-term interbank rates are most widely used as reference points by the wider capital markets, and usually (but not always) move loosely in tandem with policy rates and the rates available on liquid bank deposits and money-market funds, the form in which cash is held in most investment portfolios.[2] In late-2014, the major money-market rates – for dollars, euros and sterling – are of course negligible, but historically they have moved in a wide range (Figure 7.1) and may become more volatile once more if our "muddle through" outlook for global growth prevails.

The "term structure" of interest rates shows how rates vary according to the length of the loan, from one day through to 30 years and more. It reflects the collective opinions and transactions of the large institutional investors and corporate treasuries that dominate the capital markets, and is usually plotted as a yield curve of government securities of varying maturities. Embedded within it is a view of how short-term interest rates will evolve over time, and these "forward rates" provide a useful starting point from which to think about the likely returns we should expect from holding

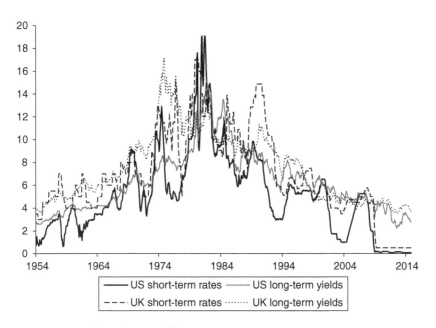

Figure 7.1   US and UK short-and long-term interest rates, 1954–2014, %
Source: Datastream.

short-term, near-cash investments over various periods. That profile has been sending a clear message recently.

At no point in the last five years have the most visible and liquid US and UK long-term interest rates (ten-year government bond yields, say) been lower than short-term rates; and because the ten-year yield is an average for the life of the loan, the short-term forward rates embedded at the furthest end of the term – three month rates in, say, nine years' time – have typically been higher again. Currently, US and UK three-month rates are roughly a half of 1%; ten-year government bonds are yielding around 2%; and three-month forward rates in mid-2023 are around 3%. The money and bond markets have thus been telling us – shouting at us – that institutional investors believe current levels of short-term interest rates are not likely to be permanent.

Institutional investors and the money markets collectively can get it wrong, of course. The slope of the yield curve – the difference between long-term and short-term interest rates – is one of the most widely-used forecasting tools, and for many US-based economists has assumed near-mystical status. An inverted or downward sloping curve, when long rates are below short rates, in particular is seen as a predictor of recession. It is far from infallible, however, and one of the key messages in this book, remember, is the need to question popular beliefs: this applies as much to interest rate expectations as it does to the demographic time bomb. Current levels of interest rates – short-term and long-term – are much lower, and have lasted for much longer, than most of us expected,[3] and as we shall see in a moment, the precise determination of rates is much more of a mystery than economists and central bankers like to acknowledge. That said, however, remember that these expectations are deeply ingrained even in a climate in which received wisdom is still defaulting to pessimism, and is expecting output growth and inflation – which usually push interest rates higher – to be lacklustre at best.

There are good reasons for thinking that in this instance the markets have got it right, and that interest rates will rebound to materially higher levels on a timescale that makes the move relevant to investors today. The current, negligible level of money-market interest rates reflects a combination of investors' short-term nervousness – even as they continue to recognise that such rates are unlikely to last – and the emergency measures taken by the Federal Reserve, the Bank of England, the European Central Bank and the Bank of Japan during the crisis and its aftermath. If we are right in thinking that the developed economies can continue to muddle through, those nerves are overdone, and the authorities will begin to normalise monetary policy (at varying speeds – as noted, in late 2014 the Bank of England and the Federal Reserve seem likely to start first). The growing global economy will itself gradually make this happen.

Interest rates are historically low, but since the massive financial write-downs that featured prominently in Chapter 4 have faded, corporate profitability has been respectable, and ongoing growth will help keep it so. As low-yielding cash accumulates on corporate balance sheets, however, it makes companies look less efficient. Their managers will eventually reinvest it in more productive business assets, and/or buy other, similarly-profitable businesses, and/or distribute more of it to their shareholders, who will in turn look to redeploy it in higher-returning assets – even, perhaps, as they continue to fret about some of the structural concerns discussed in Part I, because those are not going to evaporate overnight. At the same time, as employment grows, nervous consumers will worry a little less about the risk of losing their jobs – again, even as they continue to fret about some of those structural concerns perhaps – and will save a smaller portion of their incomes, reducing inflows to money markets and to capital markets in aggregate. These factors together reduce the flows of savings making their way into the money markets. Meanwhile, the growing economy will also be adding to the day-to-day transactional need for cash. The lubricating demand for liquidity rises just as its supply fades, and the result is that its price – in this case, short-term interbank rates – is squeezed higher as a result.

This description of the way in which growth tends to squeeze interest rates higher is of course a simplification, and one that will doubtless upset many factionally minded economists. For one thing, it assumes that the amount of aggregate liquidity is fixed, but as we saw in Part I, it is not, and can be created on demand by the collective actions of the banking system: this introduces some slack into our causal chain. For another, it also sidelines the role played by central banks, which can introduce a further degree of slack – particularly when they use unconventional measures such as "Quantitative Easing" and other more qualitative tools designed to loosen and circumvent the traditional constraints on liquidity. (That said, the conventional account likely overstates their potency: to all intents and purposes, central banks preside over, and formally validate, the general level of interest rates, rather than set them. The interaction of the economy with market expectations is key, as we saw when the best efforts of central banks failed to prevent interbank rates from surging as expectations of bank default took root in 2008.)

More importantly, the link between the real return on productive assets – the operating profitability of Global Inc., if you like – and the real return on cash is a particularly loose one, even in the ramshackle world of macroeconomics. On paper, the idea that there must be some connection between the real discount rate implicit in the collective value added by companies as they go about their routine activities, turning today's inputs into tomorrow's profitable output, and the real rate of interest in the money markets, is persuasive. The notion that capital markets somehow bring the two into line, by linking the returns available from production with savers' underlying "time preferences", is especially satisfying if you believe that capitalism requires some objective measure of the reward for waiting, a social discount rate that can serve as the ultimate benchmark for translating future outcomes into present values.[4] In practice, the level and direction of trends in corporate profitability can diverge from those in interest rates for long periods – most visibly, perhaps, after 1980, when profitability embarked on the upswing noted in Chapter 4 just as money-market rates and bond yields started upon what would prove to be a 30-year trend decline.

This may partly be because measuring corporate profitability consistently over time is not easy, as noted in Chapter 4, and in Chapter 7 below. Then there are the real-world frictions that prevent capital markets from working as neatly as textbooks suggest. In theory, for example, if a business is making a high level of profits for any length of time, it will attract competitors: capital flows to the new entrants, the industry gets bigger and its profitability is diluted, back down towards the norm. In practice, things are not that easy, as anybody who has tried to create their own Microsoft with borrowed money will testify. Brands, economies of scale, patents, discontinuities, expectations and simple inertia all combine to allow not just individual companies but business in aggregate to deliver trends in profitability that can diverge from trends in interest rates, even in the most competition-friendly climate, for a much longer period than the various theories of interest rate determination assume.[5]

Despite all these loose ends, however, there is often a link, however flexible and incomplete, between the economy's direction and that followed by interest rates. That link also offers a starting point at least from which to estimate the likely destination of rates – a reasonable expectation of the *level* that rates might gravitate towards in a "normal" economic climate. Such a climate might be thought of as one in which the economy grows steadily, unaccompanied by either a dramatic expansion or contraction of collective balance sheets of the sort which might give rise to widespread fears of unsustainability. Since the ability of borrowers to service their loans will vary according to the growth in their incomes, and since incomes collectively are simply another way of looking at the wider economy, or GDP, then the trend rate of growth in the economy is a useful benchmark against which to judge the level of interest rates. And as it happens, taking the last half a century as a whole, nominal GDP growth and long-term bond yields have been more or less in line in both the US (at roughly 7% per annum) and the UK (at roughly 8%).

For the UK, despite all the misgivings noted (and placed in context) in Part I, a reasonable projection for real economic growth over the next decade or so might be a compound annual rate of 2–3%, with projected inflation perhaps a further 2% on top of this, suggesting a nominal compound growth rate of perhaps 4–5%.[6] The profile is unlikely to be a smooth one, of course, but it is the trend that matters. Currently, as noted above, even long-term forward rates are still well below these levels.[7] Economic growth was of course well below this rate during the crisis – it was sharply negative – but it has subsequently gathered momentum, and in the last year or so has been tracking at around 3%. For the US, we might expect a broadly similar trend in nominal GDP; and for the euro area and Japan, a slower one (say perhaps 3–4%). As in the UK, most forward rates are currently well below these levels. Of course, these expectations are reasonable now, but circumstances may change over the longer term, and both lower and higher rates could at some stage be plausible.

It makes sense, then, for yield curves currently to point firmly upwards. If anything, they might be steeper still. If the developed world economy manages to muddle through and grow as it can, interest rates might yet normalise more vigorously than the markets currently expect. The clear-cut views of the money markets that rates are heading higher can indeed be reconciled with our earlier observations that received wisdom is still characterised by excessive macroeconomic pessimism.

What does this mean for likely money-market and bond returns? Taking a strategic view of the next five to ten years, say, rather than a short-term tactical view, it suggests that the returns on cash and floating-rate loan securities are likely to improve, while many fixed income securities will face headwinds from falling prices, and in each case possibly to a greater extent than is currently priced-in to markets. Most bonds are currently trading above their par values – their prices are greater than 100 – reflecting reductions in interest rates since they were issued. If rates do now rise faster than markets expect, then the average developed government bond portfolio might struggle to deliver a compounded return in line with its current yield of around 2% as prices fall faster than expected for a while – and that yield is hardly compelling to begin with, even on a pre-tax basis.[8] On this reading, many bonds are indeed expensive, and currently seem unlikely to maintain their real value, even with inflation projected at historically unremarkable levels. Pessimism makes people willing to hold even expensive bonds, of course; but if that pessimism is overdone, they may hold too many of them, particularly after that 30-year bull market. Rather than offering the "risk-free return" assumed in the modern portfolio theory textbooks, some of the highest quality bonds currently may effectively be offering "return-free risk".

The improving prospective yield on (near-)cash sounds potentially more attractive, but it will be starting from such a low level that it could take several years for floating pre-tax short-term interest rates to match prospective inflation rates. The compounded interest rate on money-market deposits might average perhaps just 2–3% over the next five to ten years (and even this assumes a faster rebound in three-month interbank rates than the money markets are currently pricing-in). Like fixed income, money-market deposits are not always held for their yield, of course: liquidity offers a high – but not complete – degree of nominal safety at times of crisis, and can be used for opportunistic forays into other assets. In the more normal business conditions that may lie ahead, however, its safe haven nature is unlikely to compensate for its lack of a meaningful return. It sounds unusual, but cash, like many bonds, is currently an expensive asset for investors to hold.

Of course, this does not mean that private investors should hold no interest-bearing deposits or bonds. We could be wrong about the economy or the geopolitical climate, and the nominal stability of cash, and the tendency of government bond prices to rise in a crisis, provides a valuable degree of insurance and ballast for portfolios.

STOCKS

Sensational forecasts for stock returns – projected booms and busts – are common, and grown men (again) seem to delight in taking quite outlandish positions on how best to value stocks, on what constitutes "fair value". Both the intrinsic return on stocks – the dividends and other distributions made by cash-generating companies – and their valuations fluctuate much more than do the returns on cash and fixed income, and the proportion of a portfolio that should be invested in stocks is the single biggest investment decision to be taken, so the wide range of views can be unsettling. Remember, however, the points made in Chapters 4 and 5: not all the views may be serious or disinterested.

As we saw in Chapter 6, the expected total return on stocks is a combination of the initial dividend income and a projected capital gain. The latter reflects not a systematic and complacent bullishness on the part of investors but simply the expected growth in the dividend as corporate profits rise over time: if share prices did not rise in line with dividend growth, dividend yields – the dividend as a proportion of the share price – would rise without limit. This total return can, and usually does, exceed the rate of growth in the wider economy, but again, this does not make it in some sense unsustainable.

Not all companies pay dividends. Profits themselves are highly volatile. Growing businesses may not yet be profitable, or may feel the need to retain profits for reinvestment or to minimise their shareholders' liability to income taxes; many finance directors prefer to keep payouts flexible, to maximise their room for manoeuvre; there can be cyclical or other short-term interruptions to profitability. Bank dividends of course were cut sharply or suspended during the crisis. For many years Microsoft paid no dividend, but this did not prevent it becoming one of the most valuable companies in the US stock market; in 2010 BP temporarily stopped paying a dividend, and eventually resumed payments at a much reduced rate, in the face of the costs incurred in the Gulf of Mexico spillage; in late 2014, Tesco has cut its dividend as a result of poor profitability and accounting problems.

Nonetheless, a company that was believed unlikely ever to be able to generate cash for its investors would have little value. The cash need not be paid out as a formal dividend: in the US in particular, it has become routine for many companies to distribute cash to their shareholders by buying-back some of their shares, to the extent that the stated dividend on the S&P 500 index in recent years has effectively understated significantly the regular payments being made to shareholders.[9] Most buy-backs are paid out of earnings, but at current stock valuations and interest rates, it pays many companies to borrow to do so. Of course, if share buy-backs were big enough, there would be nothing left to invest in, and it is often argued that such distributions are a sign of a lack of imagination – or a failure to identify attractive reinvestment opportunities – by the companies' managements. In practice, however, the flexibility and tax advantages that buy-backs can offer, and their effect on the value of the remaining bulk of the stocks outstanding, can make them an attractive source of incremental return. It is, however, one that is almost always overlooked when valuing the market as a whole.

Investors often focus on corporate earnings – profits after depreciation and taxes are deducted – instead of dividends as a guide to the potential pay-out that a company might deliver.[10] In using earnings data it is most common to quote the yield calculation upside down, as it were: the resultant "price to earnings", or PE, ratios show the number of years' earnings, at current levels, that can be bought at today's prices, and are probably the most widely used stock market valuation measures. Earnings are usually bigger than dividends, because they capture the total net income generated by companies and owned by its shareholders, not just that which is paid out formally as a dividend, but they are much more volatile. Moreover, whereas there is little ambiguity in the definition of dividends, there is a lot in the case of earnings.

In practice, the various data providers who collate and publish stock market indicators follow different approaches to defining and measuring earnings, reflecting for example the varying treatment of one-off or non-recurring gains and losses (such as exceptional and extraordinary items). To further complicate things, earnings can be viewed both on a "trailing" basis, that is, the latest twelve months' reported outcome, and on a "forward" basis, using analysts' collective expectations for a specified period ahead (usually 12 months, again). The latter approach is obviously subject to forecast error, and analysts more often aim too high than too low (despite the tendency to macro pessimism discussed at length above), but it can help to smooth the data by incorporating an expected rebound – or fall-back – after an unusual year. None of this stops market commentators talking of "the" PE ratio, but the inconvenient reality is that there are many, and pundits often forget to compare like-with-like when using them.

Expected growth in corporate profits and dividends can depend on many different factors. Business cycles, structural growth rates and banking crises vary across countries and over time. In framing long-term expectations, however, as with interest rates, the expected trend rate of growth in the nominal economy – projected output growth and inflation together – is the most obvious anchor. Governments can drive a wedge between economic growth and growth in the quoted corporate sector's earnings by changing taxes, by directly manipulating (for example) utility prices, and/or by reshaping competition policies. The various accounting authorities can have the same effect. Company managements can also drive a wedge between profits growth and dividend growth, as noted. Unless such developments are material, and capable of being predicted accurately, however, the most straightforward assumption is to expect that the long-term capital gain on stocks, like the long-term rate of interest, will loosely match long-term nominal economic growth: that is, around 4–5% in the UK and the US, and perhaps 3–4% in Continental Europe and Japan.

We suggested above that trend economic growth also represents the natural level towards which interest rates might be expected to gravitate. If equilibrium interest rates and the capital gain on stocks are equal, then the extra return to be plausibly expected from owning stocks rather than interest-bearing deposits or bonds is their dividend yield. This should not be viewed as a "risk premium", however, a necessary compensation for taking the added risk, but simply as a reasonable long-term projection.

Dividends currently are equivalent to around 3% of stock prices in the UK and Continental Europe. In the US, the dividend distribution is around 2%, but the ongoing stock buy-backs suggest a total distribution at least as large as that in Europe. In Japan, the dividend is around 2%. This suggests that expected long-term returns for the US and the UK might be 7–8% (the nominal GDP growth rate cited earlier of 4–5%, plus the starting payout of 3%); for Continental Europe, 6–7% (3–4% nominal GDP growth plus the 3% dividend); and for Japan, 5–6% (3–4% nominal growth plus the 2% dividend). Arguably, these estimates may be a little conservative, because a significant and increasing proportion of the profits made by developed companies comes from the faster-growing emerging markets, where nominal GDP growth might be 3–4% per annum faster than that in the UK and US.

Again, these expected returns might need to be modified if the starting point is one of obvious over- or under-valuation (either of which might yet develop between late-2014 and publication). If starting yields are excessively low, we might expect them eventually to rebound, which might require stock prices to lag behind the growth in dividends for a while (or vice versa). This effect would need to be deducted from (or added to) the prospective long-term return. Yields might be low because earnings and dividends are unusually depressed, in which case some upward rebound might be expected and built into projected future growth, and this might be sufficient to bring the valuation back down, leaving stock prices where they are. Alternatively, they might be low because stock prices have simply run too far ahead of earnings and dividends, in which case the expected return to more normal valuation levels is delivered by lower prices, unaccompanied by any spurt in earnings.

In practice, the difficulties associated with trying to decide whether the latest reported levels of earnings and dividends are sustainable, and so can be viewed as an appropriate starting point onto which to splice our long-term return projections, are big, and dwarf the theoretical niceties associated with equity valuation (another warning against spurious precision). The notion of a natural level of profitability, which might govern some sort of "normalised" mean to which earnings must eventually revert, is seductive, but impossible to anchor with any confidence – not least because the various measures of earnings noted above can give very different answers. In late-2014, for example, your view of the sustainability of US corporate profitability depends on whether you use an underlying measure such as operating earnings, or a more volatile measure such as the "as reported" series that delivered in full the dramatic roller-coaster ride described in Chapter 4 (and shown in Figure 4.2). The cyclically-adjusted measures of earnings that we will discuss shortly offer one way of trying to cut through this ambiguity, but an unconvincing one, not least because even a ten-year average of "as reported" earnings, for example, can tell a very idiosyncratic story – and not necessarily the one that investors have collectively priced-in. Over long periods, changes in the sectoral composition of the market indices can further complicate the picture.

Even if we could splice our projected growth rate smoothly and convincingly onto the recent past, we would not be able easily to see whether it was the one implicitly embodied in current stock prices. Whereas with interest rates and bond yields we can compare the forward rates priced into the markets with our expectation of economic growth, we cannot do that with stocks. There are no explicit yield curves for stocks – there don't need to be, because as undated securities they all have effectively the same, indefinite and potentially perpetual lifetime – and the calculation of a market implied future expected path for earnings and dividends is difficult. Effectively, in order to know what the market's implied paths for earnings and dividends might be, we need a discount rate – known as the "cost of equity" – to translate future equity cash flow back into present values. If we knew that with any confidence, we could calculate the implied growth rate priced into the market and compare it with our expectations for what that growth will turn out to be. Unfortunately, we don't – and the relevant calculations are highly sensitive to that discount rate.

Modern portfolio theory suggests calculating the cost of equity by adding an equity risk premium to a riskless interest rate, but as we have seen, neither of these things have an obvious real-world counterpart, and even if they did they would not be easily measurable. In particular, the long-term historical excess return delivered by stocks, often seen as the equity risk premium, is better viewed as a happy accident, and one whose scale has depended on what is meant by "long term". As noted, over some relatively lengthy periods – up to 20 years, for example, in the case of the US and UK – it has occasionally even been negative. Other, more ingenious methods for extracting expectations from market data have been proposed, such as using the actual paths followed by earnings and dividends as a guide to what "rational" expectations might have been, the idea being that long-sighted, perspicacious and unbiased investors would not have made systematically incorrect forecasts. Such methods raise more questions than they answer, however, and are arguably more sophisticated than the world they are trying to explain.

In practice, then, the valuation of equity markets is a much less precise affair even than the valuation of bonds. The less dogmatic one is, the better: rather than focus on a single measure or time period, the most useful approach is to look at a mix of widely watched and simple metrics such as dividend yields (a higher number indicating cheapness), and PE ratios and price-to-book ratios (which compare stock prices with the historical value of the shareholders' funds invested in the business – as with PE ratios, lower numbers indicate cheapness), and to look for material divergences from trends.

Context is important. A trailing PE ratio can be alarmingly large – as in 2009, for example – not because stock prices are crazily high but because earnings have temporarily collapsed, in which case it should probably be disregarded (in contrast to the situation in early 2000, when a high forward PE ratio reflected strong stock prices and indicated genuine overvaluation). Interest rates can be important: equity and bond valuations can be linked, formally so in modern portfolio theory, and informally in any analysis in which future cash flows – and/or the returns on competing assets – shape current equity values. Their role can be overstated: the so-called Fed model,[11] which took as a starting point an apparently stable relationship between earnings yields and government bond yields, broke down under the weight of the financial trauma of the 2000s. But the steady decline in rates, alongside the structural improvement in corporate profitability, had helped make stock markets look inexpensive through the long upswing of the 1980s and 1990s.

Given the unavoidable ambiguity surrounding the valuation of stocks, the strong convictions seemingly held by some pundits can be difficult to understand (they could of course be marketing ploys, remember). In recent years, two relatively esoteric measures in particular have gained some vocal and high-profile advocates: cyclically-adjusted price to earnings ratios (CAPEs, often referred to as "Graham & Dodd" PEs, after the two authors who first suggested such an approach) and Tobin's Q (James Tobin being the economist who baptised the idea, with "Q" standing for quotient). The ideas date back many years – Graham and Dodd introduced theirs in the 1930s – but had been largely forgotten until they were retrospectively found, by modern-day advocates, to be good forecasting tools.[12] Their merits have however been overstated, and private investors should keep them at arm's length pending corroboration from more straightforward measures. Their use illustrates again the way in which the financial debate can be sidetracked by the search for an elusive True Model, and by the elevation of Historical Data to almost mystical status.

The CAPE ratio has some intuitive appeal. Rather than use a single year's earnings, it takes a moving average of earnings over a much longer period, usually ten years, in an attempt to smooth away the volatility of the business cycle to arrive at an estimate of underlying earnings. Because earnings grow over time, an average of the last ten years' earnings will usually be lower than the latest year's, and so a CAPE will typically be higher than a conventional PE ratio. But the important comparison is with its own longer-term history. CAPE ratios are said to have been very successful in predicting returns – high levels relative to trend being followed by poor returns, and vice versa.

The CAPE idea is a good one, but its practical usefulness is limited. For one thing, as noted in Chapter 4, the further back in time we go, the less useful the historical earnings data become. More importantly, the statistical role played by the smoothing process in "explaining" market moves has been overstated. A CAPE takes a noisy series (stock prices) and divides it by a much less noisy one (the smoothed earnings series), and on closer inspection, unsurprisingly, it is the noisy component that actually does most of the statistical explaining. It has to: a variable that doesn't move around much can't account for much of the movement in one that does. In other words, the alleged predictive capability – discovered only after the event, remember – of CAPE ratios derives largely from stock prices themselves, and simply reflects the tendency of prices to fall back after a dramatic surge, and to rally after a collapse (Figure 7.2). That predictive capability has in any case been overstated, particularly in recent years, and as noted is retrospective – the ratios were not in use at the times of some of their alleged successes, for example in 1929. Finally, current levels of the CAPE are likely to fall markedly in the years ahead – making stocks look better value – even if profits stay flat at today's levels, simply because those crisis-depressed earnings numbers are going to drop out of the ten-year calculation: in this particular instance even the ten-year perspective may not be long enough to smooth earnings effectively.

Tobin's Q is flawed in design as well as execution. It is calculated by dividing the current value of the stock market by an estimate of the replacement cost of the assets – the plant, machinery and equipment – of the companies in it. If the ratio is above one, and stock market values exceed the cost of corporate assets, capital will supposedly shift from holding stocks to new business creation, and vice versa. In practice, Q has averaged less than one, suggesting – if taken at face value – that the stock market has been undervalued for most of the last century. Nonetheless, its proponents argue that its variation around that average can still be a useful guide to valuation.

But even if the notional replacement cost of assets was a good guide to what it would cost to build today's businesses from scratch – or if today's stock market value was indeed a good guide to the capital that could be realised by selling it all in one go – the value of a business does not depend on the value of its assets alone. The advisers who promote Q would not dream of charging for their own services on such a basis. One of the reasons for wanting to invest in a business is that as a going concern it can have a value that is greater than the sum of its parts. This surplus may not be tangible, but it is real, and reflected in such quantities as customer and supplier networks, brands, know-how and goodwill. This was true even in Tobin's time, and as the service sector in particular has grown, it has become even more important.

Moreover – and by now you will have guessed what's coming next – the available data are simply not good enough for us to have much confidence that we are indeed measuring what we think we are, or to compare national markets or even sectors carefully with each other. The available asset value numbers are obscure US macro data, which include unquoted private companies along with the stock market sector. The older historical figures for

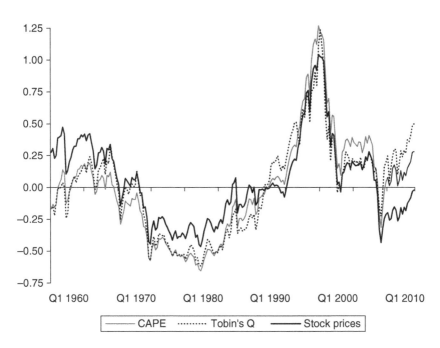

Figure 7.2   What do they tell us that stock prices don't? US stock prices, CAPE and Q ratios: deviations from trend. See text

Source: Robert Shiller's home page, Federal Reserve Bank of St Louis, author's calculations.

Q in particular are arguably even more questionable than the older earnings data. If most markets cannot have Q ratios calculated for them, and if most US investors don't look at Q, its practical worth as a valuation metric must be limited. Finally, as with the CAPE ratios, the bulk of the statistical work done by Q is done by its noisy numerator: the replacement cost of assets is relatively sluggish, and incapable of "explaining" much movement in anything (Figure 7.2 again).

Other esoteric valuation measures exist. Some analysts zealously focus on what they call the cash flow return on invested capital, comparing it with what seems (to them) to be priced into the market; others focus on a looser measure of economic value added, and again compare it to what might be priced in. The massive financial sector, however, does not easily lend itself to this sort of analysis, and measures that have little to say about the biggest sector in the developed world stock market – and are almost as obscurantist as Q – are of limited use.

There are no short cuts, no hidden secrets, no uniquely right answers, in valuing stocks. As noted, the best advice is to stay open-minded, and to compare a selection of simple, readily available measures with historically meaningful trends, and to be aware of the margin of error (or, since there is no single right answer, of the sheer scale of uncertainty). Most of the time, valuations are not the main drivers of capital markets anyway. Sometimes, they are a consequence rather than a cause: as noted earlier, at times of stress, panicking investors may dump cheap stocks to buy expensive bonds because the latter are a safer investment, in the process making stocks even cheaper and bidding bonds prices up to even higher levels. The even more distorted valuations that result represent an investment opportunity for longer-term investors, but it can take many months or years even for the wider investor community to share that view and make it a profitable one.

As noted, this uncertainty about stocks' value can be daunting. When dividend yields are just 3%, half a percentage point's difference in estimating a divergence from trend is proportionately a big deal, representing one-sixth of the value of your investment, or roughly two to three years' worth of the expected intrinsic return should yields normalise by this amount while you are invested. Nonetheless, for private investors whose investment policy allows them to take a long-term view, and to tolerate short-term volatility, equity risk can be worth taking (though again, there is no *guarantee* that it will be). As Part I tried to show, growth is the norm, not the exception, and the longer your time horizon, the bigger the chance that your equity dividend will not just represent a useful source of income in itself, but will support a materially higher stock price.

If you easily worry about missed opportunities, if you want to avoid losses at all times, or if you strive for perfectibility, the volatility in stock markets will be a source of regret, concern and frustration. If however you are able to disengage from the day-to-day noise, and are happy to wait patiently and allow the expansion of global business slowly to underpin and augment the real value of your investment while you get on with your life, then the valuation debate may not matter so much, uncertain as it is.

Of course, if that selection of simple valuation measures shows trailing and forward PEs, and price-to-book ratios, to be perhaps a couple of standard deviations above their (say) ten-year moving averages, with dividend yields a similar distance below theirs, at the same time as interest rates and bond yields are looking similarly elevated, then better opportunities to enter the markets may lie ahead. That has not been the situation since 2008, however (at least, to late-2014), and for the time being, the expected return on stocks may not need to be modified by any expected change in valuations. Figures 7.2–7.6 show developed stock market PEs, price-to-book ratios and dividend yields to be unremarkable by the standards of recent (post dot.com) years.

A backdrop of rising interest rates would often be expected to be associated with higher earnings yields (and lower PEs), but the general idea of

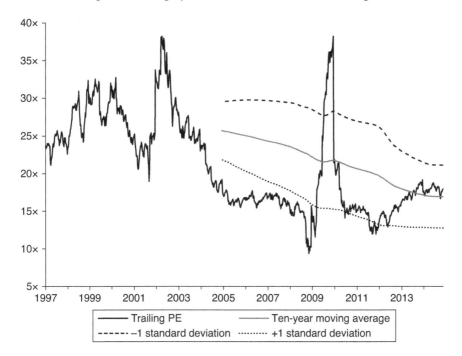

Figure 7.3   Developed stock markets: trailing PE

Source: Bloomberg, author's calculations.

Figure 7.4   Developed stock markets: forward PE
Source: Bloomberg, author's calculations.

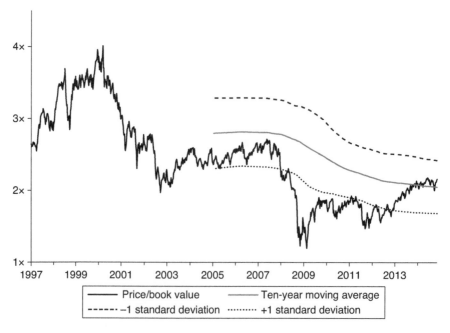

Figure 7.5   Developed stock markets: price/book value
Source: Bloomberg, author's calculations.

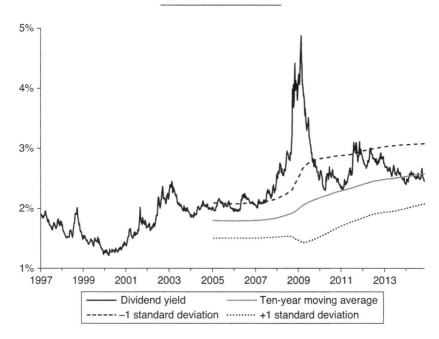

Figure 7.6 Developed stock markets: dividend yield (lower value = more expensive)

Source: Bloomberg, author's calculations.

rising rates is already deeply ingrained in investors' minds – as we have seen – while trend profitability may not be. Forward PE ratios in late 2014 are a little above their ten-year moving averages, but trailing ratios, price-to-book ratios and dividend yields are close to trend.

The expected real returns on other asset classes most of the time will fall somewhere between those on cash and government bonds, and those on stocks, as these are the two polar extremes: the perceived safe haven of a fixed-term loan to the banking system or government on the one hand, and the open-ended nature of undated business ownership on the other. Real estate returns are a case in point (we suggested in Chapter 6 that few other assets are "must-haves" for most private investors: real estate was the most plausible exception). On a long-term view, rental income might be expected to keep pace with infla-tion at least, but the prospects for real rental or capital growth from a specific building will depend on the wider economic backdrop, and in particular the outlook for population, household and (for commercial property) employment growth, in the number of households and (for commercial property) in employ-ment, together with any changes in the supply of competing buildings. As with stocks, the expected growth in rental income needs to be added to the current yield to give the expected total return: with inflation uplift only, and current commercial yields perhaps around 6% (it is difficult to generalise, as the market is so fragmented), a plausible expected total return might be around 8%. The yields on commercial real estate in particular are often compared with those on government bonds, but on a long-term view the prospects for real returns are probably better, particularly at today's bond yields.

This discussion of prospective asset class returns has been deliberately broad-brush, has focused only on the assets that we think private investors need to hold, and has ignored many regional and other sub-asset-class level subtleties (including any attempt at predicting or hedging exchange rate fluctuations, in line with the earlier comments in Chapters 5 and 6). The range of possible economic and valuation scenarios that could unfold is of course huge, particularly if you take into account the room for greater regional differentiation, but the details do not alter the main point: expectations of long-term returns should be loosely anchored by expectations of trend economic growth, modified according to whether the asset is obviously cheap or dear. Currently, interest rates and bond yields are well below those suggested by our muddle through view of prospective trend growth in the big developed economies, suggesting that cash and bonds look dear, while stock market valuations look unremarkable.[13]

WEIGHTING IN VAIN

We have suggested that private investors need to own four broad assets: cash or similarly liquid money-market instruments; government bonds; stocks; and real estate. As of late 2014, plausible compound returns on these assets over (say) the next five to ten years might be around 2–3% per annum for UK and US cash and money-market instruments; perhaps just 2% or so for British gilts and US Treasuries; perhaps 7–8% per annum from UK and US stock markets (European and Japanese markets may offer less, but emerging markets more); and perhaps 8% from real estate. Viewed in the context of most media commentary, those projected stock returns in particular may seem optimistic, but economic growth and market valuations are as likely to surprise positively as negatively.

This assumes that cash and bonds are currently expensive, and that their interest rates and yields will move back towards a notional fair value of 4–5%, which is our best guess as to where trend compound growth in nominal GDP will be; that stocks are more or less fairly valued, and that their prospective total return is in line with a 3% initial dividend distribution growing in line with the nominal local economies at 4–5%; and that real estate is similarly unlikely to see a material change in valuation, and that its prospective total return is a mix of a starting yield of 6%, plus inflation of around 2%, assuming no real growth.

There is a large and mathematically sophisticated academic and industry-based body of asset allocation research that discusses how a mix of assets such as these might best be combined. It is built on the foundations of modern portfolio theory, in which as noted a key assumption is that there is a trade-off between risk and return. This trade-off is reflected in the notion of an efficient investment frontier. This is a smooth (and usually hyperbolic, downwardly concave, rather than straight) upward sloping line plotted with the standard deviation of returns (a measure of volatility) on the horizontal scale and expected returns themselves on the vertical scale. It shows the varying mix of assets that maximises portfolio return for a given level of risk (or which minimises risk, for a given level of return). A portfolio fully invested in stocks, for example, might have highest expected returns and volatility; a portfolio invested fully in cash might have lowest expected returns and volatility. Points in between the two extremes would reflect the returns and volatilities obtained by blending the two assets, and by including other less polar assets with different covariance and return characteristics, in varying proportions. All the investor has to do is to decide, from the ranges on offer, how much volatility or prospective return they would like, and the frontier will tell them the mix of assets that will produce the highest return or lowest risk consistent with that objective. This is their optimal portfolio.

Constructing the efficient frontier, and optimising the mix of assets, is not as straightforward as it sounds, however. As noted, it needs to take into account not just prospective asset class returns, as we have done, but also their volatilities and covariances (the extent to which the assets tend to move together). It is difficult enough to arrive at a view on likely compound returns for our four core assets: the discussion above took a long-term outlook, and our conclusions were deliberately rounded, and intended to convey plausible orders of magnitude rather than precision. The convictions we have about likely volatilities and co-movements will be smaller again.

We know that equities are likely to be the most volatile asset, and cash the least; we also know that when economic or geopolitical concerns flare up again, and push equity prices down, bonds may rise in value, and vice versa. A quantitative forecast of these correlations and covariances will however always be (even) less convincing than our return forecasts, for which the likely rate of compound economic growth at least offers a plausible if approximate anchor.[14] Contexts and valuations vary: in "normal" times, and when stocks and bonds are unremarkably valued, it is quite common to see equities and bonds move together, not in opposite directions (indeed, this was the norm for much of the 1980s and 1990s). When we have primed our database with assumptions about all these things, the calculation of the efficient frontier itself is complex, involving iterative, or trial-and-error, processes and sophisticated computational expertise. And when the optimal mix of assets is found, the results turn out to be extremely sensitive to small changes in those largely arbitrary input assumptions: "corner solutions" emerge in which the optimal portfolio can swing suddenly from having no position in a particular asset class to having a very large one, a move that most investors would feel rather suspicious of if their advisers were to recommend it.

Various attempts have been made to improve the optimisation process. Rather than place so much weight on independently estimated expected return data, one popular approach in recent years has been to take the aggregate market values of each asset class as a guide to their portfolio weights, and to use their historic volatilities and covariances to work out what rates of return might be embedded in that market portfolio. The resultant returns can then be compared with the investment adviser's own expectations, and the results tweaked accordingly. A problem with this approach is that in some cases it is in fact extremely difficult to say with any confidence how much of the total market value of each asset class is being held primarily as an investment – for example, cash, real estate and commodities can each be held for other reasons. In the case of cash, for example, many bank deposits will be held for transactional and working capital purposes, not as investments, and the total supply of money might exaggerate its aggregate importance in a portfolio context.

Other modifications that can help make the optimisation process more practical include recognising that volatility is not synonymous with risk (few investors worry about asset prices going up unexpectedly), and making allowances for the fact that there are many more potential combinations of returns than those seen historically, which may need to be simulated and incorporated.

Less tractable problems, however, include the fact that the assets whose weights are being "optimised" are not all equally liquid, and have risk and return characteristics that are known with much less exactitude than is required by the carefully calibrated optimisation process (the foreign currency component of stock returns, for example). Volatilities and covariances change hugely over time, and as noted are more difficult intuitively to get a grip on than expected returns. Most importantly, as we saw earlier, in practice there need be no relationship at all between risk and volatility, and so the underlying premise of a systematic trade-off between the two that underlies modern portfolio theory is mistaken. As an investor, you are *not* necessarily paid for taking risk: if you were, it wouldn't be risk. And there are no such things as fully risk-free assets.

Indeed, talk of optimisation itself is misleading in this context, as we argued earlier. There are so many unknowns, and the raw data is so questionable, that investors should think not in terms of the best, or optimal, out-turn, but in terms of an acceptable or satisficing one. There will be many available. The idea that there is a single, right portfolio is mistaken. Someone has to come top of the various investment league tables and performance rankings, but the results owe more to luck than we like to admit, and the number of differently weighted portfolios and products that exist reflects a financial services industry that has excess capacity, and a misplaced hunger on the part of investors for precision, rather than a smoothly perfectible world. In this, as in economics and public affairs generally, the popularity of such obviously over-engineered processes as portfolio optimisation is attributable to the fact that their mathematical content provides a satisfying impression of confidence and precision missing from the messy real world. It is an illusion, and much weighting is in vain.

The temptation to rush into complex but misplaced precision can be seen by the gap between the extensive discussion of initial portfolio optimisation, and the relatively perfunctory discussion of the periodic need to rebalance that portfolio. If an asset does better than others, its effective weighting will gradually rise, and eventually will become meaningfully bigger than its optimal level – even if the return is in line with what was expected and built into the optimisation process. To avoid having all the investment eggs gravitating to this one basket, the weight will need to be trimmed back to the optimal level. How best to decide on the level, or a timetable, at which it should be rebalanced, is an important practical issue, then, but one that has received relatively little attention – precisely because it depends on questions of tactical market timing, about which the most sophisticated statistical and mathematical techniques, however satisfying, can have little to say.[15]

This does not mean that we should say nothing about how much of our suggested core assets should be held, or that we need to default to advising equal weights. We have our muddle through vision of ongoing economic growth and our plausible prospective returns, after all. And if we seem to be ignoring risk by not quantifying it, we aren't really.

Whether you are paid for taking risk or not, an asset that delivers a return without big fluctuations, and which tends to do well when other assets are doing badly, will be attractive. The investment journey it offers will be smoother, and if you are not paid for taking risk, it may even deliver a better return than a more volatile asset, taking you to a better destination. In practice, however, the likely volatilities and correlations of individual assets will depend on the specific scenarios that unfold, and about which we can say little in advance (and remember, many investment advisers suggest using more than the four core assets we suggest). The best way to deal with uncertainty is to take as long a time horizon as you can, and to try to ignore the short-term twists and turns of the business and valuation cycles along the way. Once an investor has decided that their investment policy allows them to take equity risk, for example, they have effectively decided to look beyond the short-term bumpiness of the journey and to focus on the ultimate destination.

The weighting issue is also made a little easier by the fact that for many private investors the practical issue is not whether they should have 49%, 50% or 51% in stocks, but whether they have any at all. Despite the best efforts of the financial sector's marketing teams, many savers own few or even no stocks, and hold mostly cash. The message in this book is that to stand a chance of benefiting from a growing economy, getting involved – simply showing up – in the wider investment markets is the important thing. Allocating (say) 20% of a long-term investment portfolio to stocks may not be statistically or mathematically "optimal", but it is much better than a weighting of zero. On a long-term view, some is better than none.

There are some intuitive reasons for thinking that in practice, the bulk of a genuinely long-term investment portfolio should be held in the form of stocks. Again, this assumes that the investor's personal investment policy can tolerate and afford the ownership risk that comes with that.

First, we might think of adult life, the time when we stand on our own two feet financially, as comprising two phases: the period spent at work, during which we save and accumulate assets, and the period when we have stopped work, and are drawing on those accumulated assets to pay for our retirement share of the output produced by those still in work. Stocks are best placed to share in the accumulation possibilities provided by economic growth, while bonds and cash offer the higher short-term predictability and (usually, though not recently) income needed in retirement. Real estate might be equally attractive in each phase: it offers opportunities for both wealth accumulation and income. Broadly speaking, the accumulation phase (from age 20 to age 60, perhaps) is twice as large as what we might think of as the stewardship phase (age 60–80, say). Over an adult lifetime, then, you might expect to allot twice as much portfolio space to the accumulation motive as to income and wealth preservation.

This could be achieved by holding only stocks (and real estate) during the first phase, and only bonds and cash (and real estate) during the second. However, there is no guarantee that the relative performance of stocks will be best during your personal accumulation phase, or that bonds and cash will be the best store of real wealth during your retirement. Rather than put almost all your eggs into one basket, and then switch them abruptly on retirement, it might make sense to continuously hold assets in the relevant lifetime proportions throughout your adult life. This is at odds with much current practice, whereby many schemes do indeed reduce stock weightings as retirement approaches, but in the UK at least that practice has been largely shaped by the requirement – now ended – that many defined contribution pensioners buy an annuity (a requirement which in turn has been shaped by the way in which pensions have been taxed). The possibility of passing wealth on to children too argues in favour of keeping portfolio weightings more or less constant.

Second, we might also want our investment portfolios loosely to reflect the broad pattern of economic activity. Stocks are most immediately backed by the private sector's productive capability; government bonds and cash are backed by the public sector's creditworthiness, with real estate again straddling both (some of the most attractive commercial tenants are government agencies). Historically, the private sector represents the bulk of the economy: public spending in the UK and US has been around one-third of GDP (a bit more in the UK, a bit less in the US), and less again if we focus on final government spending (that is, excluding redistributive transfer payments).

Third, as time horizons lengthen, the big uncertainties in investing apply increasingly similarly to all assets, as we have noted. It is difficult to imagine that an economic, geopolitical or natural disaster would have no effect on the real value of bonds and cash, for example. If all assets are ultimately similarly at risk, the asset class with the highest prospective returns should account for the lion's share of long-term investment portfolios.[16] Its higher return is not a unique risk premium but reflects its different economic characteristics.

In broad terms, then, someone with "average" risk appetite whose investment policy permits them to take a long-term view should think in terms of an investment portfolio that has perhaps twice as much in stocks as it does in cash and bonds together. Real estate's appropriate weighting is more difficult to judge. We have suggested that it is a core asset, and one that offers both the potential for accumulation and disbursement: its likely total return exceeds inflation, and its yield is meaningful. It is not as liquid as our other core assets, however, and as noted it is not easy for most investors to distinguish between their investment holdings and their personal holdings of property. Moreover, its prospective return is likely smaller than that on stocks. In round numbers, a portfolio weighting of 10% would be meaningful, but not so large as to materially reduce the liquidity and return of the overall portfolio. An acceptable long-term portfolio might thus be weighted 60:30:10 in terms of stocks, cash and bonds, and real estate respectively. Excluding real estate, the weightings would be two-thirds stocks, one-third cash and bonds.

The split within the interest bearing cash and bonds segment might be broadly equal if all the investor's non-essential holdings of cash (those not needed for transactions or rainy day funds) are included, but otherwise, even at current yield levels, bonds should be the bigger portion, given their stronger diversification qualities (that is, the fact that their prices can rise as stock prices fall). Even a long-term portfolio needs some active insurance against short-term, non-life-threatening accidents, some ballast to smooth the investment voyage.

These suggested weights are not in fact that different to the "optimised" conclusions presented by many investment advisers. They have been derived, however, intuitively, without any suggestion that we are following some mythical best practice, and our conclusions – as with expected returns – are presented in a heavily rounded fashion. At valuations prevailing in late 2014, a portfolio constructed along these lines, with the core assets delivering the returns suggested, could reasonably be expected to produce an overall return of roughly 6% before charges, compared to the 2–3% that we think UK and US cash alone might deliver over the next five to ten years. As we said in Chapter 5, investment is not about getting rich quickly, but these reasonable returns comfortably exceed the projected inflation that currently seems likely. Even after tax, for most people this approach stands a good chance of allowing wealth to grow in real terms, and is still worth paying a modest amount for.[17]

8

CONCLUSION – POSTMODERN PORTFOLIO THEORY

A good mathematical theory dealing with economic hypotheses (is) very unlikely to be good economics.

– Alfred Marshall[1]

I can calculate the motion of heavenly bodies, but not the madness of people.

– Newton

DON'T LET THE GLOOM AND THE GEEKS PUT YOU OFF

Received wisdom is too pessimistic about our economic prospects, and is likely to stay so. This is not a new development.[2] At the same time, investment advisers are too optimistic about their ability to analyse markets. Many savers are caught in the middle, fearful of the future and distrustful of the over-confident claims made for unnecessarily complicated and expensive investment products.

This book has shown why the economic gloom is overdone, and has argued that the perfect should not be the enemy of the good when it comes to the investment process. Remember, it is not arguing that some golden period lies ahead, only that doomsday may not. Debt, demography, decadence, depletion and danger are less pressing concerns than feared, and the constraints on growth that they represent are being routinely overstated. But even as the macroeconomic debate has been characterised by lazy thinking and sloppy logic, the investment process itself has been over-engineered by financial analysts keen to demonstrate their mathematical and statistical credentials. In practice, however, investment is about satisficing, not optimising. There are many different portfolios capable of doing a similarly good job for most savers, and the time – and management fees and dealing costs – saved in not agonising over imprecision, constantly changing covariances, unknowable foreign exchange exposures and the like can be better spent elsewhere.

Our approach to investing is not completely without its complications. It is not always easy to avoid the temptation to try to time the market: even long-term portfolios require some short-term maintenance, such as the periodic rebalancing noted in Chapter 7, and investors just starting to diversify out of cash face the daunting issue of when and how exactly to take the first step. There is also that decision as to whether to use advisers and/or fund managers, or to do it yourself.

NOT SO FAST: MARKET TIMING REVISITED

The better-performing assets in your portfolio will gradually account for a growing proportion of it. The effect can be muted – by choosing not to automatically reinvest any income generated, for example – but if assets deliver systematically different long-term price returns, as we expect, their effective weights are going to drift away from the starting point. If returns vary across assets in the way that we suggested in Chapter 7, and we start with a portfolio weighted 60:30:10 in stocks, cash and bonds, and real estate respectively, with income reinvested automatically in the assets that generate it, then after ten years the weights will have drifted to 70:21:9. If this process is allowed to continue unchecked, the stock weight will of course approach, but never quite reach, 100%. If income is not reinvested, but allowed to accumulate as cash, the weightings would be 58:34:8 after ten years.[3]

A higher stock weighting that has arisen in this way would hardly be a disappointment: after all, it is effectively telling us that the pattern of returns we expected has come to pass. It may no longer suit your investment policy, however: we have warned against overly precise notions of what the right weighting might be, but having almost all your eggs steadily gravitating towards one basket is probably not a good idea. And if stocks have unexpectedly underperformed the other assets, pulling their effective weighting down, you'll likely feel less happy about things: the pattern of returns will have been unexpected, and your original portfolio weights will be a source of regret.

Unfortunately, despite the massive literature on portfolio construction, and the huge amount of time devoted to asset allocation by professional wealth managers, relatively little has been written and said about the rebalancing of portfolios (as we noted in Chapter 7). Yet the discussion of how and when to rebalance is really the asset allocation decision revisited in a shorter-term timescale: how to decide if a position is too large or small, and whether this is a good time at which to trim or add to it, could reopen all the issues so carefully put to bed in an investment policy and portfolio construction process.

There are two broad ways of dealing with it: first, stipulate a level of divergence that will automatically trigger a rebalancing; second, use your (or your adviser's) discretion. The first has the merit of seeming objective: it does not require any explicit attempt to time the markets, and so might best be utilised by long-term, strategic approaches to investing such as the one outlined here. It is not completely objective, however, because there is no easy way of deciding what those trigger points will be. Should they be expressed relative to the portfolio as a whole, or relative to the weight (or perhaps the volatility) of the asset class whose movement is making the rebalancing necessary? A large rise in real estate values, for example, might not matter much if it was only 10% of the portfolio to begin with. Meanwhile, a wholly discretionary approach re-opens the vexed issue of tactical asset allocation: calling the twists and turns of the business cycle, and deciding the best day to sell stocks, or to buy them if their weighting has fallen below the desired long-term level, is not easy.

Similarly, an investor considering putting their cash to work in the wider capital markets has to decide when exactly to dip a toe in the water. The constructive view of the long-term economic outlook presented here suggests getting involved – showing up – in the capital markets sooner rather than later. Switching your life's savings from cash into the more balanced portfolio suggested here, however, the day before a shock change in monetary policy causes double-digit setbacks in stocks and bonds, or just as stocks crest another dotcom boom, would be deeply upsetting – particularly if, as often happens, the initial disillusionment and regret causes you immediately to step back out of the markets and into cash, only to see the markets rebound in your absence.

Choosing when to make the first step into the markets, like rebalancing, unavoidably brings us face-to-face with day-to-day market conditions and the paradox that we can't take a long-term view without making some short-term moves. It is one thing to carefully and determinedly sit-out the effects of market volatility on your portfolio ("don't just do something, stand there"), but quite another to deliberately go into the marketplace to trade amidst that daily noise. There is no foolproof way of picking the best times to act – if there were, we wouldn't need to advocate a long-term buy-and-hold strategy – and the best advice is to try to reduce the scale of the decisions being made. When rebalancing, use rounded trigger-points (divergences of five portfolio points, say, rather than smaller divergences that might trigger more frequent trading), and avoid discretion. When building-out a balanced portfolio for the first time, do it in instalments, not all in one go: as the saying goes, even the longest journey starts with a single step. And while there are no infallible short-term trading rules, or valuation guides, it doesn't hurt to be aware of the context into which you are stepping.

A surge in stocks with prices rising increasingly quickly, and charts having an upward facing concave slope, is often a "wait and see" signal. So too is positive market commentary (it does occasionally happen) and/or new jargon in the big financial broadsheets. Unusually high valuations can also suggest caution, but valuations can stay rich or cheap for remarkably long times, so you should check to see whether they have become so rapidly and recently – and even then, they may not matter. As noted, a good time to buy stocks can sometimes be when their trailing PE ratio has risen dramatically as a result of a big fall in earnings, because that fall is now behind you, and stocks may in fact be poised to benefit from recovery (forward PEs are not immune to this effect, because analysts' earnings projections are often shaped by a sharply reduced starting point).

There can be occasions when market volatility and the business cycle unearth opportunities and threats which even long-term investors might understandably be tempted to play. With hindsight, it would have paid handsomely to sell stocks in early 2000, and more so again in 2007. The reason for the first collapse was an obviously unsustainable surge in valuations driven by overly-optimistic groupthink about the new wired and weightless world; the reason for the latter was a less obvious but more profound mispricing not of stocks themselves but of mortgages and credit risk (as per Chapters 1 and 2). Having got out of the market, though, in each case it would have paid equally handsomely to get back in (at least, as of late 2014). The immediate catalysts for the rebounds (in 2003 and 2009 respectively) were less obvious, however.[4] Many of the advisers who spotted the signals to sell subsequently missed the following signals to buy, and found themselves missing the recovery train and effectively giving back the profits they had made from selling. And investors who sat tight through each episode will have eventually seen stock returns more than make good the downturns.

Big falls are not always followed quickly – they might not be followed at all – by rallies. But this book has, I hope, shown why economic growth can be more resilient than feared, and overly pessimistic market moods can result in depressed prices that favour opportunist investors able to act on a long view. The long-term investing odds are tilted in favour of assets that can benefit from economic growth. In looking at a market crisis, a good stance to take can be to be mindful, in the words of a Bangalore-based colleague in early 2009, when stocks had not yet decisively rallied, that "this will pass".

Economic growth is no guarantee of investment returns, but it helps: it is probably a necessary condition, not a sufficient one, for stocks to perform over the long term. This does not always show up in statistical analysis: the links between GDP and stock market returns are very loose, both over time and across countries.[5] This might be because econometric techniques are looking for a stable quantitative relationship when the link is likely fluid and qualitative in nature – it may even be a simple occasional and directional one, perhaps. It might also be because in some countries, governments play a very active role in their national economy, by subsidising and controlling prices, and/or directing capital spending and bank lending. This helps explain why, for example, China's internationally accessible stock market has so dramatically underperformed that of the US these last two decades, even as its real GDP growth has been roughly 7–8% per annum stronger: the profits made by its quoted companies have lagged far behind what its reported economic growth would have suggested.

Ongoing economic growth may not be linked rigidly to corporate profits and stock prices, or to the level of interest rates, but it at least creates the right climate for respectable profitability and positive real interest rates. Many savers own no stocks, and are interested in absolute returns, not performance relative to market benchmarks and other investors. Professional investors and the adviser community fret about the precise proportion of a portfolio that should be invested in equities, and how best to top the short-term performance tables, but those problems have no objective answers, and need not concern us. The key messages from this book for a private investor are that: (1) a patient, long-term view gives you the best chance of capturing some of the ongoing growth in global prosperity that is still eminently feasible; (2) owning some stocks is better than owning none; and (3) low single-digit real annual returns – that is, net of inflation – are a satisfactory outcome.

PERFORMANCE IS UNCERTAIN, FEES AREN'T

If you decide, in getting invested, to use a wealth adviser, or to own some collectively-managed funds, you are likely to pay fees and charges to somebody (and you will not be able to avoid charges completely even if you opt for a mostly do-it-yourself approach – of which more below). Intermediaries' fees and management charges are not however a guide to likely investment performance. In some cases for sure, fees are automatically higher if your funds do well. Hedge funds, as noted, typically take an explicit share (often one-fifth) of any profits, in addition to a sizable annual charge. In such cases, though, the fund's performance is what determines the fees, rather than the other way around. You do not have the option, in advance, of specifying a high-fee, high-return outcome.

Marketing teams may suggest that their high-charging firms are more likely to generate a better outcome, and use some strong historical perform-ance data to infer as much, but with the exception of some very narrow and short-lived investments, future performance is highly uncertain, while fees aren't – hence the disclaimer that the regulators insist be applied to mar-keting literature stating that "past performance is no guide to the future". Most fees and charges are set as a proportion of assets under management: as absolute amounts they do go up and down with the level of the assets, but they are a fixed percentage of those assets, come what may.

As a result, it is worth being aware what you are paying for with those fees. Advisers and fund managers can promise, and deliver, a particular level of ongoing service: the execution and clearance of transactions; safe custody; the reassurance or status that might come from having your savings looked after by a big name brand; clear and prompt reports; an ongoing market nar-rative; and the simple but valuable service of diversification if that is what you want. All these services might come under the loose heading of "stew-ardship", and can be worth paying for.

Investment performance, however, is largely in the lap of the gods. This applies to actively-managed funds trying to pick individual securities in an attempt to beat the various market indices, but also of course even to the market indices and their associated passive or tracker funds, since the future is so profoundly uncertain. It is the expenses of the first group however, that attract most attention, because active management fees are much higher, of course – security selection and extra dealing expenses have to be paid for – and there is a lot of evidence showing that many funds do not deliver per-formance to match, at least over short and medium-term time horizons.

As we discussed in Chapter 5, the active-versus-passive debate is not quite the walkover it is usually made out to be. Comparisons are not always made on a like-for-like basis: tracker fees are not zero, and they sometimes track their indices imprecisely. These considerations are not always taken into account by studies that simply compare active funds with the market indices. The differing levels of stewardship noted above are also ignored. If passive funds were to dominate markets completely, corporate governance might suffer: shareholders are supposed to exercise a degree of active scrutiny and discipline over the companies in which they invest, and a wholly passive investor base indifferent to what it holds in its tracking fund is unlikely to do so. Completely passive ownership would likely carry within it the seeds of its own demise as a result. Things are unlikely to get so polarised to begin with. Many investors value the option that active funds have of deciding to sell out of stocks, whether they successfully use it or not, whereas tracker funds are *designed* to closely follow the market down as well as up.

Some savers may also value the opportunity to have their money managed by one of the industry's star performers. Of course, the laws of probability alone would suggest that out of the many thousands of fund managers in the business, a handful will deliver performance, and in a seemingly persistent fashion. But who is to say that those stars – usually pretty smart people – have really just been lucky, rather than skilful? Some star managers follow the sort of long-term approach in picking stocks that we have advocated here in thinking about the wider market – but not all.

Finally, the statistical evidence suggesting that active funds do not perform is couched mostly in terms of stock selection: it may pay to have an adviser make some sectoral, regional and asset class selections. Moreover, an active manager of a balanced portfolio is at least going to keep an eye on that routine rebalancing for you, something that a wholly passive implementation approach will not do.

For these reasons, then, the argument in favour of passive funds is not quite as one-sided as it often seems: many investors will believe – or will want to believe – in fund manager and adviser skill, and will pay for a hands-on service. Nonetheless, the case for using lower-cost passive products to populate a big part of a balanced portfolio is a strong one. Whether you do it all yourself, or pay an adviser to do it for you, will depend not just on your thoughts about these points, but also on the extent to which you have the time and inclination to get involved. Just as we might be able to redecorate our living rooms, sometimes it's easier, if we are lucky enough to be able to afford it, to pay someone to do it for us.

The new technology that drives much long-term economic growth is currently working very visibly in favour of private investors. It is becoming easier and cheaper to deal directly in the investment markets, and intermediaries' charges – those levied by wealth advisers and fund management companies – are falling steadily as a result. Low-cost online platforms are offering access to an increasing range of individual securities and collective funds, both active and passive, and one-stop balanced portfolios are available. In late-2014, it is possible to buy even an emerging market Exchange

Traded Fund – a passive, tracking investment that will closely shadow a widely-used emerging stock market index, and which until recently was beyond the reach of many private investors – for an annual charge of 0.2%, with no upfront fee.

This is good news for savers. The days of paying more than frictional dealing fees on transactions in individual stocks, and of up-front charges of several percentage points for actively managed funds, are limited. Shaving half a percentage point from annual charges of (say) 1.5% levied on an investment portfolio growing at 5–6% per annum would represent a proportionate improvement in net annual returns of more than one-tenth, and of course add a little over 15% to your investment after 30 years. And it need not always be bad news for the industry: if lower charges and greater transparency attract more inflows, there may eventually be more business to go around.

If you decide to construct a 60:30:10 portfolio yourself, inexpensive ETFs or other tracker products should allow you to target ongoing annual charges amounting to perhaps half of 1% of your portfolio (the cost of your time is of course not taken into account here). If you opt for a completely delegated, discretionary approach in which you pay an adviser and allow them to use as many actively managed funds, or as much stock picking, as they deem fit, you should be targeting 1%. Both figures are likely to drift lower again over time. Meanwhile, at current prospective rates of growth they will still leave your net returns compounding comfortably ahead of inflation and the likely returns on cash. Some more expensive advisers and fund managers may do better, but you will not be able to know which ones in advance. More complex portfolios containing alternative asset classes will be more expensive, but again need not perform accordingly.

CONCLUDING THOUGHTS: THERE IS LESS TO BE KNOWN THAN WE THINK

Much of this book has focused on the shortcomings of conventional economic wisdom. The seismic events of 2008 were unexpected, and the sheepish response to them by many economists has been to assert that they must have been inevitable, and must have had long-term consequences, changing the economic outlook for the worse. As our alternative narrative – the "richness of embarrassments" – and our more constructive outlook showed, the shortcomings are not the result of technical inadequacies, but failures of common sense and observation. The analysis deployed in the public discussion of debt, demography, decadence, depletion and danger has been flawed not because it has not been mathematically and statistically rigorous enough, but because it has been based on questionable assumptions, lazy logic and misleading perspectives. Nonetheless, many economists have responded by asserting that it is our analytical tools and models that have not been complex enough, and that more "research" needs to be done.

The unspoken assumption is that if the right combination of diligence and analytical sophistication is brought to bear on the subject, the economic research programme and operating systems can move forward. Specifically, it has been suggested that the failure of economists to predict the financial crisis and its economic impact has reflected the lack of attention paid to the money supply process in mainstream analysis and statistical modelling.

There is certainly room for better and more complete data, as we noted at various points above. It would have helped if we had known more, for example, about the extent to which the financial system had become so interdependent, and the extent to which mortgage exposures had been packaged, insured and distributed – about who held what, in other words. There is also room for a more considered evaluation of the older historical data that we do have. If one is instinctively sceptical regarding, for example, the quality of banks' financial statements in 2007, how much more sceptical should one be regarding the usefulness of data that stretches back decades and centuries? Data collection and collation is no substitute for analysis, but in a headline hungry world it is often confused with it.

But diminishing returns to pure theory, and to econometric analysis and forecasting, set in a long time ago – just as they did in stock picking. Even before the crisis the economic research programme had been degenerating visibly for several decades, and not because the modern money supply process was being modelled inadequately (it can not be modelled in any other way in any case, because like so many other economic variables the money supply is driven by subjective expectations and actions). Purely abstract analysis has its place, and can be satisfying, even exhilarating, for its practitioners. Playing a complicated and testing game against the cleverest of your peers and within the framework of rigorously applied rules is a seductive pursuit – but one untroubled by messy reality.[6]

Behavioural finance has certainly offered some rich expository insights recently. It has also helped clarify which elements of conventional economics are most at odds with reality. However, it has not yet been able to replace them with more convincing, predictive assumptions, and is unlikely to. Economists will never unearth the sorts of regularities, causalities or laws akin to those in the natural sciences for the simple reason that they do not exist.

Ultimately the economy is less sophisticated than the analytical and statistical tools we use to study it. It is driven by emotions and relationships, which can be fickle and inconsistent, and far from profound. This does not mean that the mathematics that might be used to describe their effects is uncomplicated. The importance of expectations in economic behaviour means that any given setting of the key policy levers can likely co-exist with an infinite number of out-turns for the economy; equally, a given economic out-turn could feasibly coexist with an infinite number of policy settings. Representing this clearly and axiomatically is extremely difficult. But in this case, hard maths does not necessarily make useful economics. Describing something fully and accurately does not make it worthy of description. The fractals unearthed by the mathematics of chaos theory are beguiling, but may have little practical value.

For a model to be useful, it needs to have explanatory and predictive power – and in a world driven by the interaction of subjectively formed and constantly evolving expectations, such power will be elusive. Greed and fear in particular are not systematic, consistent or axiomatic generally.

The last few years have strengthened my conviction that we know less than we think we do about the practical linkages within economies and the way in which financial markets operate, but also that there is probably less to be known than we imagine. We need clearer thinking about the basics, and better and more complete data, not a more complex unifying theory. The frustrations of economic forecasting and of modern portfolio theory illustrate only too clearly what can happen when the tools available – in this case, a body of mathematical expertise – determine the job to be done.[7]

Rigorous analysis is of course important, and abstract study is valuable in its own right. I am simply suggesting, however, that the room for such rigour in practical economic matters – questions such as the correct size of aggregate financial balance sheets, the outlook for economic growth generally, or the mooted existence of "risk premia" – is limited.

To be fair, economists are not alone in over-analysing things, and in over-engineering the intellectual framework surrounding their discipline. The same is true of many areas in which people are called upon to discuss fundamentally uncertain matters in public and feel the need to dress their uncertainties and subjectivities in more objective-looking clothing. Politics for example is characterised by complex issues that cannot be resolved by careful analysis – Scottish independence, the UK's membership of the European Union, fiscal austerity, the conflict in Ukraine, the balance of power in the Middle East, to name a few topical examples – but we still hunger for analysis and reassurance that there is a right answer out there somewhere. The statistical revolution underway in the analysis of sport is another example: despite the ever more detailed analytical tools presented, pundits are no better at prediction then they were, and fate seemingly (and thankfully) delights in confounding their assertions by regularly throwing up results in which seemingly obvious winners lose, and in which successive tournament results fail to follow any logic whatsoever.

This is not to say that economics has nothing to teach us. Being aware of the simple substitution and income effects that underpin basic demand and supply curves makes analysis and decision-making better informed, in all sorts of contexts. And as I hope Part I in particular has shown, a basic all-round economic awareness can unearth some of the subtleties missed by the simplistic headlines that dominate the public debate. It can remind us that debt and money are largely two sides of the same coin, as it were, and that we may not have too much of the former, or ever run out of the latter. It can stop us fretting unnecessarily about our children's collective living standards, and help us make better investments as individuals. But it perhaps has more in common with plumbing than physics. The foundations of the global economy may be more secure than those of traditional financial analysis.

NOTES

INTRODUCTION: WHAT WE TALK ABOUT WHEN WE TALK ABOUT MARKETS

1 A term used by Herbert Simon in "Rational Choice and the Structure of the Environment", *Psychological Review*, Vol. 63, March 1956, pp. 129–138.

1 WHY IS EVERYBODY SO GLOOMY?

1 To return to that radio programme: the future is *exactly* what it used to be – namely, unknowable.

2 The consistency and completeness of an axiomatic approach has been questioned: see for example, Ernest Nagel & James Newman, *Godel's Proof*, New York, Routledge, 1958.

3 Some economic transactions are difficult to classify under the various categories of expenditure. Is DIY spending consumption or investment, for example? Spending on education? The purchase of a car by a company can be classified as investment, but the purchase of the same car by an individual may count as consumption. Arguably, by focusing so much on economic activity grouped somewhat arbitrarily under the various types of spending and incomes, macroeconomists neglect the output dimension: they just don't think as much about the industries that comprise the economies they analyse. For example, next time you see an economist interviewed and the service sector features in conversation, listen for when the journalist asks the economist to illustrate, for viewers, what is meant by a "service" industry – and don't be surprised if the answer, one of the standard examples used in elementary economics textbooks, is "hairdressing". The chances are that the economist will be working in a *bank* (UK finance sector employment approximately 1.1 million in 2012) and is talking to a journalist working for a *media* group (creative and information sector employment approximately 1.2 million). No offence is intended here to hairdressers (employment perhaps 0.3 million – source HABIA), who have not yet, as far as I am aware, contributed to the near collapse of capitalism.

4 Some economists have noted that central banks do not necessarily control rates, an early and over-looked example being *A Critique of Monetary Policy: Theory and British Experience*, J.C.R Dow and I.D Saville, Oxford, Oxford University Press, 1988. They have been a small minority, however.

5 See, for example, Andrew Ross Sorkin's *Too Big to Fail*, London, Allen Lane, 2009; and for an insider's account Timothy Geithner's *Stress Test: Reflections on Financial Crises*, London, Random House, 2014.

6 When the authoritative financial histories are written, the growth, scale and workings of the CDS market will feature prominently. At its peak, the gross amount of credit insurance outstanding globally in this format exceeded $60 trillion, a sum bigger than the amount of relevant insurable bonds. Many bonds were effectively insured several times over – partly because many sophisticated investors, mostly hedge funds, wanted to buy such insurance not because they had bonds that they wanted to insure, but because they simply wanted to bet that the value of the specified bonds would fall. As noted, in some cases they used them as a way of insuring the stocks that they held, or as a way of betting that those stocks would fall in value.

   In the field of conventional insurance, the potential consequences of over-insurance are well known. Being insured can change your behaviour – if your expensive car is insured, you'll drive it a little less carefully; if the bonds you own are insured against loss, why not borrow to buy a few more of them? In some cases, insurance can even foster the very event that is being insured against, what we term "moral hazard": for example, suspicious fires on business premises. (Short selling, in which investors sell assets that they don't own in expectation of their price falling, can raise similar concerns.)

In late 2008, at the height of the crisis, the exposure of the US government to the banking system caused investors to worry about its creditworthiness, and the price of the CDS outstanding on US Treasury bonds rose above the price of similar insurance on the bonds issued by McDonalds, the fast food company. Pundits noted gleefully that this suggested that Uncle Sam was a worse credit risk than Ronald McDonald, but it did nothing of the sort. None of the writers of CDS insurance – typically, banks outside the United States – would have been left unscathed in the sort of financial accident in which the US government would really have been in difficulties. Since governments can create money, tax, and (if need be) coerce their citizens, their creditworthiness in such circumstances is always likely to be better than that of the companies which operate in their jurisdiction. Writing CDS on US Treasury bonds was a little like offering to sell insurance against the world being destroyed by an asteroid strike. The fact that MacDonalds was viewed by the CDS market as a safer bet than Uncle Sam really just told us that we shouldn't take the market too seriously as an indicator of underlying value.

7   An overview is contained in *The Prospects for Mortgage Securitization in the UK and Europe*, K. Gardiner and R. Paterson, London, Council of Mortgage Lenders, 1999.

8   At the time of writing, the jury is still out on whether bitcoin, a virtual currency, will gain wider acceptance.

9   David Graeber argues that even gold-backed money has been less central to economic progress than the conventional accounts in the textbooks suggest. In the beginning, he argues, there was neither money nor barter, but credit – *Debt: The First 5000 Years*, New York, Melville House, 2011.

10   A conclusion reached also by Philip Coggan in *Paper Promises: Money Debt and the New World Order*, London, Allen Lane, 2011.

11   In late 2009 the new Greek government reported that its estimate of borrowing that year was almost twice as large as the outgoing government's (13% of GDP rather than 7%).

12   As noted earlier, economic measurement is not as precise as we'd like it to be, particularly at the global level, where the availability and quality of data varies hugely. Some important variables, such as inflation, can be measured in very different ways, which can in turn affect the measurement of real (inflation adjusted) variables. Some economic concepts themselves are relatively recent innovations. Formal estimates of Gross Domestic Product, the sum of all domestically generated spending, income and output before allowing for the depreciation of capital, only began to be used in the 1930s and 1940s, as pioneering national accountants such as Simon Kuznets in the United States and Richard Stone in the United Kingdom put statistical flesh on the bones of Keynesian analysis.

We often forget this when we look at particularly lengthy historical comparisons. GDP data for the nineteenth century, for example, or even the 1920s and 1930s, have been compiled in retrospect using fewer data sources than we have today. The idea of national accounts then would have been at best poorly articulated. So how can we be confident that current levels of global GDP per capita are indeed likely to be all-time highs? For relatively recent comparisons made over a shorter time span the methodological uncertainties are minor, and if the data suggest that GDP in 2012 was higher than in 2007, the margin for error is probably relatively small. For longer-term comparisons, we have to cross-check with other data sources, with qualitative historical sources, and with common sense. Infant mortality rates, life expectancy, levels of literacy, the availability of certain basic consumer products and services – all these things suggest that some earlier, better-off epoch for the global economy is not lurking beneath the GDP data from the statistically murky distant past.

A further complication is the distribution of income within a given level of GDP, whether globally or nationally. If higher average levels of GDP per capita simply reflect the better-off grabbing a markedly bigger share of the economic pie, they may be less useful as indicators of economic well-being. In the United States, census bureau data suggest that real incomes for the median household – those in the middle of the income rankings – have stagnated for a quarter of a century, but it is hard to believe that there has really been no improvement over this period in the range and quality of everyday consumer products and services consumed by typical US families. Meanwhile, China and India's rapid recent growth and huge populations suggest that global economic development may have reduced inequality across countries, if not within them. Note that most recent gloom is in any case not focused on income distribution, or indeed even on per capita analysis, but simply on whether aggregate GDP levels can rise in the face of the worries noted above.

2   AN ALTERNATIVE ACCOUNT – A RICHNESS OF EMBARRASSMENTS

1   From *On History*, Thomas Babington Macaulay, Edinburgh Review, 1828.

2   Simon Schama, *The Embarrassment of Riches: An Interpretation of Dutch Culture in the Golden Age*, New York, Knopf, 1987.

3   Readers who'd like more detail might want to look at Brian Tew, *The Evolution of the International Monetary System 1946–1988*, London, Hutchinson & Co, 1988; Nigel Lawson, *The View From No. 11*, London, Bantam Press, 1992; and Charles Kindleberger, *A Financial History of Western Europe*, 2nd edition, Oxford, Oxford University Press, 1993.

4   See his account in *The View from Number 11*, op. cit.

5   See, for example, *British Imperialism: Innovation and Expansion, 1688–1914*, P.J. Cain and A.G. Hopkins, London, Longman, 1993.

6   The Conservative government that took office in the UK in 1979 was perhaps the most obviously ideological in this respect, but parties of the left had also become more pragmatic. In 1976 the UK Labour leader and Prime Minister James Callaghan had made a bold conference speech questioning the ability of governments to manage the economy, and as far back as 1959 the social democratic German SPD had famously advocated "as much competition as possible, as much planning as necessary". This may seem unremarkable today, but remember that the economic failure of the centrally planned powers led by the USSR and China did not become fully visible for two or three decades after the Second World War, and the idea that unelected governments should directly run the bulk of the economy was not as far-fetched as it sounds today.

7   There is a very clear – and long overdue – essay on modern money and its creation in the Bank of England's Quarterly Bulletin of Q1 2014 (Vol. 54, No. 1): *Money Creation in the Modern Economy*, by M. Mcleay, A. Radia and R. Thomas.

8   This was one of the reasons why the monetarist approach to economic policy that became popular in the 1970s and 1980s was ultimately of limited use: there is little point in trying to control something that is usually driven by economic developments, rather than being the driver of them. The way in which money is created in a modern economy is subtler than the literal printing of huge quantities of bank notes that occurred so ruinously in Weimar Germany, for example. See the Bank of England essay cited above.

9   *Money Creation in the Modern Economy*, Bank of England Quarterly Bulletin, op. cit. This plain speaking would horrify many monetarists – and doubtless some ex-Bank officials.

10   See Cain and Hopkins above; also *The Great Degeneration*, Niall Ferguson, London, Allen Lane, 2013.

11   A more careful analysis would take into account all possible factors influencing growth, not just credit, because it is always possible that if an important variable is being overlooked, our reading of the contribution made by financial liberalisation may be mistaken, or statistically "biased". If something had been working to slow growth sharply, for example, the fact that growth didn't slow more dramatically might mean that the availability of credit had been playing a more potent role than is immediately visible. However, a convincing comprehensive and detailed analysis of this sort is not likely to be forthcoming – as we note also in Chapter 3 – and the more pessimistic assessments we're confronting don't consider such subtleties to begin with.

12   See Figure 3.1, and *Evolution of the UK Banking System* in the Bank of England Quarterly Bulletin, Q4 2010.

13   The Crash was sobering at the time, not least because of the first appearance of automated trading and the role played by derivatives, and it caused many commentators to predict a major slowdown

ahead. However, it could be seen – and quickly was – as a correction to a very sharp rise in stock markets in the previous year, and 1988 would prove to be a year of strong growth.

14 There is a definitive – and fascinating – account in Roger Lowenstein's *When Genius Failed: The Rise and Fall of Long-Term Capital Management*, London, Fourth Estate, 2001.

15 Lowenstein quotes a money manager warning LTCM that "You're picking up nickels in front of bulldozers".

16 One of the creditors not to take part was Bear Stearns, a decision which the firm reportedly believed was held against it when it faced its own, fatal, difficulties in early 2008.

17 The underlying principle of asset-backed bonds is older. In Germany, Pfandbrief bonds have been a significant source of mortgage finance since the nineteenth century.

3   FIVE BIG THINGS TO WORRY LESS ABOUT – OR WHY IT STILL PAYS TO INVEST IN THE WEST

1 Quoted in *Chasin' The Bird: The Life and Legacy of Charlie Parker*, Brian Priestley, London, Equinox, 2005, p. 27.

2 The Bloomberg article refers to a BIS statistic for the global amount of debt securities, which is in fact smaller than total debt since the latter includes conventional loans too.

3 A prominent economist said in 1948 that: "A variant of the false analogy is the declaration that national debt puts an unfair burden on our children, who are thereby made to pay for our extravagances. Very few economists need to be reminded that if our children or grandchildren repay some of the national debt these payments will be made *to* our children or grandchildren and to nobody else. Taking them altogether they will no more be impoverished by making the repayments than they will be enriched by receiving them" (Abba P. Lerner, "The Burden of the National Debt", in A. Metzler et al., (eds), *Income, Employment and Public Policy*, New York, W.W. Norton, 1948).

He was clearly mistaken: quite a few economists *do* need to be reminded that debt is unlikely directly to affect collective inter-generational living standards.

4 "Deleveraging? What deleveraging?" L. Battiglione et al., CEPR Geneva Report on the World Economy no. 16, September 2014.

5 Arguably, banks just got too large. Many are too big to be managed – or regulated – effectively, and are systemically dangerous. It might be easier simply to break them up than to risk introducing sand into the wheels of commerce with heavy-handed regulation.

6 The distribution of productive wealth, like the distribution of gross debt, is very unequal – but the point is that such wealth exists, independently of finance.

7 In practice, US consumers' non-recourse mortgages allow them to hand back their house keys – "jingle mail" is the result, as they are posted back to the bank – and walk away a little more easily than their UK counterparts.

8 Thomas Piketty, *Capital in the Twenty-First Century*, Cambridge (MA) and London, Harvard University Press, 2014. One of the less widely-reported aspects of his work is that he assumes that the return on investment can and likely will exceed the rate of economic growth, indirectly supporting a case for investing.

9 US President Nixon's Treasury Secretary John Connally observed to an overseas audience in 1971 that the dollar was "our currency, but your problem".

10 There are some notable exceptions to the alarmism: Phil Mullan's *The Imaginary Time Bomb*, London, I.B. Tauris, 2000 argued strongly that the social costs and economic costs of an aging population were being overstated; more recently, the March 2013 report from the UK House of Lords Select Committee on Public Service and Demographic Change, *Ready for Ageing*, struck a less than apocalyptic note but still felt it necessary to warn that: "The UK population is ageing rapidly, but we have concluded that the Government and our society are woefully underprepared. Longer lives can be a great benefit, but there has been a collective failure to address the implications and without urgent action this great boon could turn into a series of miserable crises".

11 This does not mean that we may as well turn over the administration of pensions completely to the state. Privately funded schemes maintain a link between contributions and nominal benefits at least, and many would agree with the idea that the fewer things governments do, the better. Some economists go further and suggest that privately funded pension administration in itself

materially boosts the efficiency of capital, and economic growth, but there is little evidence to support this, and the UK's experience has not been encouraging in this respect.

12 David Miles, "Financial Markets, Aging and Social Welfare", *Fiscal Studies*, Vol. 18, no. 2, May 1997, pp. 161–187.

13 This is only approximately true for an individual country, which might invest more than it saves by running a balance of payments deficit (and vice versa). Also, it is only true ex post: desired savings can exceed planned investment, in which case economic output falls to equilibrate the two (and vice versa), as noted in the text.

14 Very interested readers and students of the history of economic thought may want to take a look at the "reswitching" debate, which arguably should have been revitalised by the events of 2008/2009.

15 M. O'Mahony (1999), *Britain's Relative Productivity Performance 1959–1996: An International Perspective*, NIESR, London. Unemployment has been uncomfortably high not just recently, but for most of my working lifetime, which may explain my scepticism regarding the idea of a shortage of labour becoming a practical problem any time soon. Chance would be a fine thing.

16 A noteworthy early contribution being *Britain's Economic Problem: Too Few Producers*, R. Bacon and W. Eltis, London, Macmillan, 1976. The book suggested that government spending had been partly to blame, by "crowding-out" the private sector.

17 Francis Fukuyama, "The End of History?" in *The National Interest*, Summer 1989, and *The End of History and the Last Man*, USA, Free Press, 1992.

18 Samuel P. Huntington, *The Clash of Civilisations and the Remaking of World Order*, USA, Simon & Schuster, 1996.

19 This of course does not mean that all in the developed world is necessarily for the best. Even an optimist has to worry about the distribution of opportunities and our collective approach to education and literacy.

20 As in Lester Thurow's *Head to Head: The Coming Economic Battle among Japan, Europe and America*, New York, William Morrow & Co, 1992.

21 Martin Wolf's *Why Globalization Works*, New Haven, Yale University Press, 2004 makes the positive case for trade authoritatively. So too does the early writing of Paul Krugman: see, for example, *Pop Internationalism*, Cambridge (MA), MIT, 1996.

22 A fall in that currency's value will usually result in higher commodity prices in terms of that currency, which often causes confusion as to cause and effect.

23 Products for which demand rises *because* the price does are called "Veblen goods" (after the economist who first identified the idea of "conspicuous consumption"). Other goods – usually basic necessities – can see demand for them rise *despite* an increase in price. They are termed Giffen goods, after the economist who studied the spending patterns of the poor earlier in the nineteenth century.

24 See, for example, M.E. Porter, *The Competitive Advantage of Nations*, London, Palgrave Macmillan, 1990.

25 It is sometimes suggested that the West's access to previously unobtainable sources of carbon-based energy from (for example) shale rock may also do something to reduce the emerging world's cost advantage, but this effect is likely overstated: energy costs are much less important than labour for most manufacturers (and still less important again for most other businesses).

26 Including, yes, hairdressing.

27 See, for example, Alan Rugman's *The End of Globalization*, London, Random House, 2001.

28 Quoted in "The end of the Oil Age", *The Economist*, 23 October 2003.

29 The episode is described in a fascinating profile of the late Julian Simon (*The Doomslayer*) in Wired, 1997, and more recently and at greater length in Paul Sabin's *The Bet*, New Haven, Yale University Press, 2013.

30 Projections of "peak oil" production were successful in the US, where "Hubbert's peak" (named after the geologist who forecast it) occurred in the 1970s. Globally, however, it has proved more difficult to pin down – and improved extractive techniques for producing oil and natural gas from shale were causing a major, positive rethink of the US's available carbon-based energy supplies, even before late-2014's supply-driven decline in oil prices. See Dambisa Moyo's *Winner Take All: China's Race for Resources and What it Means for Us*, London, Allen Lane, 2012 for a sensationalist account of China's impact on natural resources.

31 Unconventional – constructive – assessments of the environmental and climate challenges include Bjorn Lomborg *The Skeptical Environmentalist*, Cambridge, Cambridge University

Press, 2001; and Nigel Lawson *An Appeal to Reason: A Cool Look at Global Warming*, London, Duckworth, 2008.

32 "Food Losses and Food Waste", Food and Agriculture Organisation of the United Nations, 2011.

33 "Dehydration Melting at the Top of the Lower Mantle", Brandon Schmandt et al., *Science*, June 2014.

34 I have been a governor since 2009.

35 The UK government published a booklet for general distribution titled "Protect and Survive" in 1980, advising what to do in the event of a nuclear strike. Elsewhere, Arthur M. Kotz, author of *Life after Nuclear War*, Ballinger, 1982, rather unnecessarily warned that "The banking system would face a particularly severe burden".

36 Stephen Pinker, *The Better Angels of Our Nature: The Decline of Violence in History and its Causes*, London, Allen Lane, 2011.

4 SOURCES OF PERSPECTIVE –
AND A TIGER'S TALE

1 In 2002, discussing the possible existence of weapons of mass destruction in Iraq, Donald Rumsfeld, the US Secretary of State, remarked "there are known knowns; there are things we know we know. We also know there are known unknowns; that is to say, we know there are some things we do not know. But there are also unknown unknowns – the ones we don't know we don't know" – US Department of Defence News Transcript, 12 February 2002. His comment may have been insensitive, but as a statement about the various categories of knowledge, it was syntactically and semantically spot on. If anything, he might have completed his point by noting that in addition to known knowns, known unknowns, and unknown unknowns, there are also unknown knowns – Mark Twain's things we think we know that "just ain't so".

2 A logarithmic scale is one in which each increment has the same proportionate significance, and is more useful than the conventional absolute scale when gauging growth rates over long periods.

3 The US Securities and Exchange Commission noted in its December 2008 report into mark-to-market accounting that: "Prior to the development of mandatory accounting standards following the Great Depression, companies had significant latitude in selecting their own accounting practices and policies". Perhaps ironically, today's mark-to-market accounting was arguably too conservative during the crisis, inasmuch as it resulted in banks using distressed and unrepresentative "market" prices to value their troubled assets, making them appear more fragile than they really were.

4 Two topical illustrations of economic historians' attempts at unearthing and compiling data for some very distant periods are Angus Madison's *Chinese Economic Performance in the Long Run*, Paris, OECD, 1998, and Sidney Homer's *A History of Interest Rates*, New Brunswick, Rutgers, 1977.

5 See Adam Ferguson *When Money Dies: The Nightmare of the Weimar Hyper-inflation*, London, William Kimber & Co, 1975.

6 An operational difference being that the Bank of Japan's earlier buying of bonds was aimed directly at raising bank reserves, a narrower transmission mechanism than the Western models would have in mind.

7 N. Crafts and P. Fearon, eds. *The Great Depression of the 1930s: Lessons for Today*, Oxford, Oxford University Press, 2013; S. Homer, *A History of Interest Rates*, op. cit.

8 In the summer of 2014, the ECB formally introduced a negative deposit rate. Some market-determined short-term interest rates had already been negative during the crisis and afterwards.

9 *Can Japan Compete?*, M.E. Porter, H. Takeuchi and M Sakakibara, London, Palgrave Macmillan, 2000, describes the planned nature of much economic activity in Japan in this period.

10 Of course, there are variants of capitalism within the West. Some Continental European models differ from those in the US and UK, for example. But even some of the less liberal European models are still more internationally open than Japan, and give more prominence to the efficient use of capital and shareholder interests than it does.

11 An early and very readable demonstration of this is contained in Burton G. Malkiel's *A Random Walk on Wall Street*, New York, W.W. Norton & Company, first published in 1973 and now in its 11th edition, an investment classic (deservedly so).

12 K. Gardiner "An Outside View of the Irish Economy", in *Transforming Ireland 2011–2016*, papers from the MacGill summer school, ed. Joe Mulholland, Dublin, Liffey Press, 2011.

13 Where their own immediate circumstances and characteristics are concerned, Daniel Kahneman in *Thinking, Fast and Slow*, London, Penguin, 2011 reports that individuals do display optimism – in matters such as starting a business, or gauging their career prospects for example.

14 On quieter days, journalists welcome any narrative at all: describing markets in anthropomorphic terms – "the market paused for breath today" – is reassuring for readers unwilling to accept that sometimes moves occur by chance, for no meaningful reason (or as JP Morgan famously quipped, because there were "more buyers than sellers" at a particular price). This is a case not of making the wrong sense of markets, but making some sense where there is none.

15 See Daniel Kahneman's *Thinking, Fast and Slow*, op. cit., for example.

16 J.M. Keynes, *A Treatise on Monetary Reform*, London, Macmillan & Co, 1923.

5   KNOW THE GAME, KNOW YOURSELF

1   In the Woody Allen film "A Midsummer Night's Sex Comedy" a character says "I help people with their investments until there's nothing left". As we discuss here, investment advisers' performance is uncertain, but their charges aren't, so be careful what you pay for.

2   A rare exception being *The Missing Risk Premium*, USA, Eric Falkenstein, 2012.

3   Milton Friedman, one of the most influential modern economists, once suggested that the realism of a theory's assumptions does not matter. I think he was mistaken in this. He used the example of a billiards player, arguing that we can describe their play "as if" they mentally calculated the precise angles and forces required for each shot. But we know that they do not do that, and a theory based on the assumption that they do, even if it predicts successfully, will be vulnerable – as is, for example, the modern portfolio theory that is predicated on the assumption that investors act rationally and focus only on maximising expected returns. See "The Methodology of Positive Economics" in *Essays in Positive Economics*, M. Friedman, Chicago, University of Chicago Press, 1953.

4   *A Treatise on Probability*, John Maynard Keynes, London, Macmillan, 1921. A US economist, Frank Knight, made the same point in his *Risk, Uncertainty and Profit*, Boston (MA), Houghton & Mifflin, published the same year.

5   Apologies for the brief intrusion of jargon.

6   Daniel Kahneman, *Thinking Fast and Slow*, op. cit.

7   Rupert Brooke asked that his epitaph be "Here lies One Whose Name was Writ in Water". Cable TV is an even more delible medium, but the Names writ upon it often have less to say.

8   It's almost always a chap.

9   The distribution of returns in practice may not be "normal": many writers favour a "fat-tailed" distribution in which more extreme outcomes happen more often. Nonetheless, standard deviation and the normal distribution have the benefits of familiarity and relative simplicity, and since a probabilistic approach to risk is itself of limited use (as we saw earlier), they are likely more useful than more complicated measures.

10 It is debatable whether the London Stock Exchange should have encouraged the UK stock market to become quite so international: the blue chip indices have arguably become too focused on the resources sector, which is why many professional investors favour the wider indices when choosing UK tracking funds.

6   BACK TO BASICS: WHAT YOU NEED TO OWN – IT'S ABOUT TIME

1   Some portfolio purists might dispute this point. An ex-colleague argued strongly in favour of holding an asset that he fully expected steadily to fall in value – and not just on a short-term basis, or as a contingency – because of the overall reduction in volatility that its predictability would impart to the wider portfolio.

2   The price advantages gained, somewhat contentiously, by high frequency traders – see *Dark Pools*, Scott Patterson, New York, Crown Business, 2012 – are tiny, and private investors do not lose out

noticeably from their actions. That does not mean that their efforts are laudable, and liquidity would not suffer greatly if some sand were placed in their wheels.

3   Equity duration is difficult to calculate, because future cash flows, and the discount rate needed to translate them into present values, are uncertain: any fixed income specialists reading this and missing the more precise estimates possible for bonds should bear with us. That said, just because it is difficult to calculate does not mean that the notion is not important. One approximation to equity duration is the inverse of the dividend yield. Currently, for the big Western markets this might correspond to around 30–40 years. Again, fixed income specialists will worry that this implies that stocks are massively sensitive to changes in interest rates, but the thing to remember is that the discount rates that investors implicitly apply to equity cash flows are not market rates, but a more stable, long-term notional rate. Equity duration is discussed more carefully in *Equities: It's about Time*, K. Gardiner, HSBC Global Research, April 2005.

4   In the UK, George Ross Goobey, the manager at Imperial Tobacco's pension fund, was particularly prominent in advancing the long-term case for stocks. Another landmark was the Trustee Investment Act of 1961, which permitted more funds to own stocks.

5   If all dividends were reinvested, the long-term rolling-up of total returns might lead to a situation in which the aggregate worth of stock market investments begins itself to dilute economic growth by encouraging over-investment, and this could in turn lead to a smaller total return, but this is not the point that the sceptics make. They have simply forgotten that in comparing a total return with economic growth they are not comparing like with like: you can draw an income from a business at the same time as the value of that business grows.

6   *Global Investment Returns Yearbook* (Misc), London, London Business School/Credit Suisse.

7   *Equity Insights*, HSBC Global Equity Strategy Team, 4 December 2008. In an earlier study in 2005 for the UK's FTSE100 Index – a list of companies chosen not because of their long-term growth characteristics, but simply because they were included in the index at its initial formulation in 1984 – we found that only three companies had failed outright, two of them because of fraud by dominant shareholders who had previously been proprietors. No UK government bonds – gilts – failed over this period (or any other), of course; but nine-tenths of the bonds trading in 1984 had ceased to exist.

8   Currencies are best viewed as characteristics of a particular asset, not assets in their own right. If you take a view on (say) the dollar/euro exchange rate you have to decide whether that view will be implemented by holding cash, bonds, stocks or other assets. Most currency analysis and advice is couched in terms of money-market instruments: cash is the asset and the currency simply designates the denomination in which you choose to hold it. The foreign exchange markets are perhaps the most efficient of all: it is extremely difficult for economists and advisers to beat the market when making forecasts, simply because an informational or analytical edge is so hard to get in such a public, macro context dominated by the constantly trading treasury departments of big, multinational companies. Private investors are best advised not to trade foreign currency markets actively, but to have some foreign currency exposure through their holdings in stocks – though that exposure can be tracked only loosely, as we noted in Chapter 5.

9   See for example *Facts and Fantasies about Commodities Futures*, G. Gorton and K. Geert Rouwenhorst, Yale International Centre for Finance Working Paper, June 2004.

10 The Undertakings for Collective Investment in Transferable Securities (UCITS) Directives allow for the free operation across the EU of a fund authorised to trade in one member country, and are part of the attempt to unify the EU capital markets.

11 See for example *The Hedge Fund Mirage: The Illusion of Big Money and Why It's Too Good to Be True*, Simon Lack, New Jersey, Wiley, 2012.

12 Remember also that mortgage payments are made from post-tax income. When grossed-up, they are often bigger than the likely returns on financial assets, and the best financial advice for many tax-paying investors with mortgages and investable cash can be to reduce the mortgage.

7   PUTTING IT ALL TOGETHER – WEIGHTING IN VAIN?

1   President Clinton's political adviser James Carville's reminder to Democrat activists about what mattered most during the 1992 presidential election campaign.

2   The manipulation of some key interbank rates by banks during the crisis may make these rates a little less important in future, but other proxies are readily available (such as three-month Treasury bills, for example).

3   In late 2014, the UK policy rate has been at 0.5% since March 2009. In relatively recent history, rates were more stable for a longer period only in the 13 years to 1952, when capital markets were much less liquid and open (and with the Second World War accounting for six of those years).

4   Some economists refer to a "natural" rate of interest. At the risk of offending the various factions – most obviously perhaps the followers of the "Austrian school" – the theoretical nuances pale into insignificance alongside the difficulties of making any interest rate model work neatly in practice.

5   All these factors also suggest that a given level of interest rates might be compatible with many different ways of organising production, and vice versa – a seemingly innocuous observation here, perhaps, but one that was once hotly contested, as in the "reswitching" debate referenced above.

6   The figures are deliberately round, and couched in terms of a compound growth rate, to avoid spurious precision. The 2% inflation assumption corresponds to the Bank of England's target, though we know of course that the Bank may not necessarily be successful in hitting it (inflation has more often than not exceeded the target in recent years).

7   The yield on the undated UK War Loan gilt-edged bond was back above 4% in late 2013 and early 2014, but in late 2014 was at 3.7%, at which level the government was reportedly considering redeeming it.

8   A ten-year gilt held to maturity will deliver the current redemption yield, since that yield incorporates the decline in price implied by market expectations of a rising interest rate profile. If those interest rate expectations are too low, the price will at some stage fall by more, and investors would be better off waiting before buying it. Investors holding longer-dated bonds for the same ten years face greater uncertainty, as the prices of their bonds can languish for longer, while those holding shorter-dated bonds face less.

9   It is difficult to judge how much of the buy-back is sustainable, and it must be viewed as (even) less dependable than a conventional dividend payment as a result, but a conservative estimate based on the last decade or so would suggest adding at least a percentage point to the regular dividend on this account.

10   A further refinement adds back depreciation and deducts the ongoing capital spending on new plant and equipment needed to sustain operations in order to more accurately proxy underlying pre-distribution cash flows. These "free cash flow" measures are more difficult to obtain, not least because measures of maintenance capital spending are subjective, and vary hugely across sectors.

11   The "model" was a (then) long-standing rule of thumb, christened informally by analysts after the Federal Reserve referred to the apparent stability of the earnings/bond yield ratio in its market commentary in 1997.

12   *Security Analysis*, Benjamin Graham and David Dodd, New York, McGraw-Hill, 1934; "A General Equilibrium Approach to Monetary Theory", James Tobin, *Journal of Money Credit and Banking*, Vol. 1, no. 1, 1969, pp. 15–29.

13   A comprehensive analysis of the issues encountered in gauging prospective asset class returns can be found in Antti Ilmanen's *Expected Returns*, Chichester, John Wiley, 2011.

14   The research literature tends to gloss over a related point concerning the measurement of returns themselves. Whereas intuition leads us to think of economic growth – and investment return – as a compounding process, in practice much investment analysis deals not with compounded, or geometrically-averaged, returns, but with arithmetically-averaged returns. The difference can be easily illustrated: an asset that falls by 50% and then doubles has returned to its starting point, and its compounded (geometric) average return is zero. Its average arithmetic return has however been +25% (half of –50% and +100%). Arithmetic averages are larger, and the gap between the two measures depends on volatility, which is why the debate about expected returns can sometimes get confused: to take a view on the likely arithmetic returns offered by an asset requires taking a view on volatility, a view which, as noted, most of us are unlikely to hold with any conviction. Some computational methods can only work in terms of arithmetic averages, while some assume that the investment process is limited to a single period. Again, a rush to mathematical optimisation has perhaps moved much of the investment debate away from practical usefulness.

15   Someone once said that the focus of much economic analysis is a little like looking for your lost wallet at night under the streetlight: you look there not because that is where it is likely to be, but because that is where you can see.

16   The so-called golden proportion found in many natural phenomena is 1.6:1 – or approximately 3:2.

17   UK investors can of course receive tax-free returns on investments in New Individual Savings Accounts.

8   CONCLUSION – POSTMODERN PORTFOLIO THEORY

1   In a letter to A. L. Bowley in 1901, quoted in *Reconstructing Political Economy: The Great Divide in Economic Thought*, London, W.K. Tabb, Routledge, 1999.

2   Julian Simon, the American economist who won the bet about commodity prices noted in Chapter 3, offered the following outlook 20 years ago: "This is my long-run forecast in brief: The material conditions of life will continue to get better for most people, in most countries, most of the time, indefinitely. Within a century or two, all nations and most of humanity will be at or above today's Western living standards... I also speculate, however, that many people will continue to *think and say* that the material conditions of life are getting **worse**". *The State of Humanity*, ed. Julian Simon, Oxford, Wiley-Blackwell, 1995.

3   These weightings ignore most taxes, which may if anything understate the likely drift towards stocks because a higher proportion of their prospective total return is accounted for by a (more lightly taxed) capital gain than income.

4   Market turning points can and do often occur without an obvious trigger or catalyst – perhaps because if the conditions are right, the actions of one or two large institutional investors, made for their own reasons, can be enough to set the ball rolling.

5   See, for example, E. Dimson, P. Marsh and M. Staunton in *Global Investment Returns Handbook 2005*, ABN Amro, 2005.

6   The seductiveness – and, in the appropriate context, the value – of abstract analysis is captured in *The Glass Bead Game*, the 1943 novel by Hermann Hesse: "These rules, the sign language and grammar of the Game, constitute a kind of highly developed secret language drawing upon several sciences and arts, but especially mathematics".

7   In February 2009, Warren Buffett put it more succinctly: "Beware geeks bearing formulas". Berkshire Hathaway Letter to Shareholders, February 2009.

Printed and bound in Great Britain by
CPI Group (UK) Ltd, Croydon, CR0 4YY